Teaching
Information
Literacy Online

Edited by THOMAS P. MACKEY and
TRUDI E. JACOBSON

Neal-Schuman Publishers, Inc.

New York   London

Published by Neal-Schuman Publishers, Inc.
100 William St., Suite 2004
New York, NY 10038

Copyright © 2011 Neal-Schuman Publishers, Inc.

Printed and bound in the United States of America.

The paper used in this publication meets the minimum requirements of American National Standard for Information Sciences-Permanence of Paper for Printed Library Materials, ANSI Z39.48-1992.

Library of Congress Cataloging-in-Publication Data

Teaching information literacy online / edited by Thomas P. Mackey and Trudi E. Jacobson.
     p. cm.
   Includes bibliographical references and index.
   ISBN 978-1-55570-735-4 (alk. paper)
   1. Information literacy—Study and teaching (Higher) 2. Information literacy—Web-based instruction. 3. Information literacy—Study and teaching—Case studies. 4. Research—Methodology—Study and teaching (Higher) 5. Research—Methodology—Web-based instruction. 6. Research—Methodology—Study and teaching—Case studies. 7. Academic libraries—Relations with faculty and curriculum. I. Mackey, Thomas P., 1961- II. Jacobson, Trudi E., 1957-

ZA3075.T427 2011
028.7071'1—dc22

                                                    2010050753

Dedication

To Trudi for being an excellent collaborative editor and author.
To my mother for great advice and support.
And to James for a sense of humor and adventures in travel.

—Tom Mackey

To Tom. It is an absolute pleasure working with you
on research and academic projects and dreaming up new ones.
And to John, the light of my life.

—Trudi Jacobson

Contents

List of Figures, Tables, and Appendixes

APPENDIXES

Foreword

Although the oft-cited quip that the *web changes everything* may not be true in a literal sense, it certainly has changed the role and function of teachers and academics, the function of libraries, and the work of librarians. This change has been derided by some as creating an ecology of interruptions that trains our brains to process only the inconsequential and that at surface levels only (Carr, 2010). More optimistically, web pundits such as Clay Shirky (2010) have argued that the Net affords the creation of a "cognitive surplus" that has created and will create more powerful tools and contexts that exponentially expand human creativity and productivity. Regardless if one views this cup of knowledge as half full or half empty, all agree that information production, storage, and distribution is undergoing radical change. It follows, then, that need for harnessing the tools and techniques of the new learning technologies requires corresponding new literacies and new ways to help each of us acquire these literacies.

The authors of the chapters in this text are at the forefront of this often-disruptive change. They quite rightly note that the relationship between students and libraries has changed due to the ubiquitous accessibility of the most-used library resources. They also describe how the relationship between faculty and the library has changed from one in which libraries and librarians served to assist faculty in accessing and storing discipline-related texts to one in which librarians act as cocreators, media aides, mentors, distributors, literacy instructors, and colearners with faculty members. But perhaps most important are the references in this text to the changing nature of knowledge itself. From a knowledge-scarcity model, we are moving to one of information abundance, where knowledge resources are not only available in vast quantities but at very low costs and encapsulated in multiple formats and media. Knowledge is also much more deeply networked to other objects and to humans, such that a deep ecological context of mutual dependency among producers, users, and owners emerges. These changes and related increases in complexity cry out for explanations, observations, case studies, and examples that guide our actions and attempt to properly use these resources. While these chapters do not yet provide universal best practices, much less predictive theories of use, they help us understand and develop interventions that allow us to learn more effectively and more efficiently.

As the title of the text indicates, each of the chapters struggles with instructional designs that are rooted in developing new forms of information literacies. It is easy to argue that most students of today are digital natives (Prensky, 2001) and thus their familiarity and comfort operating networked tools makes them experts. However, when one goes beyond the sensationalistic literature of pundits to empirical research studies, one finds that students today have mostly surface-level understandings of how these technologies work and even less capacity to evaluate and create their own digital artifacts (Kennedy et al., 2009). The chapters in the text and the summaries and overviews of the editors demonstrate the need for the types of collaborative (librarians plus subject matter expert) interventions and instructional designs in this text. But you will also find that most of the interventions described and evaluated here walk the talk and are designed to be delivered fully online or in blended learning contexts. Beyond the obvious "learning by using," which online contexts necessitate, is the efficiency, accessibility, and, it is hoped, reusability that online learning resources afford. Thus, the reader benefits not only from the ideas; by examining the digital artifacts created and the evaluation surveys and tools presented, this text helps each of us implement and evaluate our own information literacy projects—online.

Unlike the latest versions of popular Web 2.0 books with their focus on the wow factor, the chapters in this text are grounded with real technologies, the real expectations and responsibilities of teachers and students, and the real (if emergent) reconceptualizations of disciplinary knowledge. Thus, in the chapters that follow you will glimpse the way that the visions of the networked society are being instantiated in real learning contexts—to the benefits of the actors and hopefully by extension into your own learning contexts.

Many of the authors frame their teaching and their personal learning in constructivist frameworks in which individuals and groups work to create and re-create knowledge structures in relevant and personal contexts. However, peeking through, and partially as result of the affordances of the powerful networking tools used, is an even newer conception of knowledge building and sharing based on connectivist ideals (Downes, 2006; Siemens, 2005). Connectivism brings constructivism to the networked era by noting the necessity of connecting ideas, resources, and humans in networks of knowledge. These networks are then nourished, sustained, and enhanced in formal courses to become lifelong learning assets beyond graduation.

Many of the chapters in the book focus on the evolving definitions and function of information literacy and its attendant skills. Obviously, information literacy retains the traditional librarian role of helping learners to locate and decode information. It goes beyond the postmodern task of helping learners identify voice and critically examine the inherent bias in all information resources. We see librarians helping scholars and students create and re-create knowledge resources and, just as important, how to share and contribute their insights back to networked and collective knowledge. Further, in this text we see the emergence of librarian functions that help scholars devise means by which information flows (and not in fire-hose-size dosages) to learners rather than students searching for information. Finally, we see examples of librarians creating resources with disciplinary colleagues that persist beyond formal educational use to make knowledge freely available for lifelong learners, those without access to institutional resources, and to the growing number of amateur scholars working outside institutional walls.

If any readers harbor doubts as to the ongoing relevance and need for librarians in an era of "google anything," these notions will be disabused by reading this text. The roles of librarians have become much more complex in a networked era but have also become much more interesting. The collaborations, partnerships, resource building projects, and Web 2.0 technology demonstrations so aptly described in this text will provide not only inspiration but also practical ways in which the work of a networked library has come to life in a diverse and international set of postsecondary institutions.

It is common to end a foreword such as this by noting the audience who will gain the most from reading the chapters that follow. I won't disappoint the publisher by concluding that everyone should read this book! But that "everyone" obviously includes two target audiences: First are those, like the chapter authors, who are professionals working in libraries and teaching and learning centers in formal education and in corporate training contexts. A second and larger audience is teachers, professors, academics, and trainers from diverse disciplines who are looking for help and insight into ways to use networked tools to enhance their teaching but, more important, to enhance the learning of their students. If you have not yet been challenged to develop an online or a blended learning course, it is only a matter of time. It is true that death and retirement sometimes allow our colleagues to avoid mastering new information literacies, but it is little fun waiting for either to happen! Be assured that members of at least these two major target audiences will find the theories, literature reviews, cases, stories, learning objects, and evaluation tools detailed in this text to be invaluable aides to their personal and professional growth and enjoyment.

Terry Anderson
Professor and Canada Research Chair in Distance Education
Athabasca University

REFERENCES

Carr, N. 2010. *The Shallows: What the Internet Is Doing to Our Brains.* New York: W. W. Norton.

Downes, S. 2006. "Learning Networks and Connective Knowledge." IT Forum Paper 92. http://it.coe.uga.edu/itforum/paper92/paper92.html.

Kennedy, G., B. Dalgarno, S. Bennett, T. Judd, and K. Gray, et al. 2009. *Educating the Net Generation: A Handbook of Findings for Practice and Policy* Melbourne: Australian Learning and Teaching Council.

Prensky, M. 2001. "Digital Natives, Digital Immigrants." *On the Horizon* 9 no. 5: 1–6. http://www.marcprensky.com/writing/Prensky%20-%20Digital%20Natives,%20Digital%20Immigrants%20-%20Part1.pdf.

Shirky, Clay. 2010. *Cognitive Surplus: Creativity and Generosity in a Connected Age.* London: Penguin.

Siemens, G. 2005. A Learning Theory for the Digital Age. *Instructional Technology and Distance Education* 2 no. 1: 3–10. http://www.elearnspace.org/Articles/connectivism.htm.

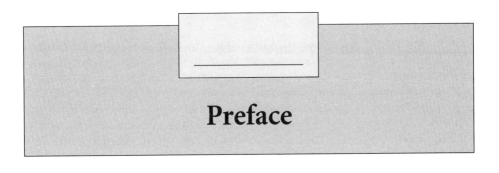

Preface

As online learning continues to expand in scope and influence, faculty and librarians are working collaboratively to design innovative programming in blended, hybrid, open, and fully online modes. The strength of these partnerships contributes to effective teaching practices, allowing for an exchange of ideas about emerging technologies, pedagogical theory, disciplinary perspectives, and student learning outcomes. While there are many challenges to faculty and librarians working together, including institutional barriers, differences in technology experience, and changing notions of library instruction, collaborative approaches to online learning lead to innovation and renewed practices.

This book presents eight original models for teaching information literacy online. Each chapter is coauthored by a faculty-librarian team and describes successful online strategies for collaborative information literacy instruction. The author teams provide theoretical frameworks for real-world practice, presenting disciplinary and institutional contexts, as well as essential details about program planning and assessment. Each team describes multiple technologies to engage students online, including reusable learning objects, Web 2.0 resources, learning management systems, open wiki environments, online portals, and the virtual world of Second Life. This book provides a global perspective from the United Kingdom's Open University and the University of Manchester, in addition to the six U.S. institutions such as the University of Central Florida, The University of Massachusetts Dartmouth, and Indiana State University. The disciplines are represented at the undergraduate and graduate levels and include business and accounting, computer and library science, history, English, women's studies, education, social work, as well as curriculum instruction and media studies.

In his book *Theory and Practice of Online Learning*, Terry Anderson argues that "the challenge for teachers and course developers working in an online learning context is to construct a learning environment that is simultaneously learning centered, content centered, community centered, and assessment centered" (Anderson, 2004: 54). Anderson defines an interrelated set of concerns, from content to learning outcomes, that instructors and designers must address in an integrated manner. In well-designed online learning environments, students actively explore content in dialogue with one another using a range of interactive technologies. According to Anderson:

> There is no single, right medium of online learning, nor a formulaic specification that dictates the kind of interaction most conducive to learning in all domains with all learners. Rather, teachers must learn to develop their skills so that they can respond to student and curriculum needs by developing a set of online learning activities that are adaptable to diverse student needs. (Anderson, 2004: 54)

This is a flexible and diverse approach to online learning that considers the needs of learners within a range of curricular contexts. We see this methodology demonstrated in this book as well, as faculty-librarian teams from multiple disciplines analyze the design of learner-centered assignments and courses in online environments. The collaborative approaches vary from blended and hybrid to open and fully online, with a primary emphasis on how to engage students in critical thinking and information literacy. As Anderson (2004: 42) asserts, "the greatest affordance of the Web for educational use is the profound and multifaceted increase in communication and interaction capability that it provides." This enhanced level of interactivity is integral to developing information literacy online, continuously connecting learners with one another and the instructor while challenging them to create and produce in these environments as informed citizens and lifelong learners.

TRENDS IN ONLINE LEARNING

We have seen the rapid expansion of online programs at community colleges, four-year institutions, universities with graduate- and doctoral-degree programs, through nontraditional adult education programs, and via international distance-learning initiatives. According to the report *Learning on Demand: Online Education in the United States, 2009*, coauthored by I. Elaine Allen and Jeff Seaman (2009: 1), "Online enrollments have continued to grow at rates far in excess of the total higher education student population, with the most recent data demonstrating no signs of slowing" (see also Allen and Seaman, 2010). In support of this assertion, the same report argues that "over 4.6 million students were taking at least one online course during the fall 2008 term; a 17 percent increase over the number reported the previous year" (p. 1). In addition, a report by the U.S. Department of Education (2007) argues that "sixty-one percent of 2-year and 4-year institutions reported offering online courses, 35 percent reported hybrid/blended courses, and 26 percent reported other types of college-level credit-granting distance education courses in 2006–07" (p. 2). This report identified a widespread and growing use of online courses and programs. Based on these trends, online learning is having a significant impact on teaching and learning, and the term itself continues to be defined and redefined in multiple ways.

One of the key findings from a meta-analysis of online research studies by the U.S. Department of Education (2009: xiv) is that "students who took all or part of their class online performed better, on average, than those taking the same course through traditional face-to-face instruction." This finding indicates that online learning is more than an enhancement to traditional classroom practice and must be taken seriously as a pedagogical approach in its own right that impacts student learning in a positive way. This report challenges some of the assumptions about face-to-face instruction as better than online learning because it asserts that "learning outcomes for students who engaged in online learning exceeded those of students receiving face-to-face instruction" (p. xiv). At the same time, this research also promotes blended models that combine in-class and online teaching by arguing that "instruction combining online and face-to-face elements had a larger advantage relative to purely face-to-face instruction than did purely online instruction" (p. xv). According to Scott Jaschik (2009) from InsideHigherEd.com, this finding "could be significant as many colleges report that blended instruction is among the fastest-growing types of enrollment." Overall, online learning continues to advance, not only the number of courses and programs, but also in the way this form of education positively impacts student learning and how it is perceived as an effective and diverse form of pedagogical practice.

INFORMATION LITERACY ONLINE

Technology considerations have been addressed to some extent through the development of information literacy in higher education, and more recently we have seen stronger connections between online learning and information literacy. Initially, the American Library Association's (1989) "Presidential Committee on Information Literacy: Final Report" acknowledged the ongoing development of technology by suggesting that in the future "one would see more information technology than is evident today, and it would be important to people not only in itself but also in regard to its capacity to help them solve problems and create knowledge." Although this document does not mention online learning specifically, it does acknowledge the impact of technology on information literacy and focuses on the problem-solving capability of information-literate citizens.

The Association of College and Research Libraries (ACRL) made a key point related to distance learning by stating that "the challenge for those promoting information literacy in distance education courses is to develop a comparable range of experiences in learning about information resources as are offered on traditional campuses" (2000: 4). Distance-learning courses and programs have progressed considerably since 2000, but this assertion about developing comparable experiences for students in distance-learning environments continues to inform how these courses and programs are developed and perceived. It reinforces the idea that online learning must be as effective as face-to-face, and that the traditional classroom is the baseline for comparison. This perspective does not fully address the unique dimensions of online learning and how teaching online is an innovative and effective practice.

The Middle States Commission on Higher Education (MSCHE) supports the design of comparable educational programs for distance-learning environments. In the document *Characteristics of Excellence in Higher Education: Eligibility Requirements and Standards for Accreditation*, MSCHE (2006) reinforces the relationship between the library and distance learning initiatives as a consideration for accreditation by arguing that "learning resources fundamental to all educational and research programs and the library, are adequately supported and staffed to accomplish the institution's objectives for student learning, both on campuses and at a distance" (p. 10). The accreditation standards address information literacy in online modes by requiring institutions to show "evidence of how the institution assures that students and faculty have sufficient technological skills and those information literacy skills that are necessary to access and to use effectively the information resources available at a distance" (p. 59). By recognizing the emergence of distance and distributed learning modes, accrediting agencies such as MSCHE support the overall learning objectives for critical thinking and information literacy in these online environments. Distance learning is also addressed by MSCHE (2002) in the guidebook

Distance Learning Programs: Interregional Guidelines for Electronically Offered Degree and Certificate Programs, but the references to information literacy in this document are somewhat brief. Institutions are encouraged to provide library resources for "training in information literacy including research techniques" (p. 16), but this statement does not define a highly substantive or synergistic connection between the two concepts. The actual standards for accreditation, however, at least acknowledge the presence of distance and distributed learning and the need for comparable support.

In *Standards for Distance Learning Library Services* (2008), ACRL emphasized the importance of "access entitlement" for all library users by stating that "every student, faculty member, administrator, staff member, or any other member of an institution of higher education, is entitled to the library services and resources of that institution, including direct communication with the appropriate library personnel, regardless of where enrolled or where located in affiliation with the institution." ACRL acknowledges how online library services have blurred the lines between brick-and-mortar institutions and online endeavors since students have access to information online in any context. In addition, ACRL emphasizes the importance of collaboration in these environments by arguing that librarians and administrators need to collaborate "with teaching faculty in distance-delivered programs to integrate information literacy into courses and programs in order to foster lifelong learning skills."

Information literacy instruction has built a presence online, especially with ongoing changes in technology and increased institutional support for these initiatives. Online programs advanced in numbers and influence in the 1990s, as illustrated in the extensive annotated bibliography *Library Services for Open and Distance Learning: The Third Annotated Bibliography*, by Alexander L. Slade and Marie A. Kascus (2000). The authors of this book presented more than 750 publications related to library services and online learning between 1995 and 1999. In 2005, a book titled *Exploring the Digital Library: A Guide for Online Teaching and Learning* by Kay Johnson and Elaine Magusin included three chapters that address faculty-librarian collaboration, and one of those three chapters examines information literacy specifically. In 2007, ACRL published *Information Literacy Programs in the Digital Age: Educating College and University Students Online* by Alice Daugherty and Michael F. Russo. This book presented more than 24 case studies about information literacy in a variety of online modes. Although these two books do not focus on faculty-librarian collaboration, the expansive scope of each volume demonstrates how widespread these initiatives have become.

BOOK ORGANIZATION

This book is divided into two main sections—Part I: Blended and Hybrid Learning and Part II: Open and Online Learning. Each part of the book includes four chapters that explore at least one of these format types, although there is some overlap in terminology throughout the volume. All of the chapters are organized in a similar way, with a detailed literature review and discussion of institutional context and disciplinary perspectives. The authors describe their collaborations, including the challenges they overcame and the specifics of program planning. Each chapter presents an online learning model with a discussion of the impact on student learning and assessment strategies. We begin both sections with an introduction that explores key themes and summarizes the unique contribution of each chapter.

Part I: Blended and Hybrid Learning

We start the book with a chapter coauthored by John Venecek and Katheryn Giglio from the University of Central Florida. This faculty-librarian team describes the development of an interactive open wiki environment in a hybrid course that integrates information literacy and Renaissance literature. Their goal was to engage students through an inquiry-based project to develop online research guides. Students became active producers of online information through the collaborative course wiki. In the next chapter, Matthew C. Sylvain, Kari Mofford, Elizabeth Lehr, and Jeannette E. Riley, of the University of Massachusetts Dartmouth, write about a program they developed to meet the needs of nontraditional students who are not on campus, as well as more traditional students interested in instruction at times and in places that meet their own needs. They developed reusable learning objects (RLOs) to teach information literacy in a range of contexts and describe the use of these RLOs in a course within the multidisciplinary liberal arts major.

Andrew Whitworth, Ian Fishwick, and Steve McIndoe of the University of Manchester in the United Kingdom collaborated on a postgraduate course, "Media and Information Literacy," which is part of a program that includes both full-time, on-campus students and part-time students who might be on or off campus. The course, taught both online and on campus, holistically incorporates information literacy instruction, rather than teaching information literacy as a discrete set of skills. The fourth chapter in the section describes a collaborative venture in the field of history, undertaken at Morehead State University in Kentucky. Kristina DuRocher and Lisa Nichols assigned students to use primary resources in an online research game revolving around people's fates during a particular twentieth-century period. This game was used, with necessary variations, in both face-to-face and online iterations of the course.

Part II: Open and Online Learning

The second part of the book starts with a chapter coauthored by Clarissa Gosling and Ingrid Nix from The Open University, United Kingdom. This faculty-librarian team describes a "supported open learning" model for students to work at their own pace while integrating information literacy and information, communication, and technology (ICT) skills. This chapter explores open and online learning to prepare work-based students who are seeking professional qualifications in the field of social work. The next chapter in this section is written by Jenna Kammer and Tracey Thompson from New Mexico State University (NMSU). The authors examine the virtual world of Second Life as an online environment to promote resource-based learning and service learning. Students actively explore Second Life via Aggie Island, a virtual library and information commons designed especially for this institution. This chapter illustrates the transformation of a course initially focused on technology skills to a broader interdisciplinary and virtual service learning experience through the integration of information literacy concepts.

We close the book with two chapters that address online learning in graduate courses. David Lavoie, Andrew Rosman, and Shikha Sharma from The University of Connecticut

(UConn) write about a Resource-Enriched Learning Model (RELM) developed for the Master of Science in Accounting (MSA) program. This approach is supported by an expanded team that includes faculty, librarians, a curriculum and instructional designer, media specialist, and students. The authors describe a holistic approach to information literacy that is informed by constructivism and integrated into an asynchronous online learning environment. The last chapter in the book is coauthored by Susan M. Frey and Rebecca L. Fiedler, a faculty-librarian team from the Bayh College of Education at Indiana State University (ISU). In this model, an information literacy course is designed for working professionals pursuing graduate degrees at a distance through the department of Curriculum, Instruction, and Media Technology (CIMT). The authors offer a compelling argument for faculty-librarian collaboration built on trust and the need to rethink traditional professional roles.

ONLINE LEARNING AT YOUR INSTITUTION

While the institutional contexts in this book may vary from your own setting, the techniques explored and lessons learned are portable to many different learning environments. Your college or university may be investing in different technologies from those described here or making the choice to move in the direction of open source. In addition, we continue to see rapid changes in emerging technologies, which makes it difficult for some institutions to keep pace with such revolutionary transformation. The models in this book, however, transcend any particular application or system because the focus of each chapter is on teamwork and inventive instructional design while being grounded in good teaching practices.

This is not to suggest that the technology itself is tangential to the learning experience. Technology is integral to each model and will inspire new ideas using other formats. For instance, in the first part of the book, the use of open wikis may inspire assignments at your campus that require collaborative narratives using Twitter or even text messaging. Similarly, the application of reusable learning objects (RLOs) may generate ideas about ways to incorporate portable modules using mobile apps, handheld devices, e-book readers, or iPads. In the second part of the book, the synchronous world of Second Life may inspire explorations in simultaneous web conferencing, gaming, virtual modeling, or digital animation. As we close the book, the discussion of student-centered fully online courses may encourage your faculty and librarians to explore the next generation learning environments that move beyond any particular learning management system to feature single sign-on, social networking, micro blogs, or cloud computing. We are certain that readers will appreciate all of the models presented in this book and then adapt the collaborative approaches to their own institutional contexts and technology environments.

As a significant trend in higher education, online learning is continuously moving forward, intersects all pedagogical considerations, and enhances information literacy efforts. Through the advance of technology we see the refinement of online learning formats, such as blended and hybrid, as well as open and fully online. Regardless of the particular format, the online learning models in this book demonstrate that faculty-librarian collaboration is especially beneficial in the design and implementation of information literacy endeavors. This work will continue to move forward through faculty-librarian partnerships that effectively fuse the pedagogical, disciplinary, assessment, and information theory and practice online.

If you have questions for the authors or editors, contact information with e-mail addresses is available toward the end of the book.

REFERENCES

Allen, I. Elaine, and Jeff Seaman. 2009. *Learning on Demand: Online Education in the United States, 2009*. The Sloan Consortium. http://www.sloan-c.org/publications/survey/pdf/learning ondemand.pdf.

———. 2010. *Class Differences: Online Education in the United States, 2010*. The Sloan Consortium. http://sloanconsortium.org/publications/survey/pdf/class_differences.pdf.

American Library Association. 1989. "Presidential Committee on Information Literacy: Final Report." American Library Association. http://www.ala.org/ala/mgrps/divs/acrl/publications/whitepapers/presidential.cfm.

Anderson, Terry. 2004. "Toward a Theory and Practice of Online Learning." In *Theory and Practice of Online Learning*, edited by Terry Anderson and Fathi Elloumi, 33–60. Athabasca University. http://cde.athabascau.ca/online_book/.

Association of College and Research Libraries (ACRL). 2008. *Standards for Distance Learning Library Services. American Library Association*. http://www.ala.org/ala/mgrps/divs/acrl/standards/guidelinesdistancelearning.cfm.

Association of College and Research Libraries (ACRL), "Information Literacy Competency Standards for Higher Education." 2000. American Library Association. http://www.ala.org/ala/mgrps/divs/acrl/standards/standards.pdf.

Daugherty, Alice, and Michael F. Russo. 2007. *Information Literacy Programs in the Digital Age: Educating College and University Students Online*. Association of College and Research Libraries.

Jaschik, Scott. 2009. "Inside Higher Education: The Evidence on Online Education." Inside Higher Ed. http://www.insidehighered.com/news/2009/06/29/online.

Johnson, Kay, and Elaine Magusin. 2005. *Exploring the Digital Library: A Guide for Online Teaching and Learning*. Jossey-Bass Online Teaching and Learning Series. San Francisco: Jossey-Bass.

Middle States Commission on Higher Education (MSCHE). 2002. *Distance Learning Programs: Interregional Guidelines for Electronically Offered Degree and Certificate Programs*. Middle States Commission on Higher Education. http://www.msche.org/publications/distguide 02050208135713.pdf.

Middle States Commission on Higher Education (MSCHE). 2006. *Characteristics of Excellence in Higher Education: Eligibility Requirements and Standards for Accreditation*. Middle States Commission on Higher Education. http://www.msche.org/publications/CHX06_Aug08REV March09.pdf.

Slade, Alexander L., and Marie A. Kascus. 2000. *Library Services for Open and Distance Learning: The Third Annotated Bibliography*. Englewood, CO: Libraries Unlimited, Inc.

U.S. Department of Education. 2007. "Distance Education at Degree-Granting Postsecondary Institutions 2006-2007." National Center for Education Statistics. http://nces.ed.gov/pubs2009/2009044.pdf.

U.S. Department of Education. 2009. "Evaluation of Evidence-Based Practices in Online Learning: A Meta-Analysis and Review of Online Learning Studies." U.S. Department of Education. http://www.ed.gov/rschstat/eval/tech/evidence-based-practices/finalreport.pdf.

Acknowledgments

We acknowledge the impressive contributions of our faculty and librarian author teams who describe their collaborative models for teaching information literacy online. We appreciated the opportunity to work with you on this book and we gained new knowledge about this topic by editing your chapters.

We greatly appreciate the involvement of Terry Anderson, Professor and Canada Research Chair in Distance Education at Athabasca University, who wrote the book's exceptional Foreword. Terry brought his well-known expertise in open and online learning to his contribution, and he was our first reader of the book.

As always, we value the exceptional support we received from the outstanding team at Neal-Schuman Publishers, including Charles Harmon, Vice President and Director of Publishing, and Amy Knauer, Production Editor.

Blended and Hybrid Learning

SECTION INTRODUCTION

In this first part of the book, the terms *blended* and *hybrid* are used interchangeably to describe online learning efforts that combine face-to-face and online instruction. According to the report *Learning on Demand: Online Education in the United States, 2009*, "blended (sometimes called hybrid) instruction is defined as having between 30 percent and 80 percent of the course content delivered online" (Allen and Seaman, 2009: 4). A course developed in a blended or hybrid format "typically uses online discussions, and typically has a reduced number of face-to-face meetings" (Allen and Seaman, 2009: 4). Blended and hybrid courses have also been defined by teaching practices that integrate multiple technologies, although the intersection between in-class and online is a primary consideration.

The faculty-librarian teams in this section explore four different collaborative models to engage learners with online content. In some instances, learners also actively produce online materials. A common element among most of the examples in this section is that the instruction was offered both face to face and online, providing blended approaches that could be adapted to differing situations. This section covers ventures for specific courses, as well as related components such as online tutorials, Web 2.0 resources, and learning objects that were designed for disciplines at the authors' institutions. Each example provides an excellent start for considering the approaches that might allow instructors to incorporate information literacy instruction into courses with some online elements. The author teams also include ideas that will inspire curriculum and instructional design revisions for courses that might be undergoing transitions from face-to-face to online.

This section features courses taught at the undergraduate and graduate levels, in disciplinary and interdisciplinary contexts that include the humanities, liberal arts, education, and history.

In "Shakespeare Is Not a One-Shot Deal: An Open Wiki Model for the Humanities," John Venecek and Katheryn Giglio of the University of Central Florida delve into one of the Web 2.0 applications that can be used to engage students. They developed an information-literacy component in several undergraduate Renaissance literature courses, first offered face-to-face and then in a hybrid format, in which students developed online research guides that were designed for continuing use in future semesters. These guides were designed in collaborative wikis and included both primary and secondary sources. The wiki environment proved to be extremely effective for both modes of instruction and also increased the opportunities for students to collaborate and to engage in deep critique. The authors conducted a citation analysis to assess the quality of the sources in the information literacy component of the project. They determined the percentage of scholarly sources used by students and found that their results compared favorably to a similar study. They identify areas that need strengthening in the future, including additional database and catalog instruction.

The next chapter, "Reusable Learning Objects: Developing Online Information Literacy Instruction Through Collaborative Design," written by Matthew C. Sylvain, Kari Mofford, Elizabeth Lehr, and Jeannette E. Riley of the University of Massachusetts Dartmouth, describes a project in which the authors wanted to meet the needs of a campus that increased the number of online courses. The University of Massachusetts Dartmouth has both a residential student base as well as students who rely upon blended and online courses. Two librarians, working as part of a multidisciplinary team, created the reusable learning objects (RLOs) to support a new liberal arts program and major. The collaboration analyzed in this chapter concerns a 200-level course in this new major (LAR 201), although information is provided from the RLOs' use in six different courses in the liberal arts. The faculty member teaching LAR 201 was concerned that students' lack of key skills may be more evident in the online setting. In addition, the course requires students to conduct research using both primary and secondary sources, and to cite these sources correctly. Information literacy instruction would be critical to help students succeed. The planning team's goals included the ability to develop RLOs that could be employed in settings beyond this course and the fully online setting, including use in both face-to-face and blended courses. To encourage their broad application, the team designed the RLOs to be flexible. Topics include primary and secondary sources, truncation, Boolean operators, and understanding citations in online databases. The authors discuss the impact of the RLOs on student learning and include results from a student survey that addressed the content of the tutorials, their ease of use, and their effectiveness.

Andrew Whitworth, Ian Fishwick, and Steve McIndoe of the University of Manchester in the United Kingdom contribute "Framing Multiliteracies: A Blended and Holistic Approach to Digital Technology Education." Their collaboration emerged from the Media and Information Literacy (M&IL) course in the master's level digital technologies, communication and education program. This course addresses the need for a holistic integration of information literacy within the multiple literacies defined as important for this context. Students taking the M&IL course may be in the School of Education or other programs, and some are full-time on-campus students, while others may study part time and/or online. Therefore, the program's courses are delivered in a hybrid format to meet the varying needs of the students. MI&L is a self-paced course, offered both on-campus (through weekly meetings) and online. Librarians at John Rylands University Library and faculty in the School of Education are now developing a revised, shortened version of the course with the objective of meeting the information literacy learning needs of a broad spectrum of University of Manchester students at all levels.

The authors report on the course's impact on students' learning using an assessment of students' work and the results of an e-mail survey.

In the fourth chapter in this section, students have the opportunity to research their fates based on a persona that they are given in the History 201 course at Morehead State University in Kentucky. Kristina DuRocher and Lisa Nichols collaborated on this two-week project, which originally included an online component in a face-to-face class and then moved to a completely online project. This research game, which currently supports the course section on the Vietnam conflict, requires students to use both primary and secondary sources. The students provided positive feedback on the project, and the authors note that they became more engaged with the topic and the historical context of the assignment. The authors discuss the challenges of their collaborations and the changes that were implemented over several iterations of the course. The assessment of student learning changed over time as well, with self-assessments, student surveys, and comments students submitted with their completed assignments.

The authors of these four chapters raise several key points that are worthy of consideration by faculty and librarians who are developing information literacy instruction for blended or hybrid settings. One theme that emerges as a prominent concern is the need for flexibility. This is a critical design principle for implementing information literacy online and may determine its continued success. Readers will note that many of the items in the list below are not unique to the blended learning environment: they are elements of carefully considered instructional design.

- Consider whether the instructional components developed might be used in multiple courses and by different faculty members. If it is possible to create instruction that can be implemented in a number of courses, everyone will benefit.
- Think about the possible transition from using some online elements to a fully online course. Might the instruction be designed in a way that it can be used in both environments? Is it possible to adapt these techniques without extensive changes?
- Design with flexibility in mind, allowing for the integration of emerging technology formats and for the inclusion of students with different learning styles.
- Use a team approach where possible. Librarian-faculty collaborations can be enhanced by the participation of technology and instructional design specialists.
- While assessing student learning is not unique to this type of instruction, the possible methods for conducting it might be broader than for courses without an online component. Again, plan for methods that will continue to work should the program or course become fully online.
- For blended courses, determine which information literacy learning objectives are best met using which environment. Even elements that might immediately be thought of as face to face, such as a tour of the library, might appropriately be addressed through online means, such as using a virtual tour, streaming video, or Second Life.
- Specifically ask students about the method of presentation used, and consider revising those that did not successfully meet their needs. It might be possible to

present some material in more than one format, allowing students to select that which best meets their needs and learning style.

Each chapter in this section presents a unique situation with many examples and suggestions that provide readers with novel ideas to explore on their own. The models introduced here are adaptable to other collaborations and institutions, especially for faculty and librarians interested in moving forward with blended and hybrid learning initiatives.

REFERENCES

Allen, I. Elaine, and Jeff Seaman. 2009. *Learning on Demand: Online Education in the United States, 2009.* The Sloan Consortium. http://www.sloan-c.org/publications/survey/pdf/learningondemand.pdf.

1

Shakespeare Is Not a One-Shot Deal

An Open Wiki Model for the Humanities

John Venecek and Katheryn Giglio

INTRODUCTION

Many academic libraries are currently reassessing how to better support teaching and research in the digital age. The advent of interactive Web 2.0 technology offers a unique opportunity to engage faculty in ways that not only support their research, such as through the creation of open-access repositories, but can add a new dimension to information literacy instruction as well. In a recent article for the *Publications of the Modern Language Association of America* (*PMLA*), Cathy Davidson discusses the potential impact of Web 2.0 on scholarly communication within the humanities and makes a number of points concerning new possibilities for interdisciplinary collaboration and, by extension, information literacy instruction. Regarding the advent of open access resources and collaborative archives, she says:

> An open repository challenges the borders between disciplines as well as between professionals and amateurs, between scholars and knowledge enthusiasts. It raises questions of privilege and authority as well as ethical issues of credibility and responsibility, privacy and security, neutrality and freedom of expression. (Davidson, 2008: 711)

Davidson further adds, "Humanities 2.0 is distinguished from monumental, first-generation, data-based projects not just by its interactivity, but also by an openness about participation grounded in a different set of theoretical premises, which decenter knowledge and authority" (p. 712). It is the interactive, collaborative nature of Web 2.0 applications, she hopes, that will lead to a sort of "Big Humanities," where the focus is on the process, not the product. "There is a latest version," she says, "but never a final one" (p. 713).

These ideas of "openness" and "interactivity" will be familiar to anyone with any experience using blogs, wikis, or any other social networking tools. The point Davidson makes that is most relevant to the project at hand is the idea of "decentering knowledge" and how this will affect our notions of authority, expertise, participation, interdisciplinarity, and other concepts that are prevalent throughout academia. The changes she foresees will not only impact how scholars conduct research, share information, and teach, they will also affect the role of librarians within this ever-changing environment.

Some of the traditional notions of authority and control that Davidson looks to eschew have often been barriers to librarian/faculty collaboration. Breaking through the "faculty culture" where time-strapped instructors cherish their autonomy and are wary of external involvement in their classes has been a long-standing challenge for academic librarians. Larry Hardesty addresses this point in his study of the relationship between faculty culture and bibliographic instruction:

> In other words, faculty members who hold to the values of faculty culture (a feeling of lack of time; emphasis on content, professional autonomy, and academic freedom; de-emphasis on the applied and the process of learning; and resistance to change) are not interested in "bright ideas" from librarians about bibliographic instruction. (Hardesty, 1995: 356)

William Badke, writing ten years later, argues that many of the concerns expressed by Hardesty still prevail: "We are locked within an environment in which discipline-specific instruction is the norm, professors cling to their turf, and the powers that be will release neither personnel, funding nor curriculum space to enable a wider information literacy to take root" (Badke, 2005: 71). But instead of accepting this apparent vicious cycle, librarians looking to take a leadership role in promoting information literacy might do well to play off of the changes, or challenges, that Cathy Davidson suggests. In a follow-up interview to her article for the *PMLA*, she talks about the idea of "collaboration by difference." Where much of the literature about collaboration deals with "shared goals, and shared methods or shared areas of expertise," Davidson says she "became interested in this much looser way of learning, kind of mash-up learning, where people may or may not share credentials" (Bass and Schlafly, 2009). As will be discussed in greater detail, "participation" and "difference" are both key components of Web 2.0 technology, and both can help break through the confines of faculty culture that have long been barriers to librarians and proponents of information literacy.

The project discussed in this chapter is an example of a collaboration undertaken by a literature professor and humanities librarian at the University of Central Florida that incorporated many of Davidson's ideas of shared authority in the creation of knowledge by merging our areas of specialization—Renaissance literature and information literacy—while embracing our differences. By having our students use wikis to create online research guides, our goal was to design an engaging, critical, and theoretically reflective project wherein theory would emerge "naturally" as students experienced a full range of written and visual texts pertinent to the vaster understanding of our given time period. The interactive nature of wikis provided a unique venue through which our students were able to make original and meaningful connections with both literary and historical material even as they struggled with one another's interpretations of primary and secondary sources. The inquiry-based design of our project brought to light deeper and compelling questions regarding historical narratives. This approach, we hoped, would alleviate some of the humanities' disengagement from the "real world" that many have been suggesting of late. This, in turn, would allow our students—the future generation of researchers—to explore important questions regarding collaborative analysis that are likely to arise as we begin working on the larger Humanities 2.0 projects called for by Cathy Davidson.

RECENT LITERATURE

While articles about information literacy and Web 2.0 are starting to emerge, most are of the "what we did and how we did it" variety and only a few pertain directly to the humanities. In a recent article, however, Robin Farabaugh writes about using wikis to establish a discourse community in her own Shakespeare courses. Farabaugh makes a key point regarding her choice to use wikis, one that can be applied to any class project being conducted in an online environment:

> Our choice of the software may either teach us how we think, or keep us from thinking freely. Highly structured course software, with delivered formats, could eliminate a crucial element in language education. (Farabaugh, 2007: 44)

The decision to conduct a similar project using Blackboard or WebCT would have different implications for student involvement and expected learning outcomes. Farabaugh argues that "elaborate course software programs may be said to teach us their language" (p. 44). With wikis, however, instead of formatting entries to the template that a specific type of software provides, students are given the opportunity to "experiment with different languages to determine not only how they want to say things, but also what they want to discuss"; in other words, "they are responsible for creating their own body of knowledge, rather than merely receiving it" (pp. 45–46). Unlike the course management systems previously mentioned, students working in this environment play a more active role in shaping both the form and content of their projects. As a result, they have a personal stake in deciding what to include in their wikis, which encourages them to envision the larger context of the works being studied and reaffirms the idea that context is a source of constant negotiation.

To illustrate this point, Farabaugh discusses a section of a wiki in which a student asks about the role of the audience as possible coconspirators in a play. Since the audience (as is often the case) knows more than the other characters, the student wonders if the audience carries some responsibility for a character's actions. Farabaugh notes that the student has engaged in a "metaquestion" about the "nature of form and its ability to convey meaning" (2007: 54). She continues, "In this fashion students are given an opportunity to recognize that language meaning, like learning, is influenced not only by the words we use, but the forms we use to contain them" (p. 54). Much like a theater audience, wiki users play an active role in determining what these resources should be and, in so doing, they add value and create meaning through their continued interaction with these resources.

While it is true that the student may have come to this realization in another way, the point about form and meaning illustrates how wikis differ from other types of educational software. With an emphasis on flexibility, wikis encourage users to make their own connections instead of relying on the types of structured templates that are common with content management systems such as WebCT and Blackboard. Instead, wikis provide an outlet through which users can customize information and create contexts that emphasize flexibility in a way that is relevant to the current culture of information. James Hilton speaks to this point when he compares current trends in the information-seeking behavior of college students to what he calls the "rip, mix and burn" era of music: "Today's students want to be able to take content from other people, they want to mix it, in new creative ways—to produce it, to publish it, and to distribute it" (Hilton, 2006: 60).

Students raised in the digital era tend to think of value in terms of their ability to remix and personalize information, a point that is addressed by Calandra and Lee in their article about the Digital History Pedagogy Project (DHPP), which was designed to promote active learning through exploration of the ever-growing number of primary sources being made available online.

> Digital historical resources should enable learners to actively construct their own under-standings of the past, using authentic resources, but these understandings must also be reflective of discrete and universal knowledge and scientific processes for attaining knowl-edge. (Calandra and Lee, 2005: 325)

These authors go on to cite Richard Mayer, who suggests that "a learner can be viewed as a knowledge constructor who actively selects and constructs pieces of verbal and visual knowledge in unique ways" (p. 325). Calandra and Lee further add that "meaningful learning occurs when learners select relevant information from what is presented, organize the pieces of information into a coherent mental representation, and integrate the newly constructed representations with others" (p. 326). In the same vein as James Hilton, they encourage "physical manipulation of digital media by the learner that supports active, meaningful learning; but that also produces tangible, shareable knowledge representation created by the learner" (p. 326). Their emphasis on manipulation and active learning speaks directly to our project and our encouragement of students to explore a variety of resources to construct their own understanding of the past as it pertains to the life and times of Shakespeare.

Although it does not deal specifically with information literacy as such, Schroeder and den Besten's recent article about the Thomas Pynchon *Against the Day* wiki echoes a key point made by Cathy Davidson. The authors here are concerned with whether it is possible for an online community to use a wiki to complete a finalized annotated "edition" of Pynchon's novel. Like Davidson, they suggest that the value of this project lies more in the process than the final product. In other words, these projects seem to have more value when they "adopt a more playful approach which treats texts as having endless scope for further work" (Schroeder and den Besten, 2008: 183). They further add that wikis promote "competition to complete the task," which would not occur if the entries were organized alphabetically or by topic as in a traditional scholarly bibliography (p. 184). The unevenness of the entries and the open-ended nature of the medium expose gaps in knowledge and encourage users to fill in those gaps and make new associations. Wikis seem to be most effective, then, in projects that rely on *interpretive* rather than purely *informative* entries and "where endless detective work is called for, and this may apply to other areas of e-research or online collaborations" (p. 184). Based on our experience working with literature students, we know that texts and interpretations are often viewed as authoritative rather than sources in which to locate difference and expose gaps in knowledge. As a result, undergraduate researchers often focus on compiling citations from recognized authorities as opposed to pursuing genuine interaction and discourse with established ideas. Projects that employ open-source technology, however, have the capacity to release texts from what often seems like interpretive closure and, in so doing, can reopen the seeming finality of printed materials as well as historical narratives.

INFORMATION LITERACY AT THE UNIVERSITY OF CENTRAL FLORIDA

The University of Central Florida is a large metropolitan university located just outside downtown Orlando and is one of 52 "space-grant" universities in the country. Founded in 1963 as Florida Technical University, the school's original mission was to train personnel to work at the nearby Kennedy Space Center. The size and scope of the university grew, and the name was changed to the University of Central Florida in 1978. As of 2011, UCF ranks as the third largest university in the United States, consisting of nearly 54,000 students and more than 10,000 faculty and staff. The university offers 214 degrees from 14 colleges and special programs. The College of Arts and Humanities consists of seven departments, which collectively offer 75 undergraduate and graduate programs. The English Department alone offers 15 different programs at the graduate and undergraduate levels.

The Department of Information Literacy and Outreach (ILO) was created in 2006 and consists of 12 librarians who teach an average of 400 face-to-face instruction sessions each year. Most of these are traditional one-shot sessions, but librarians are also working with an increasing number of online and hybrid courses for various departments. The role of librarians in these types of classes depends greatly on the needs of individual instructors, but responsibilities typically include providing online instruction, creating and grading assignments, and providing feedback on discussion board topics. Librarian involvement with online classes has increased from 40 to 58 classes in the past four years, reaching a total number of 2,100 online students in the 2009–2010 academic year. These numbers are consistent with the rate at which online courses have increased during the same time.

UCF librarians are also expanding the scope of the instruction program by creating a series of information literacy modules that can be used in both online and face-to-face classes. Modules generally include guided instruction with a follow-up quiz that can be graded as a stand-alone assignment. Current modules include citing sources, maximizing Google Scholar searches, recognizing a research study, creating a search strategy, and avoiding plagiarism. Other endeavors are the use of Adobe Captivate streaming-video tutorials, creation of LibGuides that can be tailored to specific classes, development of a liaison program, workshops given at orientation sessions, and the marketing of instruction services to all courses that include a research methods component.

Despite the range of these efforts, the ILO Department remains fairly traditional in that a vast majority of librarians' involvement with classes remains the aforementioned one-shot instruction sessions or their online equivalent. Although librarians are always thinking creatively about how to move beyond this limited model, one key barrier is the sheer size of the university. Reaching out to nearly 1,700 teaching faculty and providing integrated instruction to 54,000 students creates a number of daunting challenges. As a result, collaboration has been difficult and generally limited to small groups of librarian–faculty teams such as the one described in this chapter.

INTERDISCIPLINARY PERSPECTIVE

Over the past decade, the idea of interdisciplinarity has received a lot of attention in academia. However, as Julie Thompson Klein has noted, "There is a general uncertainty about the meaning of the term," which often places the onus of definition on the immediate body of individuals or individuals having to work within it (Thompson Klein, 1991: 12). Loosely stated, the goal of interdisciplinarity in the humanities has been to examine interconnected, complex ideas or problems in congruence with multiple disciplines. In some ways, interdisciplinarity is the logical outgrowth of early postmodern critique, which applauded the death of the author and the opening of the text to the rest of the world. Under the vague enchantment of interdisciplinarity, as in the theory of Barthes, Foucault, Greenblatt, and others, the reader no longer turns to Shakespeare as the single source to understand how the playwright constructed his world. One must also turn to church sermons (religion), theories of Renaissance childhood and selfhood (psychology), government and authority structures (political science), as well as music, art, and recipe books to appreciate even the smallest textual details. While interdisciplinary scholars have produced breathtakingly rich and thorough considerations of single topics, the jury is still out on how well we are achieving this goal in the undergraduate classroom.

With respect to the project at hand, we sought to achieve the previously stated goals by asking our students to explore Shakespeare's world through an interdisciplinary lens. Further, we strove to put into practice some of the key principles discussed by Cathy Davidson—specifically to use this collaboration as an opportunity to decenter the discipline-specific approaches to our own areas of expertise. Although we were somewhat idealistic at the beginning of the project, this task proved more difficult than originally anticipated and, as a result, we often found ourselves falling back into our familiar domains, an issue that may have had as much to do with comfort and control as it did with subject expertise. We will discuss more about the nature of humanities research in the following section, but it's worth noting here that, despite the effect that emerging technologies are having on scholarship across the curriculum, there will always be an aspect of research in any field that requires more discipline-specific expertise, a point that has significant implications for librarians who strive for more collaboration and a more integrated approach to information literacy instruction. Many of the changes we have been discussing have created new opportunities for librarians, many of whom regularly work with students and faculty from different disciplines and are proactive about incorporating new technologies into their instruction. As Miriam Conteh-Morgan points out, "Librarians have an even more pivotal role to play to bring together, in a coherent and cohesive whole, the seemingly discrete strands of the multi-canon, intercultural, and interdisciplinary mosaic" (Conteh-Morgan, 2004: 169). Quoting Pelster and Baker, she further adds that, "Having historically responded to and supported the academy's enshrinement of the Great Books, librarians may now need to participate in enlarging the canons" (p. 169). This objective can be accomplished by becoming more actively involved with curriculum development and by becoming "co-creators of the curriculum" (p. 170).

However, taking an active role in curriculum development requires a high degree of subject-specific expertise as well as the keys to common institutional barriers. This brings us back to the point made earlier about faculty culture in which instructors are often reluctant to relinquish sole authority of their subjects and allow curricular input from the nonspecialist. Department culture can be equally unwelcoming in that classes are traditionally taught by a single expert who is reviewed by departmental chairs on the quality of his or her teaching *alone*. As a librarian–faculty team working together on a small number of classes, we were able to overcome some of these barriers and gain a certain degree of autonomy within the realm of our project. However, even within this relatively controlled setting, we found that our goals would be a source of constant negotiation as we learned to work together and keep the project moving forward in a way that was beneficial both to us and to our students. One example of this negotiation is the realization that, even though we had a shared interest in using technology in the classroom, this project held a different level of significance for each of us. For the librarian, this was a major project—an opportunity to be involved with curriculum development from the ground up and to use this class to showcase the benefits of embedded information literacy instruction. For the instructor, however, the project always remained a secondary priority that often took a backseat to more pressing issues related to promotion and tenure as well as other administrative duties.

COLLABORATION IN THE HUMANITIES

In addition to the points previously made, collaboration can be particularly difficult in the humanities, which is still viewed as a very traditional and often solitary discipline. Brockman and colleagues address this point when they note that, while humanities scholars do share ideas "through the grapevine" and at conferences, and that these endeavors may add a social dimension to their scholarship, they nevertheless rarely coauthor books or articles. "Research projects in the social sciences and hard sciences are commonly funded and executed by a team and presented in articles coauthored by team members. By contrast, individuals write virtually all articles and books in the humanities" (Brockman et al., 2001: 13). They further add, "When the scholars in our study spoke of libraries, they conceived of them first as collections and second as places in which research—in the purposive sense—takes place" (p. 13). Brockman and colleagues also conclude that humanist scholars tend to build larger personal collections than do those in the social and hard sciences, and they work from a smaller collection of "core texts" that are central to their research; the texts they work with also tend to be older and contain a high degree of "nebulous and symbolic" language that may make searching in databases and other online sources more difficult.

Since their study was first published in 2001, there have been many changes in the types of technologies that have had an impact on scholarship across the curriculum and have prompted scholars like Cathy Davidson to call for humanists to adopt these changes and start thinking beyond the prescribed boundaries of traditional humanities research. This call can be seen as an opportunity for librarians to define new roles and areas of expertise that can lead to enhanced information literacy instruction. In this particular case, the librarian's willingness to take on the role of managing the technological aspect of the wikis was a key factor in moving the project forward. Without this modification, the project likely would not have gotten off the ground because the instructor would not have been able to devote the time necessary to manage the technology in addition to teaching the course content. Although this was a very practical solution to an early barrier, it was nevertheless an opportunity to expand upon the role that librarians usually play and, as a result, to advance the project beyond the planning stage. Further, while the librarian's presence was a critical part of face-to-face class time, an added benefit was his availability to students who wished to stop by his office or stay in e-mail contact for either technical or research support, a convenience that the professor's two weekly office hours did not offer them. This created an extra layer of support throughout the semester and helped personalize the online portions of the class. This approach helped us bypass some of the obstacles that have been described and show the library in a different light. Rather than simply being the place where books are stored, the library became an important extension of the class and a place where research—in the purposive sense—takes place.

PROJECT OVERVIEW

This project is the result of a conversation that occurred during a conference at UCF's Faculty Center for Teaching and Learning. The original idea centered on the desire to create more research guides and finding aids that could be tailored to meet the needs of individual courses. However, instead of the librarian and instructor creating these together, it became apparent that there was great potential for this idea to be carried out as part of a student project. During the course of the following four semesters—in two face-to-face and two hybrid classes—students were charged with creating online research guides that could continue to be developed in future semesters. This process would allow us to embed information literacy instruction into the fabric of the course by asking students to select which resources would be most appropriate for inclusion in the course research guide. This open-ended approach, in turn, would provide insight into the information-seeking behavior of our students, learn what they value as emerging researchers, and identify gaps in their skills that would help us develop better research projects in the future.

From a literary point of view, we hoped this project would engage students in thinking about the historical context that lay behind the creation of some of Shakespeare's most famous characters and, through students' investigations of these figures, come to experience the interpretability of all historical writing, including their own. The project, then, had two complicated but ultimately interconnected literary goals. The first was to gain a basic sense of the social identities Shakespeare playfully tinkered with in the creation of his figures. Sir Toby Belch, from *Twelfth Night*, and Sir John Falstaff, from *Henry IV*, Parts I and II, are literary (albeit comical) interpretations of knights in the early modern period, just as Juliet, from *Romeo and Juliet*, and Miranda, from *The Tempest*, are interpretations of daughters. Knights and daughters—as well as kings, witches, servants, slaves, and anyone else we are likely to meet upon the Shakespearean stage—were identities laden with high social expectations. In fact, after the arrival of the printing press in England in 1476, there was an increasing number of printed sermons and courtesy and conduct manuals available for knights, daughters, princes, and the like, advising each to act within the parameters of certain behaviors. The sheer number of behavioral prescriptions and advice manuals suggests that social roles, or "identities," were rigorously scripted. The instructor's thinking here was that by reading primary source material as well as secondary literary analyses and then building wiki entries focused on identities, students would truly come to appreciate the comic and tragic literary nuances of Shakespearean figures.

Because the course was geared towards junior- and senior-level students, we felt we could enact the second goal as well, one that moved students beyond literary appreciation into the realm of deeper critique. It may seem long ago that Fredric Jameson urged readers to "always historicize," but this 1981 sentiment-turned-historicist-slogan is a perfectly relevant expectation of student engagement for a new medium in a new century. For Jameson and others, everything can be seen through the lens of historical context— including nonliterary historical texts *and* historical interpretations. We wanted students to become aware of the "historicity" of the plays and sources they were using as well as the critique they were generating online. More than just presenting a list of disembodied facts and findings to one another in a shared website, students would forge important connections between historical acts and literary representations as a negotiating group. By working together to create one cohesive entry, each group would be producing an interpretation that had to encompass each individual's take on the early modern period. In other words, students would be taking the same kind of postmodern intellectual risk of historians whose work "inevitably entails taking a stand on key theoretical issues" and is "an intrinsically theoretical as well as empirical enterprise" (Fulbrook, 2002: 4).

Wikis turned out to be the perfect medium through which to achieve these goals, thanks in large part to their easy-to-use editing functions and relatively low learning curve. They are also effective tools for collaboration in a variety of environments—an important feature considering that we would be working both with traditional and hybrid courses and would need to create a project that would be equally effective in either environment. The initial phase was conducted in the fall of 2007 in a Shakespeare Studies course, which took place in a traditional face-to-face environment. Early in the semester, the class was broken into twelve groups of three to four students, and each group was assigned an identity that would recur throughout the assigned texts. These identities included "Men," "Women," "Nobility," "Servants," "Religious Types," "Professionals," "Magicians and Witches," "Colonizer and Colonized," "Fools," "Poor Folk," and "Villains." Each group was then charged with creating a wiki based on the identity it had been assigned. The wikis would include an array of primary and secondary sources that would serve as a research guide—a customizable course-specific database—that this and future classes could consult and continue to develop.

An introductory session was dedicated to forming groups, setting up wiki accounts, and familiarizing students with the wiki's key editing functions. During this session, students were also given a list of expectations for their online creations (see Appendix 1.1). We intentionally created loose guidelines to allow the groups as much freedom as possible to explore and decide what should be included in their wikis while keeping the material task relevant. After some initial apprehension from students who, after having been instructed not to use wikis (or Wikipedia) as part of their research in previous courses, were surprised that we were asking them to create their own. However, this apprehension allowed for a useful discussion about the changing nature of research, scholarly communication, and intellectual presentation more generally. In creating a historicist study guide for future researchers, our students would be gaining an insider's view of scholarly production.

In addition to the early introductory session, a number of instruction sessions led by the librarian were scheduled throughout the semester. One of these classes was devoted to an overview of library resources (including key literature databases such as MLA International Bibliography) and another to finding primary sources with a focus on Early English Books Online (EEBO). The librarian's heightened presence in the classroom added to the information literacy element of the project. The instructor, like most, was not an information specialist and was too time-restrained by facilitating regular classroom practices (group discussions, formal lectures, impromptu acting) to concentrate on the intricacies of finding, assessing, and accessing materials appropriate for the wiki project. The primary database resources, such as MLA and EEBO, are highly specialized and required additional support by the librarian than what was allotted to him in the syllabus. Students sought his guidance on their own time through e-mail and real-time online consultation as well as in-person office visits. The building of a "big humanities project," even in the small-scale context of a single humanities class, required both the librarian and information literacy to become an integral part of the classroom's culture.

PROGRAM PLANNING

One of the other benefits of working in this medium is the general ease with which the project could be implemented and the low rate of problems related to access and control. After a comparison of several wiki services, we decided on the standard free version of PBworks, which comes with 2 gigabytes of storage and can facilitate up to 100 users. Other features are relatively common to the free versions of most wiki services, including easy setup, public and private options, e-mail notifications to help monitor changes, history pages, and some customizable features. The privacy controls allowed us to make the wikis viewable only to members of individual groups while they were in progress, then open them to the entire class at the end of the semester. Although an option to open the wikis to the public is also available, and there was some debate about this issue, most students seemed more comfortable keeping the project within the realm of their own class.

In addition to the class session described, the collaborating librarian was available throughout the semester to provide technical assistance. The goal was to make learning and using this technology as stress free as possible so that students could concentrate more fully on completing the project without worrying about technical and access issues. We also made an effort to include one student in each group who was comfortable with HTML coding which, though not required to use wikis effectively, is helpful for more advanced formatting.

Also worth mentioning is that a student who was enrolled in the first Shakespeare Studies course won an undergraduate research grant based on his own inquiry into the impact that wikis had on the research process from the student's perspective. He applied the money he received to the second phase of the project, conducted during a Milton Studies class, which we used to upgrade to a more advanced type of wikis. The upgrade included more customizability, more storage space, the ability to manipulate the HTML and add multimedia plug-ins. This improvement allowed students to create more sophisticated pages, many of which included embedded video and audio but, as will be discussed further on, was not always to the benefit to their scholarship.

LEARNING OUTCOMES

Given the interdisciplinary nature of the project, final assessment had to take each of our goals into account. This proved to be more challenging than initially anticipated, primarily because much of the value of the wikis is tied to the experience which, in turn, makes assessment more subjective than would be the case with a traditional research paper. While we considered these to be intellectual projects, we also recognized that they were more discovery than thesis based, which made it difficult to determine whether the students were actually constructing arguments rather than just exploring resources and points of view. While it was clear that most students were engaged with the project and thinking creatively—not only about how to build their wikis but also about how to seek and organize their resources—many of the wikis lacked a cohesive perspective or clear conclusions about what had been learned.

From a literary/historicist perspective, we were able to determine that the wikis effectively encouraged students to contend with many of challenges inherent in post-modern knowledge production. Our emphasis on primary source research and on challenging established interpretations of those resources helped students look beyond the Shakespeare they knew as a prepackaged cultural icon and appreciate him as a uniquely talented but always politically and socially invested individual. While these are goals that could also be achieved with a more traditional research project, we found that the fluid nature of wikis helped illustrate the equally fluid nature of literary and historical interpretation and, in turn, helped students recognize gaps inherent in knowledge acquisition. As a result, our students grappled not only with issues related to historical and literary interpretation but also with the breadth and scope of what they could hope to achieve in one semester. Echoing points made earlier by Schroeder and den Besten, our response was to focus on quality over completeness.

With respect to the information literacy component, we decided to assess the quality of sources used by conducting a citation analysis. There have been a number of recent citation studies that have drawn conclusions about the apparent decline in quality of undergraduate research, perhaps most notable is the Davis and Cohen (2001) study which analyzed research papers in an introductory-level microeconomics course at Cornell University from 1996 to 1999. Their findings showed a fairly significant decrease in the number of "traditional" scholarly sources (books and journals) used by students during this time. "In general, students cited fewer books in 1999 than they did in 1996. Comprising nearly one third (30%) of total citations in 1996, book citations dropped to less than one fifth (19%) in 1999. This translates into a decrease from 3.5 books per bibliography in 1996 to 2.2 in 1999, with the median citation number dropping from 3 to 1" (Davis and Cohen, 2001: 311). Although they did not analyze the type or quality of web documents cited, one might surmise that a general increase in Internet usage during this time played a factor in the shift away from books and journals. As a result, the authors conclude that, since students are "very literal" when it comes to requirements, instructors should be more prescriptive with the types of resources they would like to see students use (p. 313).

To test this hypothesis, Davis conducted a follow-up study in 2000 in which he implemented three recommendations based on results from his earlier study. Those recommendations were stricter guidelines about what types of sources students should be allowed to use, the creation of scholarly portals to guide students to "authoritative" sources, and more instruction about how to critically evaluate sources (Davis, 2002: 53). However, even after implementing his recommendations, Davis's second study yielded no new results:

> The results of the 2000 update suggest that the professor's verbal instructions had little (if any) effect on improving the scholarly component of research papers. The number of traditional scholarly materials cited this year was similar to previous years. Bibliographies grew, but only in respect to additional web sites and newspapers. When viewed as a percentage of total citations, the "scholarliness" of bibliographies continued to decline. (p. 59)

Davis's response to these disappointing results was to suggest that "a possible crisis in undergraduate scholarship is at hand" and that librarians and professors should work together more closely and "provide more clearly defined expectations in their assignments" (p. 59). While a full analysis of the state of undergraduate scholarship, especially as it pertains to information literacy instruction, is beyond the scope of this chapter, it is our contention that the best approach is to provide targeted, prescriptive instruction while continuing to promote one of the key components of information literacy: self-reliance. As the culture of information continues to evolve and become more complex, and lines between library resources and the Internet become increasingly transparent, distinctions between what counts as "scholarly" and "nonscholarly" will also become less obvious. In such an environment, emphasis should always be placed on the ability to seek, access, and assess quality information, but this should be done in a way that accounts for the wide variety of new and emerging sources of information.

Our analysis of the first semester's results found that, while the average number of citations in our project is on par with the Davis and Cohen study (12.3 per wiki to their final result of 11.9 per paper in 1999), the ratio of "scholarly" materials used (books and articles) in each project was much different. While Davis and Cohen saw a decline from 30 to 19 percent in three years, we recorded a much higher 43 percent of total citations from books and 22 percent from articles, for a combined total of 65 percent. After weeding out books and articles that were from popular or otherwise nonscholarly publishers, we were left with 48 percent from scholarly books and articles. In addition, 9 out of the 12 groups consulted primary sources for a total number of 13 citations among those 9 groups. We included these in the scholarly category primarily because they demonstrated proficiency using an academic database (EEBO). Along with a few academic web citations, this brought our final scholarly versus non-scholarly totals to 59 percent versus 41 percent.

Web citations in general proved to be the greatest area in need of improvement. Of all citations recorded, 24.5 percent were from the Internet, which averaged to about three Web citations per wiki. This number is not overwhelming, especially considering we were working in an online medium, but only 4 of these 36 citations were academic (see Appendix 1.2 for a complete breakdown of the citations).

While these results were encouraging, especially for the initial phase of the project, there were several areas we sought to improve upon in future classes. Key among those were the following: greater emphasis on substance over style, more evenness of content throughout the wikis, and more pointed instruction regarding such areas as database and catalog use. We also decided to require that all wikis have a stated focal point that, while it did not necessarily have to be a formal thesis statement, would be something around which the wikis could be built, thereby improving focus and evenness and making assessment easier as well. In addition, we enhanced our instruction program by adding two informal workshop-style sessions toward the end of the semester so that students would be free to ask questions that were more specific to their own projects. These changes were implemented during the next year in three more classes: Milton Studies, Renaissance Women Writers, and Women in Shakespeare. The first two of these—Milton Studies and Renaissance Women Writers—posed an extra challenge because they were conducted in a hybrid format in which the students met once weekly in person and once online. This alternative classroom structure would test the ability of wikis to serve as a tool for collaboration and extend the boundaries of the traditional classroom setting.

We thought that the hybrid format would create extra challenges to what we had already started, but the wikis, in fact, proved to be as effective in this environment as they were in the more traditional face-to-face setting. Further, our citation analysis of the final semester shows that there was a continued progression both in the type and quality of resources being used by students in both the Milton Studies course and subsequent classes. More specifically, the results show positive gains in the number of scholarly books, articles, and primary sources consulted and significant decreases in the number of general Internet citations and nonscholarly books. These outcomes show that, with the adjustments described, we had begun to strike a better balance between embedding research methodology into the fabric of the course while maintaining an open, explorative environment. However, it is worth noting that although these numbers do provide a snapshot of the research done in this class, there will always be a more experiential component in which users add value and meaning through their interaction both with the resources and the wiki itself.

ASSESSMENT OF ONLINE LEARNING

When considering wikis or any other Web 2.0 application as a learning tool, it is important to think about how these technologies differ from other course management systems, such as Blackboard and WebCT, as well as the potential impact they will have on learning outcomes. As previously stated, we chose to employ wikis primarily because of the ease with which they can be implemented and their easy-to-use "what you see is what you get" (WYSIWYG) editing functions. As such, wikis can capably facilitate collaboration and, based on the results described, are equally effective in traditional face-to-face classes as in hybrid and online environments. While other course management systems may include some of these features, such as discussion boards where students can respond to one another's posts, students in these settings don't feel the same sense of ownership that they do when they are an active contributor to a blog or wiki. As Barbara Schroeder points out, "Course management systems are structured for teacher-created and directed content" (Schroeder, 2009: 183). In other words, while students working in Blackboard may be able to create and facilitate their own discussions, there is always the perception that their work is being monitored and, to some extent, controlled by the teacher. The instructor may, of course, monitor the development of a wiki as well, but the perceptions of space and ownership vary greatly from one to the other. The decision to employ wikis "also requires a shift in pedagogical perspectives and theoretical frameworks, with learning being more student-centered" (Schroeder, 2009: 189).

Yoany Beldarrain speaks to this point when she states that "technology is responsible for distorting the concept of distance between learner and instructor, and enabled learners to access education at any time and from any place" (Beldarrain, 2006: 139). She further adds, "Teaching models that integrate technologies such as blogs and wikis may afford more learning control, and thus be more effective at delivering instructional strategies that support knowledge construction" (p. 142). To accomplish this shift, greater emphasis needs to be placed on customization rather than on a prescriptive mode of delivering course content. Bruns and Humphreys note,

> Much of our educational system remains based on the idea that the teacher/lecturer will impart their knowledge to the student through a one-way communication system, such as lectures or text books. For reasons of convenience more than pedagogy, academic delivery is often structured in a linear fashion—papers present an argument which builds from instruction to conclusion; subjects offer a series of lectures which present content in weekly installments over the course of a semester. (Bruns and Humphreys, 2005)

Teachers, they argue, still play an important role in the realm of the wiki, but "this kind of pedagogical design is based on the idea that, in order to learn, students have to create." They add, "This kind of pedagogy is construction based, in that it builds on existing knowledge of the learner as well as interaction with the environment" (Bruns and Humphreys, 2005).

These are all points we considered seriously as we designed and began to implement our project. As stated, two of our classes—Milton Studies and Renaissance Women Writers—were taught in the hybrid format in which classes met in person once a week and online once a week. We felt strongly that WebCT, the course management system that was already in place, would not be sufficient to meet our goals. Projects conducted in this sort of environment are bound to a fairly rigid template that does not allow the same level of flexibility and creativity that we were trying to emphasize. Here it is worth recalling points made earlier by Robin Farabaugh, who drew a distinction between open-source technology and other types of course management software that "teach us their language" (Farabaugh, 2007: 44). She also made the argument that "language meaning, like learning, is influenced not only by the words we use, but the forms we use to contain them" (p. 54). Providing students the power to create and customize their own learning spaces, we hoped, would encourage them to take more ownership of their projects than would typically be the case with another course management system, which, in turn, would provide us with some insights into what students value as emerging researchers and humanist scholars. There was a concern that our students in the hybrid courses would view the wikis as an add-on to WebCT and that working with two different technologies in the same class might create a whole new set of problems. The wikis proved to be flexible enough to alleviate anxieties that may have existed early on, and students came to view them as a bridge between the face-to-face and online components of these courses. As a result, and as was noted in our citation analysis, there was no perceptible difference in the overall quality of the wikis that were created in the hybrid class as compared to the traditional face-to-face classes.

Having said that, we did observe that many of our students struggled to break free from the familiar research-paper model and adopt a new style of writing that would be more appropriate for an online medium. Even though we made the guidelines flexible enough to encourage them to make the wiki space their own, most of the groups settled on a style that was based on the one wiki with which they were most familiar: Wikipedia. The result was that most of the wikis were constructed as long, single-paged encyclopedic entries. This approach is not only familiar to anyone who has read a Wikipedia entry but is one that has proven to be an effective way to create pages that can be easily built upon and revised by other users. As a result, while we were happy with the overall quality of the resources being used, many of the wikis contained some of the same faults for which Wikipedia is often criticized. Setting aside the debatable issue of reliability, other concerns we faced were a lack of an authentic voice, a clear point of view, unevenness, and an occasional lack of audience awareness. These particular issues stem from the collaborative nature of the project and the way the workload was divided by section, which led to entries that were not quite as consistently developed as we would have liked.

TEXT AND IMAGE

One key way in which the wikis created for this project differed from Wikipedia entries is that our students made much greater use of images. But this was interesting not so much for the number of images used (there were, in fact, images used in just about every section of every wiki) but for the limited range of those images. The group focusing on the Nobility in the first Shakespeare Studies class, for example, chose to include images of Elizabeth II's bejeweled crowns and lush nineteenth- and early-twentieth-century paintings, such as John Waterhouse's *Miranda*; in other words, they featured works that were visually pleasing but ultimately did not support their textual analysis of what they saw as the playwright's struggle to appease the crown. Many groups chose to include images of movie posters featuring contemporary adaptations, such as *She's the Man* (2006) and *10 Things I Hate About You* (1999), both of which fail to illustrate their historically based arguments and speak instead to the sustained and general interest in Shakespeare's works today. Ideally, students would engage with both text and image to develop more accurate representations of each identity, but visually, the result of the final wikis is one of topical disconnection and, to our surprise, sometimes degradation. The first page of the wiki dedicated to women was, at the last moment, emended with a cartoonish representation of Shakespeare under which one student in the group added the comment, "Yes, he was just that sexy," a superfluous if not comical remark made as if the student recognized that the image of the male author misrepresented their topic and even devalued the analytic work therein.

The apparent disconnect between text and image created an unexpected and interesting dilemma. Our initial reaction was that many groups had fallen into the trap of emphasizing style over substance. Many English majors have primarily been trained in textual rather than visual analysis, which is still an emerging area of English studies. This problem was most apparent during the Milton Studies course in which we received a grant to upgrade the wiki service we were using to a version that allowed for more customization. During this semester, many of the groups did some creative work with the wikis, including embedding videos, slideshows, and even acting out portions of *Paradise Lost* for inclusion in their wiki. Although these endeavors showed a great deal of creativity and interest in the course, they veered from the original intention of the project: that the wikis would serve as research guides both for this and future classes. This issue demonstrates how our students were both negotiating this new technology and struggling to define an appropriate audience for the work they were creating. For many, the Internet is primarily a site to engage in social interaction and the consumption of popular culture, a place to converse with peers rather than serious researchers with whom they may not yet feel authorized to speak. Notably, most pictures were situated throughout the pages in the upper halves of each field or used as dividers between topic sections—those places where a viewer would immediately encounter new written analysis and might expect, magazine style, an image to hook their interest. If, as John Zuern suggests, "the most complicated and ultimately most productive aspect of the transition from word to image in teaching is the capacity of images to do more than simply restate verbal messages, to resist, in fact, any mere repetition of the verbal statement," then the images the students chose resisted the sociopolitical analysis and the historical temporality in which they were urged to engage (Zuern, 2004: 51). For the students' imagined audience, images suggestive of a nostalgic sense of heraldry, lovelorn young heroines, and contemporary Hollywood actors, instead of being mere decoration, had the power to attract potential readers by maintaining some of the sentiment with which Shakespeare is popularly associated.

These issues get back to a point made earlier about ownership and the shifting roles of teacher and learner in these new spaces. Especially in the turbulent early stages of this project, we were able to observe our students negotiate the terms of this new medium and experiment with a less linear and less thesis-based form of writing than they were used to. As M. C. Morgan states in his notes on the rhetoric of wikis, "Writers need to unlearn, relearn, or adapt hard won practices from paper" (Morgan, 2004: under "Introduction"); wikis, he continues, "encourage and support a dialogical, collaborative, essayistic or associative rhetoric over a monological, thesis/support rhetoric. The openness of the wiki makes it difficult to lock it down to a final, authoritative, complete, single-voiced version." Where students have been trained to defer to the authoritative ideas of experts, the flexible "perpetually beta" nature of wikis effectively illustrates the fluid and dynamic nature of knowledge itself. Primarily by encouraging students to recognize and fill in gaps, wikis encourage students to take an active role in knowledge production and acquisition. As Bruns and Humphreys point out, this differs from other online course management systems in that "its social, interactive, collaborative and dynamic features encourage learning in more complex ways than an 'e-learning content delivery'-style application can" (2005). One of the key differences between the two, again, is the sense of ownership that students feel. As an anecdotal case in point, students continued to add to their wikis even after the semester had ended and final grades had been submitted, thereby expanding the learning experience, and the practice of information literacy, beyond a single course or semester.

CONCLUSION

It is our hope that this case study can serve as a model for librarian–faculty teams interested in collaborating on embedded information literacy projects, especially those that employ Web 2.0 technologies. We have attempted to highlight some of our own successes as well as the challenges we faced during the two years of this project, with particular emphasis on issues that are relevant to the humanities. We discovered that the prevalence of these new technologies and the emergence of online collections of digitized primary sources and other nontraditional research materials is impacting how humanist scholars conduct research, which, in turn, has created new opportunities for interdisciplinary collaboration. Librarians can seize upon these advancements to move forward new areas of expertise and help alter the landscape across the curriculum and challenge preconceived notions of authority and control. In so doing, we can impact the next generation of humanities scholars who will enter the profession with a greater degree of proficiency both in using these collaborative technologies and in navigating the ever-changing world of information. However, these changes can be hard-fought, as our notions of authority and expertise are firmly entrenched throughout the academy. Cathy Davidson's point about "collaboration by difference" is worth mentioning one last time. While we were encouraging our own students to read literature through a historical lens as a way to unlock classic texts and open them to a greater array of possibilities, we did not always follow this model ourselves. Pursuing collaboration from a point of difference rather than consensus, however, helped us rethink our preconceived notions of authority and expertise and ultimately allowed our project to flourish.

REFERENCES

Badke, William B. 2005. "Can't Get No Respect: Helping Faculty to Understand the Educational Power of Information Literacy." *The Reference Librarian* 43, no. 89: 63–80.

Bass, Randy, and Theresa Schlafly. 2009. "Participatory Learning and the New Humanities: An Interview with Cathy Davidson." Academic Commons, January 7. http://www.academic commons.org.

Beldarrain, Yoany. 2006. "Distance Education Trends: Integrating New Technologies to Foster Student Interaction and Collaboration." *Distance Education* 27, no. 2 (August): 139–153.

Brockman, William S., Laura Neumann, Carol L. Palmer, and Tonyia J. Tidline. 2001. "Scholarly Work in the Humanities and the Evolving Information Environment." Washington, DC: Digital Library Federation and the Council on Library and Information Resources.

Bruns, Axel, and Sal Humphreys. 2005. "Wikis in Teaching and Assessment: The M/Cyclopedia Project." International Symposium on Wikis, San Diego, CA (25–32). http://delivery.acm.org/10.1145/1110000/1104976/p25-bruns.pdf?key1=1104976&key2=0706317621&coll=GUIDE&dl=GUIDE&CFID=79501342&CFTOKEN=76294818.

Calandra, Brendan, and John Lee. 2005. "The Digital History and Pedagogy Project: Creating an Interpretative/Pedagogical Historical Website." *The Internet & Higher Education* 8, no. 4: 323–333.

Conteh-Morgan, Miriam. 2004. "Reading African Women's Writing: The Role of Librarians in Expanding the Canon." *The Reference Librarian* 42, no. 87/88 (October): 163–178.

Davidson, Cathy. 2008. "Humanities 2.0: Promises, Perils, Predictions." *Publications of the Modern Language Association of America* 123, no. 3 (May): 707–717.

Davis, Philip M. 2002. "The Effect of the Web on Undergraduate Citation Behavior: A 2000 Update." *College and Research Libraries* 63, no.1 (January): 53–60.

Davis, Philip M. and Suzanne A. Cohen. 2001. "The Effect of the Web on Undergraduate Citation Behavior 1996-1999." *Journal of the American Society for Information Science and Technology* 52, no. 4 (February): 309–314.

Farabaugh, Robin. 2007. "The Isle Is Full of Noises: Using Wiki Software to Establish a Discourse Community in a Shakespeare Classroom." *Language Awareness* 16, no. 1: 41–56.

Fulbrook, Mary. 2002. *Historical Theory.* London: Routledge.

Hardesty, Larry. 1995. "Faculty Culture and Bibliographic Instruction: An Exploratory Analysis." *Library Trends* 44, no. 2 (Fall): 339–368.

Hilton, James. 2006. "The Future for Higher Education: Sunrise or Perfect Storm?" *EDUCAUSE Review* 41, no. 2 (March/April): 58–71.

Morgan, M. C. 2004. "Notes Towards a Rhetoric of Wiki." MCMorgan.org. http://mcmorgan.org/papers_and_presentations/notes_towards_a_rhetoric_of/.

Schroeder, Barbara. 2009. "Within the Wiki: Best Practices for Educators." *AACE Journal* 17, no. 3 (July): 181–197.

Schroeder, Ralph, and Matthijs den Besten. 2008. "Literary Sleuths Online: E-Research Collaboration on the Pynchon Wiki." *Information, Communication & Society* 11, no. 2 (July): 167–187.

Thompson Klein, Julie. 1991. *Interdisciplinarity: History, Theory, and Practice.* Northumberland, UK: Bloodaxe Books.

Zuern, John. 2004. "Diagram, Dialogue, Dialectic: Visual Explanations and Visual Rhetoric in the Teaching of Literary Theory." In *Visual Media and the Humanities: A Pedagogy of Representation,* edited by Kecia Driver McBride, 47–73. Knoxville: The University of Tennessee Press.

Appendix 1.1. Expectations for Online Creations

What You'll Be Doing

Together, you'll be creating a Shakespeare wiki that will work toward gathering and presenting information pertaining to William Shakespeare, his works, his life and times, and especially those social identities discussed throughout this course.

Teams of two or three will be assigned and begin to meet early in the semester. Each team will choose a topic relating to Elizabethan identities and begin to plan and craft a wiki that gives others in this class information and insight into your topic. You will, in fewer words, become experts in an area.

Minimum Criteria for This Project

- A Descriptive Title

- A Definition of Your Topic

  Do this last, after you have a chance to digest all the information that you encounter. Alternately, you can choose to create a preliminary definition but plan to continuously edit this as you become the area specialists throughout the course of your readings.

- A Discussion of Textual Occurrences

  Identify your topic and its occurrences throughout the plays we read (and any others, if you are familiar with works beyond those in this syllabus). You may wish to expand upon your definition by explaining your topic's importance in these plays.

- Historical Context

  Connect your readers to history. Information from Early English Books Online, or EEBO (one of the premier databases that makes all sorts of early modern texts on all sorts of subjects available to contemporary readers), other library databases, and the Internet can be used. Be creative with your research. You may provide direct links, post information and pictures and sound bytes from different sites, quote directly from print sources. *This wiki is limited only by your imagination and the time you spend in developing your project.*

- A List of Works Cited

  Keep in accordance with UCF's rules on academic integrity. If you quote or embed any information from the web or a printed source, you'll have to show where it came from.

- A List for Further Study

  Your wiki will be used as a research guide by students in this and future classes. Give them sites to visit and sources to use. Remember that you are the experts on your subject and you want to send your students off in the right direction as they begin to think about the topic you've spent all semester developing.

Appendix 1.2. Rate of Change			

1st semester = 12 wikis
4th semester = 9 wikis

Breakdown in percentages

Citation Source	1st	4th	Change
Book Citations	42.9	40.6	−2.3
Scholarly	27.9	31.3	+3.4
Nonscholarly	15.0	9.4	−5.6
Article Citations	21.8	24.4	+2.6
Scholarly	19.7	23.8	+4.1
Newspaper	0.7	0.6	−0.1
Magazine	1.4	0	−1.4
Primary Sources	8.8	15.0	+6.2
Internet Citations	24.5	13.1	−11.4
Scholarly	2.7	2.5	−0.2
Nonscholarly	21.8	10.6	−11.2
Other	2.0	6.9	+4.9
Scholarly	0	1.9	+1.9

- Scholarly books were defined as those published by a university press or a known academic publisher. If this could not be determined, books were placed in the "other" or "nonscholarly" category.
- Scholarly articles were defined as those published in peer-reviewed journals. No distinction between articles accessed in print or in databases was made, nor did we rank the articles according to quality or currency.
- Scholarly Internet sites were identified first by those ending in an .edu, then double-checked to make sure the links were still active and led to an original document intended for scholarly purposes. We did not rank or rate the popular web citations.
- Assigned texts or other common editions of the works being studied were eliminated from the breakdown, as were any texts that were simply listed in the bibliography but not referenced in the wikis themselves.

2

Reusable Learning Objects

Developing Online Information Literacy Instruction through Collaborative Design

Matthew C. Sylvain, Kari Mofford,
Elizabeth Lehr, and Jeannette E. Riley

INTRODUCTION

The University of Massachusetts Dartmouth, located in southeastern Massachusetts, offers undergraduate and graduate programs to a residential and commuter population. These programs are primarily traditional face-to-face courses, but increasingly programs and courses are offered as blended and/or fully online classes. Through its Division of Professional and Continuing Education, UMass Dartmouth seeks to expand its online course offerings to reach nontraditional students who are interested in continuing their education but unable to pursue courses on campus due to work or family obligations. In addition, the university seeks to reach out to on-campus students with anytime, anywhere instruction.

The university's efforts to develop online programs and courses for both nontraditional and traditional students create an imperative for the provision of online information literacy instruction. A multidisciplinary team of faculty and librarians, along with the UMass Dartmouth Instructional Development (ID) team, came together to develop new delivery mechanisms for information literacy instruction and a model for their implementation. A central component of this effort was the collaborative design, development, and implementation of reusable learning objects (RLOs) focused on information literacy skills in the online classroom.

The RLO creation process was driven by the formation of a new Liberal Arts (LAR) program and major that includes information literacy outcomes. Our approach to assist students in meeting these outcomes encouraged visual, auditory, and active learning, while our implementation model recognized the importance of supplementing the RLOs with activities that connect librarians with students, such as synchronous instruction and research log monitoring and assistance. This comprehensive design energized faculty and librarians alike, leading us to develop a collaborative process that can result in more effective online information literacy instruction. This chapter focuses on the importance of our collaboration in creating and implementing a series of RLOs, as well as the infrastructure we developed to integrate the RLOs and information literacy instruction more effectively into the online classroom environment.

RELATED LITERATURE

In their statement regarding information literacy instruction, the Association of College and Research Libraries (ACRL) asserts that the "challenge for those promoting information literacy in distance education courses is to develop a comparable range of experiences in learning about information resources as are offered on traditional campuses. Information literacy competencies for distance learning students should be comparable to those for 'on campus' students" (ACRL, 2000: under "Information Literacy and Higher Education"). Yet, as a review of the literature regarding faculty–librarian collaboration to teach information literacy reveals, there are many common concerns in the quest to provide comparable outreach to distance-learning students.

For example, some faculty may assume that the act of researching and writing a paper will lead to information literacy skills (McGuinness, 2006); at the same time, there is the assumption that if a student is in an online class, then he or she is computer literate (Owens and Bozeman, 2009). These assumptions are complicated by the world of increasing information on the web and in library databases, which makes it increasingly difficult for students to locate and evaluate information (Miller and Bell, 2005); and reaching students when they are studying and need information literacy assistance, often late at night, has become imperative (Backhus and Summey, 2003). Moreover, teaching skills to students a librarian might never see in person affects comfort level on both sides and requires a certain degree of technological competency (Gandhi, 2003). In short, technology has changed the library-student relationship (Figa, Bone, and MacPherson, 2009) and created the need for faculty and librarians to move beyond the traditional single class session to an integrated and more collaborative model (Miller and Bell, 2005).

Additional barriers impede effective informational literacy instruction online. In a 2005 survey within the California State University system, Pamela Jackson found that "librarians reported frequently collaborating with faculty to provide in-person library instruction, but almost never for courses on the LMS [learning management system]" (2007: 456). Facilitating library instruction within a LMS requires significant time and training, as well as faculty and librarian commitment. As Jackson reports, barriers to online library instruction include "the librarian–faculty relationship, meaning faculty buy in, cooperation, and willingness to include information literacy; time, staffing, and funding for the library to create content; and the technology learning curve for librarians" (2007: 457).

Yet, simultaneously, there is much discussion about the merits of a faculty, librarian, and administrator collaboration to provide quality library and information literacy instruction for students. As Shank and Bell point out, students gain access to library resources and librarian assistance; faculty save time and develop meaningful collaborations with librarians as librarian instruction moves beyond the "traditional model" of "offering as-needed, outside-of-class student assistance and the one-shot model of a single library instruction session" (2006: under "Conclusion"). Online learning experiences and tutorials "offer flexibility for use within course instruction or as stand-alone modules" (Blummer and Kritskaya, 2009: 200). Such tutorials are reusable over a period of time; thus, effective use of instructional technologies enables both faculty and librarians to manage their time more efficiently (Miller and Bell, 2005; Mardis and Ury, 2008). Most important, informational literacy is "often viewed as a library concern in which librarians are responsible for program development and instruction," which points to the growing need to "integrate the roles of faculty as full partners in a collaborative endeavor" with librarians (Mackey and Jacobson, 2005: 140). More than ever, faculty–librarian collaboration is essential to developing and delivering effective information literacy instruction online.

INSTITUTIONAL CONTEXT

The University of Massachusetts Dartmouth traces its roots to 1895, when the Massachusetts legislature chartered the New Bedford Textile School and the Bradford Durfee Textile School in Fall River. Over the years, these schools evolved and merged to create the Southeastern Massachusetts Institute of Technology (SMTI) and later Southeastern Massachusetts University (SMU). In 1991, SMU entered the University of Massachusetts system as the University of Massachusetts Dartmouth. Today, UMass Dartmouth is a comprehensive institution serving 7,749 undergraduates and 1,683 graduate students from 37 states and 35 countries. It is an important intellectual catalyst for regional economic, social, and cultural development in a region where only "16.4 percent of the region's residents have earned a bachelor's degree or higher compared to 33.2 percent statewide" (Center for Policy Analysis, 2004: 11).

Currently, 21 percent of the students entering UMass Dartmouth each year transfer from other institutions or are individuals who, after a hiatus in their education, wish to complete their degrees. The transfer and returning students' context for continuing their learning significantly differs from that of the entering first-year students because they not only bring previous higher education experience but also personal and workplace situations that influence their access to learning. Underemployed working adults in the region who seek to better their employment situations often find pursuit of a degree difficult given family and job commitments. The university's structure continues to assume that all students are a version of the stereotypical college freshman. This, of course, is not the case, as approximately one-fifth of the university's students do not matriculate directly out of high school. Nevertheless, university class schedules, faculty teaching formats, and student support services are built upon assumptions that often do not provide appropriate learning contexts for many nontraditional students.

It is in this context that the university sought to transform the bachelor of arts in humanities/social sciences degree in ways that meet the needs of the regional population through an innovative format and structure. This initiative, funded in part through an Alfred P. Sloan Foundation grant, created a new program to increase access to a degree completion program and improve an individual's economic stability. The revised program, renamed the liberal arts major, consists of online, blended, and web-enhanced classes and includes information literacy–related learning outcomes. As stipulated in the grant proposal, these outcomes would be achieved with the assistance of reusable learning objects that students could access anytime, anywhere.

INTERDISCIPLINARY CONTEXT

The librarian–faculty collaboration described in this chapter focuses on a specific course in a multidisciplinary major. Liberal Arts 201: Introduction to Studies Across the Disciplines is a foundation course in the liberal arts major at UMass Dartmouth. Major completion requirements include LAR 201, LAR 401 (Capstone Seminar in Multidisciplinary Studies), 15 credit hours in a social science concentration, and 15 credit hours in a humanities concentration.

An English Department faculty member experienced in interdisciplinary studies wrote the LAR 201 curriculum and first offered the course in a face-to-face (FtF) classroom in the spring of 2008. The intention was that the course would go fully online immediately, doing so in summer 2008. The transition from FtF to the online environment involved a new faculty member, Elizabeth Lehr, who reconceptualized the delivery of the coursework for the online environment. Several challenges were quickly identified. First, in the online environment, student skills or the lack of skills are accentuated. For example, students who are well organized perform well online because they can pace and schedule their work effectively. However, students lacking organization fall behind more quickly than in a classroom where they face the professor regularly.

Second, the FtF classroom environment facilitates the building of analytical and critical thinking skills through discussion and allows faculty to ascertain how well students comprehend the material, although some students rarely or never speak in class. Based on previous experience with online teaching, we knew that classroom discussion might be difficult to reproduce when not face to face and is almost fully reliant on discussion board postings. However, our online discussion board instructions require every student to contribute to a minimum standard set by the faculty member; thus, participation is evenly distributed among all students. As a result, faculty can easily identify students who are not learning. However, capturing the way classroom discussion teaches critical thinking is problematic online as the process is dependent on teaching online students to post developed responses typically not found in FtF discussions. For early-semester discussion boards, students receive formative feedback in terms of the substantive nature and mechanics of their postings, as well as summative feedback about content. They are taught how to interact effectively with classmates by commenting on others' postings. These primary concerns, organizational and comprehension skills, along with the student demographics described, guided the development of LAR 201 online.

As the foundation course for the major, LAR 201 introduces students to the idea that they are not only studying in more than one discipline, but that all disciplines differ in their approaches to research and ways of thinking. In the course objectives, we stipulate that we want students to be able to:

- Identify features of content, principle, and practice which characterize humanities and social sciences disciplines and which distinguish them from each other.
- Identify concerns and methods that these disciplines have in common and ways in which bringing multiple perspectives to bear can increase knowledge about a subject, inquiry, or field of study.
- Compare disciplinary perspectives by addressing subjects and inquiries through multiple disciplines in sequence.
- Identify and use the basic text, graphic, and material research tools of these disciplines, including print and online databases, scholarship, and collections.
- Use a wide range of electronic resources to explore subjects, ideas and arguments, and supporting data and materials.
- Write an entry-level academic research paper that uses two distinct disciplinary perspectives, one social science and one humanities, in a parallel discussion investigating what can be learned about the subject through each.

Early in the class, students are asked to think of themselves as scholars and to consider the different strategies they must enact to move between courses in the social sciences and humanities and for courses that integrate the two fields. We want them to identify the principles and practices of their two fields and learn to engage in a multidisciplinary approach to the development of knowledge. Additional course objectives include conducting research that evaluates and employs primary and secondary resources effectively and using appropriate disciplinary conventions for citation and documentation. These focus areas necessarily require not just an introduction to the range of library services, but also detailed instructional support to teach students how to use and search databases effectively and efficiently, how to evaluate sources, and how to integrate sources effectively into one's own work.

Students bring a variety of goals to liberal arts as a major. Many are aspiring public school teachers; others focus on the strengths a liberal arts education will provide for their as yet undetermined future employment. Online students are often full-time workers who hope for improvement in their employment situations, but some are traditional students fitting LAR 201 into busy schedules. For nontraditional students, many of whom have been away from school for several years if not longer, the range of library databases and online services may be overwhelming. Regardless of the students' goals and prior experiences, however, the concept of both multi- and interdisciplinary studies is new to them. The first concern, then, is to help students resituate themselves in an interdisciplinary environment.

As students advance through LAR 201, they are asked to read essays and journal articles in both disciplines, noting where the authors integrate more than one discipline. Discussion boards offer a venue for talking about the readings, as they examine how research is performed and reported. At first, students research and write about the disciplines separately, as they work to decipher the ways in which the social sciences and humanities differ and what they share in common.

Later in the semester, students are asked to write a final paper that incorporates both disciplines and synthesizes information from research sources into well-delineated understandings of both disciplines, as well as a single multidisciplinary merging of ideas. Students must be able to identify how all three perspectives are demonstrated in their writing and thinking about their chosen topic.

The final paper, as designed by Lehr and others in the program, includes the requirement to find and analyze a primary text in the student's humanities discipline, to find and use other authors' primary research in both the humanities and social science disciplines to support the analysis, to synthesize an understanding of the topic from the research, and finally, to reflect on the process of multi- and interdisciplinary approaches to knowledge building. To ensure success with this paper, students first need to review, and in most cases learn for the first time, how to identify primary and secondary source documents, use online library resources, and consult with a reference librarian. The model we developed utilizes the library's information literacy RLOs as part of a comprehensive instruction model aimed at helping students attain the necessary information literacy skills.

DISCUSSION OF FACULTY–LIBRARIAN COLLABORATION

It was clear from the outset that developing the RLOs would require a team approach as they required the expertise of librarians, faculty, and instructional technology support staff. Professor Jeannette E. Riley, Liberal Arts Program Director, solicited the participation of faculty associated with the LAR program and a social sciences librarian, Matthew C. Sylvain, as well as members of the Instructional Development team. Sylvain's selection was due to his experience in information literacy instruction and in using Camtasia, a screen and video capture software. This program allows users to record activity on screen and include voice-over narration. It is commonly used by librarians to produce online tutorials.

Prior to the initial team meeting, Riley and Sylvain invited newly hired humanities librarian Kari Mofford to join the team. This decision brought in additional library expertise from the humanities, which helped to address the diverse needs of the multidisciplinary program.

The deliberate selection of librarians, faculty, and instructional technologists created a team capable of designing a comprehensive RLO development plan. The faculty understood the program's learning objectives, student demographics, curricula plan, and course rollout schedule. Librarians contributed their understanding of information literacy and how best to impart the requisite skills and knowledge. The ID team brought necessary technical and design assistance to the creation of the RLOs. With the team finalized, and the broad constructs of the plan outlined, the team was ready to design and build the first RLOs for the fully online version of LAR 201.

Although initially designed to impart information literacy knowledge in a fully online environment, the team recognized that the RLOs would also have applications in the FtF and blended classrooms. This recognition required the development of versatile tools that faculty could use in multiple ways to reinforce or supplement FtF lessons. As the strategic and collaborative process evolved, it also became apparent that the RLOs could serve as an active learning mechanism in the classroom (e.g., librarians and/or faculty could use personal response systems, such as i-clickers, with a self-mastery component to stimulate conversation and gauge student understanding). The team also decided the RLOs should be available from different access points, including the campus's Blackboard Vista LMS, the ID team's faculty resource site, the library's website, and library subject and course guides.

Design and Development

Following an initial team meeting, Mofford and Sylvain drafted, revised, and prioritized a listing of tutorial topics and their respective learning outcomes. Top priorities included primary research in the humanities and social sciences and advanced searching skills, such as using Boolean operators and truncation and reading citations in an online database. The overarching goal was to help students locate and identify appropriate sources in academic databases and on the web. Evaluating Internet sources and differentiating between scholarly and popular sources were also identified as key goals. Tutorial development was then prioritized based primarily on student learning needs and the delivery of content and assignments in the course itself. Most important, the team aimed to create a series of tutorials that would be integrated into the classroom systematically, using a building-block approach to developing information-literate students. The tutorials would be used in LAR 201 to enable faculty teaching upper-level courses to build on a uniform foundation.

The first tutorial developed covers identifying primary and secondary sources. Mofford and Sylvain collaborated to create the tutorial content using Camtasia, which offered several elements deemed vital to the project, among them ease of integrating audio and visual instructions, closed-captioning for hearing-impaired students, and the ability to screencast database demonstrations.

Since the project was grant-funded, all work for the tutorial had to be completed outside normal work hours to comply with university policy. For librarians who typically stay late to catch up with day-to-day responsibilities, this required weekend meet-ups. In theory, this was not a problem; in practice, the time lag between meetings required that Mofford and Sylvain relearn some of the technological skills they had used at a previous meeting. This situation slowed the development of the tutorial and highlighted the fact that it was advantageous to dedicate blocks of time to the creation process. This realization changed the workflow as they dedicated larger blocks of time to developing the tutorials independently while reviewing and editing each other's work. After they finalized a draft, the tutorial was shared with the team as well as with external reviewers, which included other librarians and faculty.

The ID team's role in developing the tutorials also evolved during the early stages of the project. Initially Mofford and Sylvain viewed the ID team as a resource of last resort, leading them to spend time troubleshooting technical issues that could have been devoted to developing content. Through closer collaboration, the ID team provided valuable assistance with developing and editing audio files, integrating images, providing XML editing for the self-mastery components, and creating a repository in Blackboard Vista from which faculty could download the tutorials. In addition, the ID team developed the instructional materials to teach faculty how to access and use the repository. Thus, the evolution of the development process ultimately drew upon the particular skills each team member offered: curricular content from the faculty; information literacy instruction from the librarians; and technical and design assistance from the ID team. This model not only proved successful for completing the remaining tutorials but also created a more efficient development process and timeline.

Pilot Launch

Upon completing the RLOs, the team conducted a pilot launch by asking five faculty members to participate in testing the tutorials and self-mastery components. The selected faculty taught six distinct courses in liberal arts disciplines: English literature, education, liberal arts, political science (two courses), and women's studies. These courses largely reflected the content taught within the LAR major. All participating faculty used the university-supported Blackboard Vista, which allowed the RLOs to be fully integrated into course sites. The ID team provided technical support to those faculty members who needed help embedding the tutorials in the class sites.

Sylvain met with faculty members individually to discuss integrating the RLOs into their class syllabi. He worked with faculty on issues such as when to release the tutorial to the students (e.g., before or after an instruction session), which tutorials would best address learning needs, and how the faculty member wished to use the self-mastery component (e.g., percent of questions students needed to answer correctly in order to complete the tutorial).

At Riley's suggestion, Sylvain tracked RLO use in a spreadsheet, which recorded the titles used by class, research assignments, methods of integrating the tutorials into the classes, incentives for student participation, student completion rate, and use of the self-mastery components. The decision to track use in the spreadsheet assisted in evaluating student survey responses and creating a record of effective uses of the RLOs.

Implementation Model

The team's efforts to effectively implement the RLOs during the pilot launch led to the creation of a more holistic library component in the liberal arts major, which was developed through the collaboration between Mofford, Sylvain, and Lehr. Lehr intended to use the RLOs in her online LAR 201 class but wanted a stronger library component. The three discussed creating a model that not only focused on information literacy skills but also created a learning environment that was more comfortable and accessible for nontraditional students, who comprise the majority of students in LAR 201 online.

Working together, they created an infrastructure centered around the RLOs to reinforce learning objectives and help students connect with librarians. Sylvain and Mofford partnered to deliver synchronous online information literacy instruction using Wimba Classroom, a live virtual classroom which features audio communication, the ability to conduct database demonstrations, a content area for displaying handouts, and a chat feature for asking questions. They also partnered to review student research logs, create an individually tailored course guide, offer research help using Wimba Classroom and chat widgets, and provide librarian photos and biographies.

Students were required to complete the RLOs prior to the online live classroom instruction session where the librarian answered questions, reviewed key concepts, provided additional instruction, and personally connected with students. The librarians then worked with students to develop and revise their research logs using a discussion board while providing reference assistance as needed. Throughout the process Lehr, Sylvain, and Mofford encouraged students to connect with the librarians when they needed help.

PROGRAM PLANNING

The team agreed that the RLOs should do the following:

- Focus on broad information literacy goals and not be course- or assignment-specific. Such a model would increase shelf life, impart transferable knowledge and skills, and have interdepartmental applications.
- Integrate with LAR assignments and course requirements. As research demonstrates, learning objects are most effective when directly related to student work.
- Address multiple learning styles. Previous library tutorials contained audiovisual components; the team felt this approach could be improved through the addition of active learning exercises.
- Provide faculty with flexibility in implementation and use. It was the team's belief that the more flexible the tutorials were, the more likely faculty would be to integrate them into their classes. Multiple implementation options would enable faculty to choose whether to use an RLO as a graded quiz, mandatory homework assignment, or supplementary material. Multiple points of access would allow faculty to point students to a website or to embed the tutorials in their course sites.
- Demonstrate an intuitive and fairly uniform design. Once students became familiar with how to take a tutorial, they wouldn't have to learn a new module. The technology would not get in the way of learning.

The team chose to develop RLOs that consisted of two parts: an audio/visual tutorial and a self-mastery active learning component.

Planning the first tutorial, Primary and Secondary Sources (Mofford and Sylvain, 2008), involved close collaboration between Mofford, Sylvain, and the ID team as content was developed and an appropriate delivery system selected. Mofford and Sylvain started by thinking about the kind of tutorial that would best present the material, the types of examples they would include, and the approximate length of the tutorial. To be effective, the RLOs needed to re-create the experience of a face-to-face instruction session in the online environment. To achieve this goal, the librarians incorporated audio, visual, and hands-on components, which covered a wide range of different learning styles.

To create a more descriptive tutorial with text and photographic images, the team elected to create a PowerPoint presentation rather than using screencasting features to record a demonstration. This tutorial could be viewed early in a semester, which might mean that students had not yet been introduced to research databases. To keep the focus on understanding concepts, it was important to use a more basic technology that guided students through the materials. This approach allowed the librarians to clearly demonstrate the differences between primary and secondary sources. Later tutorials, such as

Using Boolean Terms and Truncations, were better suited to demonstration-based movies, generated using Adobe Flash, which showed search skills in the context of sample database searches.

Next, the types of examples were selected. Since students would be completing assignments in both humanities and the social sciences online, Sylvain and Mofford decided to include examples for both in the tutorial. Taking into account that research in each discipline might include several types of examples and student needs would vary, Mofford and Sylvain recognized that students needed to be introduced to the varying types of primary and secondary sources in detail. Mofford and Sylvain chose to focus on primary sources in the first half of the tutorial, then on secondary sources for the remainder; each half presented several different examples. This format emphasized the basic tenets of each concept, helping students develop guidelines that could be applied to other sources not highlighted. The final example was a source that could be used as either a primary or secondary source depending on the context.

Source examples in the first tutorial were chosen based on the librarians' experiences of the types of materials the students would most likely encounter, such as speeches, photographs, scholarly research articles, novels, poems, census data, and city directories. The variety of sources would also make this particular tutorial well suited to a number of courses. Callout features, zoom, and highlighting features were employed to better reinforce student learning of informational details and create a dynamic presentation.[1]

The team made the decision to include audio lecture as well as closed-captioning to be compliant with the Americans with Disabilities Act (ADA); Mofford and Sylvain cowrote the first script, deciding to use only Sylvain's voice for the audio to keep the narrative smooth and consistent. The challenge was how to convey a face-to-face feel while utilizing the benefits of a short tutorial. They purposely chose to create a descriptive, conversational audio component so they could explain concepts much the way they would in a face-to-face class, which would also benefit those students who respond to auditory learning.

Upon completion, the RLO was sent to the full team, as well as other librarians, to review. The team then met to discuss the tutorial and make suggestions for revision. This collaborative review format provided fresh eyes on each tutorial and resulted in thoughtful updates to each, among them editing for clarity and pacing, as well as for technical issues in the tutorial playback. In particular, reviewers paid close attention to the length of each tutorial. All tutorials are seven to eight minutes long, as the team recognized that maintaining students' attention spans online is difficult.

The self-mastery portion of the tutorial was the final component. The librarians worked with the ID team to create a set of questions designed to mimic real research situations where the student would need to know which sources would be considered primary or secondary. Thus, students needed to apply what they had learned and demonstrate their decision making rather than simply repeat a tutorial's contents verbatim. Sylvain worked with the ID team to add components that would allow faculty to have the quiz embedded in Blackboard Vista pages. By editing the Sharable Content Object Reference Model (SCORM) compliancy section, quizzes could be used as a graded exercise, which would automatically be entered into the Blackboard Vista Grade Book, or as a self-mastery exercise by students.

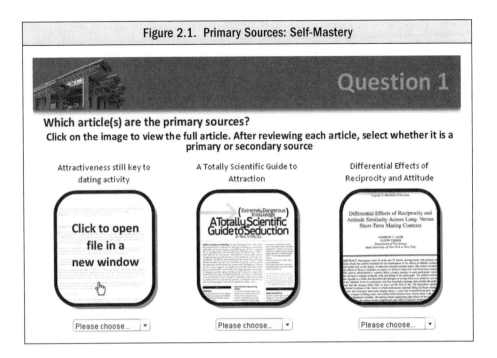

Figure 2.1. Primary Sources: Self-Mastery

A central design element for the self-mastery components is the use of branching. For example, if a student answers question number 1a incorrectly, she will be routed to question 1b, which addresses the same concept. Before receiving question 1b, the student views a brief explanation detailing why the answer to question 1a was incorrect. In all cases, faculty control the percentage of questions a student must answer correctly to earn credit for completing the self-mastery component. In addition, faculty can set up the quizzes so that students can make multiple attempts if they are not immediately successful. This technique reinforces key concepts that a more static quiz structure does not provide.

After completion of the self-mastery component, the ID team created a frame that included a photo of our library, the school logo, and school colors. This frame provides a professional look and also brands the tutorials so that students and faculty can easily recognize them as library support services. With the first tutorial completed, the librarians divided the work on the remaining tutorials to expedite the development process. Using the first tutorial as a master model, the librarians also added in their own style, which gave the later tutorials a more individualized feel. Unlike the first tutorial, which had an equal number of humanities and social science examples, the other tutorials generally used one or the other, depending on which librarian created the tutorial. This approach worked well for the screen-capture tutorials, which demonstrate searches in a particular database. Students in the liberal arts major work within both disciplines, so all examples came from resources they most typically use for research.

At the end of the process, the team had a set of RLOs (Primary and Secondary Sources; Truncations; Using Boolean Terms: AND, OR, and NOT; and Reading Citations in an Online Database) designed to help students grasp essential information literacy concepts and assist them in their research projects. One of the main goals was to bring the classroom experience to life for students in the blended or fully online environment. An added benefit turned out to be giving students a tool to receive more in-depth information and assessment opportunities that traditional classroom library sessions do not always have time to address. Often, librarians only visit a class once during the semester, and have less than an hour to cover material and allow time for students to practice using the resources before they leave. The tutorials are an effective homework assignment given before the library session, which allows librarians to use class time to provide in-depth information literacy instruction. The self-mastery portion, which can be graded, helps ensure the homework's completion.

ONLINE LEARNING MODEL

At UMass Dartmouth, we teach all fully online and blended classes using Blackboard Vista. In LAR 201 online, announcements and internal e-mail tools facilitate communication with students. The primary method of instruction is through lecture notes built into learning modules, which are organized into topic areas and include written or recorded lectures and hyperlinks to relevant websites. Textbook and academic journal readings are followed by responses to study questions and threads posted on discussion boards. Wimba Classroom provides the platform for live class sessions during which students and faculty converse in real time using microphones. Drawing upon these resources, we developed an information literacy component featuring the RLOs, discussions, and an online library guide developed for the class.

LAR faculty want 201 students to develop lifelong learning skills. To help accomplish this goal, the RLOs are a successful starting place as they offer what Larreamendy-Joerns and Leinhardt describe as the "presentational view" in distance learning through the use of multimedia to "restore to distance learning the vividness and instructional creativity of quality classroom instruction" (2006: 584). The tutorials' audio aspect and visual movement mimic the presence of the instructor, lending familiarity to students who never encounter the librarian in person. Used in tandem with other strategies in our LAR online environment, the RLOs set students on solid ground, eventually fostering personal and sustained contact with librarians and the development of a scholarly frame of mind.

In LAR 201, students are asked to *become* scholars, not just read them; in the online class, the goals for teaching information literacy are broader and deeper because the student body differs from day school. Often unable to travel to the university library, they rely entirely on electronic access to databases for research. In the online class, we encounter many transfer students from the region's community colleges who work at full-time jobs, care for children and families, and have often been out of school for a time. As Owens and Bozeman stipulate, the assumption that all online students are computer literate and able to access library-based information readily is misguided (2009: 32). In fact, the computer itself is often an educational innovation for many returning students, and learning online may be a special challenge, with or without the added burden of database research. Faculty, for whom database research has been a welcome innovation, take their use for granted; but to many nontraditional students, a database is the Excel file they use at work. Even for students in their twenties, database research may not have been part of their previous library research training. In addition, information in scholarly journal articles is difficult to access until students are taught how to read them. The team's goals with the RLOs are therefore twofold: students either learn and practice skills for the first time or refresh and further develop existing skills.

When LAR 201 went fully online in the summer of 2008, the RLOs were a natural addition. Sylvain, Mofford, and Lehr worked together to develop the complete library module, which ultimately included a sequence of events: development of a research questions; viewing tutorials and completing self-assessments; a live classroom session with Sylvain, including a demonstration of database searches and differentiating scholarly journals from popular magazines; a research log kept to fine-tune keyword searches; and discussion boards with Mofford about the log and how articles might be useful in the final paper. All elements of the module are required and students earn points towards their final grade through participation.

The RLOs are the foundation of the information literacy instruction and set the tone for the module as a whole. Lehr required students to watch the selected tutorials and complete the matching self-mastery components until each student was able to answer each question correctly, at which point the student would earn full credit for completing the assignment. The ability to keep reworking the assessments until they master the material completely, and knowing that they can eventually earn full credit, motivates students to persist. The scores are automatically reported to the instructor through Blackboard Vista.

Students completed the RLOs before attending a live classroom session with Sylvain, during which they were shown how to distinguish journals from magazines and to perform database searches. Next, they practiced database searches, keeping a research log, and spent time on a discussion board with Mofford as they reported on their searches and explained how one article might be used in their final paper. Log entries recorded the databases used, keywords attempted, and each student's interpretation of the success of hits. Students were also provided with contact information for both librarians, including an LAR 201 library guide available on the library website and linked to the course site. Students were encouraged to contact Mofford and Sylvain as they continued through the research and writing stages of their final paper. The carefully constructed sequence of events prepares students to find helpful sources, think about the use of primary and secondary research, and identify their own primary text as integral to their own primary research and their position as scholars. In addition, as they became familiar with both librarians throughout the module process, the students often turned to them for help with locating and using sources, including asking questions about documentation format.

IMPACT ON STUDENT LEARNING

Faculty and librarians teaching online must constantly remind students, and themselves, that visible benefits accrue for the online learner, but faculty and librarians must always be aware of filling the gaps of the best features found in a FtF classroom. Primary among the gaps is loss of physical interaction and the give and take as they ask and answer questions. In addition, faculty face high online attrition due to frustration with the software or inability to manage time, lack of body language and tone during discussion, and the difficulties they have assessing whether students are missing information because they do not use the software well, because they did not understand how to do the work, or because they are not reading the material thoroughly.

Web-based technology commonly found on all computers can replace some of these missing components, as they offer opportunities to teach in ways not possible in the classroom. The RLOs' online presence means they are available for students during the evening and weekend hours when they are most likely to access them. This access, in turn, increases the students' exposure to library support and fosters a connection to the librarians themselves. RLO variety also broadens the scope of library instruction to meet student needs. Visual learners see immediate results as the tutorial progresses through the lesson, and the voice of the librarian can be matched to the photos of Mofford and Sylvain found in the library guide. For faculty and librarians, who need only to reframe their pedagogy and embrace the possibilities, much can be done to enhance online learning.

The nontraditional student enrolls in online classes for the benefits found in asynchronous learning. LAR 201 online classes have ranged in size from 8 to 20 students with a full range of experience performing library research—from the ability to find a novel at the public library to substantive ability in performing academic database searches successfully. Day students who have taken their first-year English classes at UMass Dartmouth have some database experience, but transfer students often lack library research skills in an electronic medium.

The steep technical learning curve in online learning also affects individual student retention in classes. Data indicate that students leave online classes in larger numbers and earlier in the semester than in day classes (Park and Choi, 2009) often as a result of frustration with software and the need to manage their time in new ways. Pedagogical strategies that ease students into the use of software are important, as is addressing the isolation students feel. Although they are recordings, the tutorials allow students to watch and listen as the librarian ushers them through the skill set selected. They address effective learning needs, take advantage of the benefits of the asynchronous format, and can be repeated immediately or later in the semester.

Furthermore, the self-mastery components reinforce the learning by providing immediate feedback about correct or incorrect answers. For a student population inexperienced in database research, the visual and audio nature of the tutorials helps students negotiate entry into the world of electronic library research before proceeding with other aspects of a complete library module. For those who need only to be reoriented in the capabilities of electronic library research, the tutorials offer much-needed review.

Thus, because the class is a shock to many students who express dismay at the depth of analysis required and the importance placed on writing skills, the tutorials have become an invaluable resource. Being asked to think like a scholar and understand how social science research differs from research in the humanities means a fundamental shift in cognition and self-identity. The role played by the library module and the RLOs in successfully ushering students through this process cannot be overstated. They can be scholars only if they act like scholars and develop skills such as information evaluation and analysis that will assist them after they leave the university.

The results of the library module have been immediate and positive. The opportunity for students to interact with Sylvain during the live session engages them in the research process. Because there are fewer students in online classes, which are limited to 20 students versus a FtF library session that may involve 30 to 40 students, and because the online learning environment is active and eliminates distractions, every student is fully present. Students are required to use at least one scholarly article from the social sciences and one from the humanities as they argue their research question. They must discover and identify the journals, determine the articles' usefulness, and integrate the information into their scholarly work. They must also be able to determine whether a primary source is scholarly and be able to incorporate nonscholarly primary texts, such as works of fiction, into their own scholarly paper. For many students, who have had little or long-past reinforcement of research abilities, assessment of student impact demonstrates that students who completed the library module are successful at finding appropriate sources.

ASSESSMENT OF ONLINE LEARNING

The demographic features and nontraditional nature of our online student body poses a variety of learning obstacles. The effectiveness of the RLOs and the library module is highlighted when we look at what our students have to contend with to be successful in an online major. A review of one online LAR 201 class showed the following results. Only the nine students who completed the semester through the final paper are included:

- Four worked full time outside the home; two self-identified as full-time parents of multiple children; one was unemployed; and two worked part-time, ranging from 24 to 40 hours per week.
- Online classes taken previously ranged from zero to three to "many" in quantity.
- Three had taken first-year English at UMass Dartmouth; all others took it elsewhere, anytime from the year before to 15 years earlier, when databases were not in use; two did not respond to the question.
- To the question, "How often have you used databases before?", response choices were: Often (one student), Sometimes (four), Rarely (two), and Never (two).

Seven of the students successfully researched and integrated at least one scholarly journal article from a social science journal and one from a humanities journal into the final paper. Of the other two students, one was missing a humanities article and the other a social science article.

Although this is a small sampling, the numbers are consistent with other classes and represent a higher level of accomplishment in performing scholarly research than earlier in the semester and in other courses. In addition, students are able to decipher when an article is about primary research and when it is not. The ability to succeed helps build student confidence by semester's end and, in turn, improves their scholarship as they are more willing to invest in their own research endeavors.

Anecdotal accounts suggest that the students understand and appreciate the value of this intense library instruction, including the recursive use to which they put the RLOs. Students told Lehr, afterward, that they have a higher degree of ability to do future course work as a result of the library module as a whole. One student, who took the class after completing most of his other coursework in the LAR major, expressed regret that he had not been exposed to the library module earlier in his studies. Yet another student stopped Lehr in the hallway a year later to explain how important her experience in LAR 201 had been to her subsequent studies and ability to succeed, mentioning the library module specifically.

Student Survey

Soliciting student input is especially important in an online environment where informal feedback is often lacking. It is essential to understand whether students perceive instructional tools as easy to use, understandable, and helpful for developing their research skills. Furthermore, students should be given an opportunity to provide suggestions for improvement. This input must then be analyzed and used to close the assessment loop, allowing faculty and librarians to modify the design and implementation of their tools.

To supplement the data collected by Lehr in her liberal arts class, Sylvain worked with Riley to develop a survey to assess the usability and effectiveness of the RLOs. The survey was created and administered using SurveyGizmo, an online survey tool. Sylvain asked faculty who participated in the RLO pilot launch to provide their classes with a hyperlink to the survey. Students were asked 11 questions, consisting of two open-ended questions, eight multiple-choice questions, five of which provided a text box for additional information, and a fill-in-the-blank question for student names (see Appendix 2.1). Students also had the choice of submitting the survey anonymously. In all cases, faculty could see only that a student had completed the survey and could not see identifiable, individual responses. The survey included questions concerning the clarity, ease of navigation, and usefulness of tutorials and self-mastery components. The open-ended questions allowed students to expand upon clarity and ease of navigation issues, as well as to suggest other research-related tutorials that they would find helpful.

All faculty involved in the pilot launch agreed to administer the survey; however, student compliance varied among the classes. This variation appeared to be associated, in large part, with the presentation of the survey by the professor as part of a participation or extra credit grade. In classes where there was no extrinsic motivation, student participation was significantly lower. We received 110 completed surveys, with one student completing the survey twice. Approximately two-thirds of the respondents were enrolled in the Women's Studies 101 classes. The other third included students in political science, liberal arts, education, and literature classes. These classes included a broad segment of the student body, including traditional undergraduates in a face-to-face setting, returning students enrolled in a fully online class, and graduate students pursuing a master's degree in education at a satellite campus.

The results suggest that the responding students found the RLOs easy to use, understandable, and helpful to the maturation of their research skills. When asked whether tutorial content was clear and easy to understand, 86 percent of respondents replied "yes," while 14 percent indicated that the content was somewhat clear. Regarding ease of navigation, 96 percent of responding students found the tutorials easy to navigate, while 88 percent found the self-mastery components easy to navigate. All other respondents indicated that the RLOs were somewhat easy to use, except for three students who felt the self-mastery components were difficult. Student responses to the open-ended questions revealed that some of the students having difficulty navigating the self-mastery component were having trouble answering one particular question in the Reading Citations RLO. The self-mastery component required students to correctly identify the volume and issue number. Since the volume and issue number were separated by a period, some students viewed it as a single number. With the help of the ID team, Sylvain used the student feedback to modify the component so that it now highlights the element of the citation that a student clicks on. This revision seems to have resolved the issue.

Students were asked to rate the usefulness of each tutorial. As Figure 2.2 indicates, students generally found the tutorials helpful to the completion of their assignments. It is likely these numbers were influenced by RLO content as well as class research assignments and prior student exposure to, and knowledge of, the subject matter. For example when asked, "If you didn't find one or more of the tutorials helpful, please explain why," one student responded, "The primary and secondary sources and the reading citations were helpful, I just had this knowledge previously, so it wasn't very new to me." Also in one of the classes surveyed, students were not required to use library databases. Nonetheless, the survey data suggest that students perceive direct benefit from completing the RLOs. Seventy-seven percent of respondents stated that the RLOs helped them complete their research assignment, while only 3 percent indicated that the RLOs were not helpful.

Figure 2.2. Tutorial Usefulness

Please rate the usefulness of each tutorial.

ITEM	Very Useful	Somewhat Useful	Not Useful	N/A	Total
Boolean Operators	75.0% 78	20.2% 21	1.9% 2	2.9% 3	104
Primary and Secondary Sources	65.5% 72	33.6% 37	–	0.9% 1	110
Reading Citations	69.8% 74	27.4% 29	–	2.8% 3	106
Truncations	76.2% 80	20.0% 21	–	3.8% 4	105
Average %:	71.5%	25.4%	0.5%	2.6%	

CONCLUSION

Through a strategic and well-planned collaborative process, we were able to produce an effective model for teaching information literacy online. Drawing upon the strengths of our multidisciplinary team, we created RLOs that taught key information literacy concepts that were directly related to the curriculum. Our approach encouraged visual, auditory, and active learning, while also providing opportunity for formative and/or summative assessment. We improved the implementation of the RLOs by building infrastructure around the tutorials that further supported the desired learning outcomes. This infrastructure, such as live online instruction and research logs, also served to help students develop a comfort level with researching and with seeking librarian assistance. The evidence that we gathered from informal student feedback, and the analysis of student research and student survey results, suggest that our model had a positive effect on academic achievement.

The RLOs offer faculty a versatile means of imparting information literacy knowledge. We demonstrated that RLOs have various applications and can be used as preparation for live, fully online instruction sessions, as well as review material, independent study tools, and supplements to FtF sessions. Likewise, the SCORM-compliant self-mastery components can serve as graded quizzes, extra credit assignments, or mandatory homework. Thus, our collaboration resulted in reusable tools that faculty can select according to their course learning objectives and needs, while also providing students with consistent core information literacy instruction.

Despite our team's success, we face the challenge of promoting the RLOs beyond the faculty involved in the LAR program and our pilot launch. We believe our promotion must be multifaceted and recognize that the RLOs fit within the broader context of our university's general education program. The university's Integrated Student Learning Outcomes (ISLO) Statement and the General Education Task Force, whose mission it is to propose learning outcomes based on ISLO, have emphasized the centrality of information literacy to the education of all UMass Dartmouth students. This attention to information literacy may provide us with an opportunity to demonstrate how RLOs can support learning outcomes in fully online, blended, and FtF classes.

Our continued success depends on the institutionalization of the model. Unless our collaborative work becomes programmatic, information literacy education will be uneven. We must use our success to secure broad faculty support of the model. Since our model is the result of a collaboration of faculty and librarians associated with the liberal arts program, our team, with administrative support, is well positioned to move this agenda forward. Such buy-in will help ensure that all graduates of the program have the information literacy skills and knowledge needed for graduate study, employment, and lifelong learning.

NOTE

1. This work was completed by Katelyn Huynh, a senior digital media major at UMass Dartmouth. The position was funded by the Sloan grant.

REFERENCES

Association of College and Research Libraries (ACRL). 2000. "Information Literacy Competency Standards for Higher Education." American Library Association. http://www.ala.org/ala/mgrps/divs/acrl/standards/informationliteracycompetency.cfm.

Backhus, Sherry Hawkins, and Terri P. Summey. 2003. "Collaboration: The Key to Unlocking the Dilemma of Distance Reference Services." *The Reference Librarian* 40, no. 83/84: 193–202.

Blummer, Barbara A., and Olga Kritskaya. 2009. "Best Practices for Creating an Online Tutorial: A Literature Review." *Journal of Web Librarianship* 3, no. 3: 199–216.

Center for Policy Analysis, University of Massachusetts Dartmouth. 2004. "SouthCoast Facts." University of Massachusetts Dartmouth. http://www.umassd.edu/cfpa/docs/facts.pdf.

Figa, Elizabeth, Tonda Bone, and Janet R. MacPherson. 2009. "Faculty-Librarian Collaboration for Library Services in the Online Classroom: Student Evaluation Results and Recommended Practices for Implementation." *Journal of Library & Information Services in Distance Learning* 3, no. 2: 67–102.

Gandhi, Smiti. 2003. "Academic Librarians and Distance Education: Challenges and Opportunities." *Reference & User Services Quarterly* 43, no. 2 (Winter): 138–154.

Jackson, Pamela Alexandra. 2007. "Integrating Information Literacy into Blackboard: Building Campus Partnerships for Successful Student Learning." *The Journal of Academic Librarianship* 33, no. 4 (July): 454–461.

Larreamendy-Joerns, Jorge, and Gaea Leinhardt. 2006. "Going the Distance with Online Education." *Review of Educational Research* 76, no. 4 (Winter): 567–605.

Mackey, Thomas P., and Trudi E. Jacobson. 2005. "Information Literacy: A Collaborative Endeavor." *College Teaching* 53, no. 4 (Fall): 140–144.

Mardis, Lori A., and Connie Jo Ury. 2008. "Innovation—An LO Library: Reuse of Learning Objects." *Reference Services Review* 36, no. 4: 389–413.

McGuiness, Claire. 2006. "What Faculty Think—Exploring the Barriers to Information Literacy Development in Undergraduate Education." *The Journal of Academic Librarianship* 32, no. 6 (November): 573–582.

Miller, William, and Steven Bell. 2005. "A New Strategy for Enhancing Library Use: Faculty-Led Information Literacy Instruction." *Library Issues* 25, no. 5 (May): 1–4.

Mofford, Kari, and Matthew Sylvain. 2008. "Primary and Secondary Sources: Understanding the Difference." University of Massachusetts Dartmouth. http://www.lib.umassd.edu/find/tutorials/PrimarySecondarySources/index.html.

Owens, Rachel, and Dee Bozeman. 2009. "Toward a Faculty-Librarian Collaboration: Enhancement of Online Teaching and Learning." *Journal of Library & Information Services in Distance Learning* 3, no. 1: 31–38.

Park, Jye-Hi, and Hee Jun Choi. 2009. "Factors Influencing Adult Learners' Decision to Drop Out or Persist in Online Learning." *Educational Technology & Society* 12, no. 4: 207–217.

Shank, John, and Steven Bell. 2006. "A Strategic Alliance for Improving Student Learning Outcomes." *Innovate* 2, no. 4. http://www.innovateonline.info/index.php?view=article&id=46.

Appendix 2.1. Library Tutorial Survey
1. In which class(es) did you use the tutorials?
☐ ENL 258
☐ LAR 201
☐ PSC 349
☐ WMS 101
☐ MAT 610
☐ PSC 311
2. Which tutorials did you use?
☐ Boolean Operators
☐ Primary and Secondary Sources
☐ Reading Citations
☐ Truncations
3. Did you find the tutorials' content clear and easy to understand?
☐ Yes
☐ Somewhat
☐ No
Please tell us what parts, if any, were not clear or easy to understand.
4. Were the tutorials easy to navigate?
☐ Yes
☐ Somewhat
☐ No
If you found the tutorials difficult to navigate, please tell us where you had trouble.
5. Did the tutorials help you complete your research assignment?
☐ Yes
☐ Somewhat
☐ No

(Continued)

Appendix 2.1. Library Tutorial Survey *(Continued)*

6. Please rate the usefulness of each tutorial.

	Very Useful	Somewhat Useful	Not Useful	Did Not Use
Boolean Operators	☐	☐	☐	☐
Primary and Secondary Sources	☐	☐	☐	☐
Reading Citations	☐	☐	☐	☐
Truncations	☐	☐	☐	☐

If you didn't find one or more of the tutorials helpful, please explain why.

7. Were the self-assessment activities easy to navigate?

☐	Yes
☐	Somewhat
☐	No

If you found the self-assessment activities difficult to navigate, please explain why.

8. Were the self-assessment activities helpful in reinforcing the tutorial content?

☐	Yes
☐	Somewhat
☐	No

If the self-assessment activities were not helpful, please explain why.

9. What other types of research-related tutorials would you find helpful?

10. Other comments?

11. Your name:

3

Framing Multiliteracies

A Blended and Holistic Approach to Digital Technology Education

Andrew Whitworth, Ian Fishwick,
and Steve McIndoe

INTRODUCTION

This chapter describes a postgraduate course titled Media and Information Literacy (hereafter, M&IL), which is taught in the School of Education, University of Manchester, United Kingdom. A recently published paper in the *Journal of Information Literacy* (Whitworth, 2009b) describes how this course is designed as an attempt to teach within the "relational" frame of information literacy (IL) education (Bruce, Edwards, and Lupton, 2007). This chapter briefly discusses the philosophy behind the course and then evaluates its impact upon student learning, something not undertaken in the *JIL* paper. This evaluation considers whether students have adopted the course's holistic view of IL.

Since the *JIL* paper was published, the course has also been taken up by the John Rylands University Library (JRUL) at Manchester and adapted to the needs of a more general audience of postgraduate research students. We also discuss the motivation behind this project.

RELATED LITERATURE

IL is not a theory of learning. This means that "people's approaches to IL and IL education are informed by the views of teaching, learning and IL which they adopt either implicitly or explicitly in different contexts" (Bruce, Edwards, and Lupton, 2007: 37). Thus, there is scope for a great deal of variation in approach when using and developing informational resources. Any such resources are an integral part of the environment within which activity occurs (Whitworth, 2009a: 3–10). This explains the existence of a very wide range of contexts within which IL teaching, learning, and application must take place. To help with analyses of these contexts, Bruce, Edwards, and Lupton developed the *six frames of IL* model as a "conceptual tool" (2007: 39). Their interest is in how information, curriculum, learning, teaching, content, and assessment (2007: 40) are viewed in these different frames. The model helps one understand how different approaches to IL education can affect the dynamic evolution of the informational resources on which future activity must draw.

Bruce, Edwards, and Lupton (2007: 40–42) start with the "content" and "competency" frames in which IL is conceived as competencies and skills. IL education within these frames will focus on what learners know about IL, what they can do with it, and at what level of competence. Learners' skills are assessed by quantifiable and objective measures such as how well learners perform activities, such as an information search. Next, Bruce and colleagues describe more personal, subjective views. These are the "learning to learn" and "personal relevance" frames, and within them the interest is in how IL has informed learning and how it is used to approach, and then solve, educational problems. Self- and peer-assessment are preferred, in contrast to the more objective approaches used in the content and competency frames; students are encouraged to develop and evaluate their own information needs and searching methods. Finally, Bruce and colleagues describe critical and transformative views of IL. Within the "social impact" frame are those approaches in which IL is applied to help communities solve problems. This has a wider scope than in the previous, subjective pair of frames, in which the problems to be addressed do not extend beyond the boundaries of a classroom or workplace. In the social impact frame the learner becomes an activist, using information to transform practices in his or her community and, potentially, in wider society (for examples, see Levine, 2007, and Whitworth, 2009a: 195–198).

Ultimately, Bruce, Edwards, and Lupton (2007: 42) believe that information is experienced, filtered, and evaluated within all of these frames at different times. Through combining them, informational resources are built on which the individual learner and the communities of which he or she is a member can draw to solve future problems. Therefore, true literacy is multifaceted, a view supported by Beetham, McGill, and Littlejohn, who say it is wrong to "imply a single model of digital competence rather than the multiple modes of engagement, varieties of digital scholarship, and numerous specialist applications, which characterise the academic experience" (2009: 67). It is not that any of these five frames should be seen as inferior or superior to others but that all of them contribute to communicative competence (Whitworth, 2007).

These five frames—content, competency, learning to learn, personal relevance, and social impact—are accompanied by, and brought together within, the sixth of Bruce, Edwards, and Lupton's frames of information literacy: the relational frame. Broadly, this is the frame in which students "explore variation" (Bruce, Edwards, and Lupton, 2007: 51; see also Bowden and Marton, 1998: 154) in the way they think about and experience information literacy. The relational frame is that which provides the learner with the ability to move between the other frames as appropriate:

> Students experience information literacy in a range of ways that are more or less complex or powerful.... Information literacy is not a set of skills, competencies and characteristics. It is a complex of different ways of interacting with information which might also include:
>
> • knowledge about the world of information (content frame)
>
> • a set of competencies or skills (competency frame)
>
> • a way of learning (learning to learn frame)

- contextual and situated social practices (personal relevance frame)
- power relationships in society and social responsibility (social impact frame). (Bruce, Edwards, and Lupton, 2007: 43)

Table 3.1 shows the relationship between these frames, which is one of equality and interdependence on one another. The frames have been grouped by connecting them to the different schemes of valuing information presented by Whitworth (2009a: 12–15), that is, objective, subjective, and intersubjective, as well as Egan's classification of literacies (1990: 41ff.) as conventional, emergent, and comprehensive.

It is because the frames are interdependent that all are of value when it comes to constructing informational resources. Whitworth (2009b) has argued that serious pathologies will result if any one of these three forms of value is not accounted for in information processing. If *objective* value is omitted, the learner (individual or community) will tend toward what Thompson (2008) has called "counterknowledge": beliefs and mythologies, such as conspiracy theories, pseudohistory, and other irrationalities which may be widely accepted but which have no scientific validity. If *subjective* value is omitted, the learner is no longer an active cognitive agent and will tend toward what Blaug (2007) called "battery cognition." An individual who is not subjectively valuing the information work he or she does is not an active agent but a passive instrument of an organization or community: this is "groupthink" in the classic sense of the word (Janis, 1972). Finally, if *intersubjective* value is omitted, the learner will not be judging his or her work against intersubjectively developed measures of value such as morals, ethics, laws, or economic value. The pathological tendency here would be toward relativism, illustrated by Whitworth's example (2007: 99) of a poisoner seeking advice online about how to manufacture lethal gas but who might be considered an effective agent simply fulfilling informational needs, if the ethical and moral aspects of the search are not taken into account.

These are all potentially serious pathologies, and it is therefore incumbent on all teachers of IL to address each scheme of value as they strive to create information literate learners. We believe that many existing schemes of IL education do so only implicitly. The classic Association of College and Research Libraries (ACRL) definition, for instance, emphasizes subjective value almost exclusively (ACRL, 2000). The individual learner is not only the agent of the search but also its originator and evaluator. Only a final clause, regarding the ethical and legal use of the found information, saves it from relativism (Whitworth, 2007: 99); and no specific attention is paid here to how ethical practice, for

Table 3.1. The Three Domains of Value		
OBJECTIVE	SUBJECTIVE	INTERSUBJECTIVE
Macro-level	Micro-level	Meso-level
Content and competency frames	Learning to learn and personal relevance frames	Social impact and relational frames
Structural	Individual	Critical
Conventional literacy	Emergent literacy	Comprehensive literacy
Conforming	Informing	Transforming

example, can be established only with reference to the initial information need. Nor is account taken of how an individual learner is not a fully independent cognitive agent. Innate cognitive biases exist that are functions both of our sensory engagement with the world and our prior experience. For example, we are primed to receive information which confirms our prior beliefs and filter out that which challenges them (see Blaug, 2007: 30–31). This is obviously of importance to any learner who is supposed to produce original or critical work rather than just regurgitate existing dogma in a discipline. Organizations also "push" cognitive schema, or ways of thinking, at their members, whether subconsciously or overtly (Blaug, 2007). For instance, a worker in a business cannot use only his or her subjective value to establish what information is important but will have to refer to organizational goals, practices, and procedures as well. These may also require challenging if they no longer meet the needs of an organization (Argyris, 1999).

Information needs cannot therefore be established outside of a particular context, and that context will inevitably shape how the information literacy skills of the agent are applied and evaluated. Contexts are also dynamic, and the results of previous searches will change the environment within which the current search must occur. Therefore, IL cannot be taught alone but must always be connected with the *multi*literacies which the learner must exhibit in his or her particular context and which will create the information needs in the first place. IL is not a stand-alone practice but must work throughout the structures of education and wider society to help maintain the "information commons" as a healthy, open, and sustainable ecology of resources (Hess and Ostrom, 2007; Luckin, 2008; Whitworth, 2009a: 20–23).

To teach IL in this way requires a holistic course, designed and assessed in ways that encourage students to identify and connect their own individual context; the origin of the information need and hence its particular shape and form; and differences between searching and filtering strategies (see Bruce, Edwards, and Lupton, 2007: 44–50, particularly p. 48) that will therefore apply in different circumstances. A holistic approach, then, also implies that students be able to combine the different frames when appropriate.

THE INSTITUTIONAL CONTEXT OF THE UNIVERSITY OF MANCHESTER

M&IL is taught to postgraduate students at the University of Manchester, United Kingdom. It is one of a portfolio of courses primarily designed for a particular master's level program—the MA: Digital Technologies, Communication, and Education (MA: DTCE)—but in principle is available to all postgraduate students in the School of Education and in other departments. The MA: DTCE was created by combining two existing programs that were on-campus only. At its launch in 2007, the MA: DTCE program was expanded online as well. In 2010–2011, the program has around 60 registered students. Of these, 22 are full-time, on-campus students who will complete the program in one year, but the remainder study the course part-time either on campus, online, or by some mixture of the two. The online program is followed only by part-time students; however, on-campus students can take online versions of courses if they wish. The program and its component courses are therefore truly blended, delivered in a hybrid format that includes both face-to-face (FtF) and online instruction, between which students—at least as far as is practical—can move as they see fit. *Blended learning* is a term which we believe is too casually used, often indicating little more than the use of some online resources to support campus students (cf. Andrews and Haythornthwaite, 2007: 15–16). However, the MA: DTCE, through its emphasis on flexibility and equality of experience between on-campus and online students, offers a more involved, deeper view of what a blended course can entail.

Online students are located all over the world, from the Americas through the United Kingdom, Europe, and the Middle East to East Asia. Most of the part-time students are working full-time jobs while studying. The course attracts educators from primary through secondary and tertiary education, alongside corporate trainers, educational software designers, policy makers, and finally those interested in education, communication, and technology as a more general field of study. Students, therefore, come from a very wide range of contexts and have many different practical needs.

Because of this, and in line with its professional development ethos, the program's central principle is flexibility. The principal rules for course design are that all MA: DTCE units must be available to both on-campus and online students and that the two modes are considered equal; that is, online and on-campus students have the same objectives, follow the same syllabi, and are assessed in the same ways, even if teaching methods vary between the modes. Beyond this, the program does not have a set course template. Individual designers and tutors are free to develop online courses howsoever they wish. As a result, whereas some of the MA: DTCE courses are built using program-control models with fairly strict timetables, weekly synchronous sessions, and so on, others are much freer in form, offering high degrees of learner control (see Clark and Mayer, 2003: 225–245).

M&IL was developed a year after the initial offering of the MA: DTCE. By the time it was written, in 2008, student and faculty evaluations of the program's first year suggested it would be useful to incorporate in it a course which could be taken by students at any point and which was completely self-paced. There were times at which students working full-time while studying were finding it difficult to keep up with the demands of the program. Offering a self-paced course was a means of relieving some of this pressure, particularly by making it available in the summer, outside the usual UK semesters of September to Christmas and late January to May. At the same time, any such unit would have to require weekly classes offered to on-campus students.

Therefore, the M&IL course is offered in two distinct ways: as an on-campus course with a relatively high degree of program control (implied by the fact that there remain scheduled weekly on-campus classes) and as an online version (with the same syllabus and assessment but a high degree of learner control).

The wider institutional context of the University of Manchester should also be discussed. Manchester is ranked as one of the top 50 universities in the world (ARWU, 2010); in U.S. terminology, it is a Research One institution. This distinction means that although it has the largest student body of any campus university in the United Kingdom (only the Open University, a distance-only institution, has more enrollments), teaching can often feel subordinated to research work. Nor is online education a significant part of its business model. Only around 30 Manchester degree programs are available to online students; a small proportion of the university's portfolio. Support structures for online and blended learning have been enhanced in recent years through the creation of e-learning support teams, but nevertheless there remain certain tensions between the needs of the M&IL course and the availability of technologies and support from the university, which have manifested themselves in program planning.

The John Rylands University Library is one of the largest and best-resourced academic libraries in the United Kingdom. Its holdings of more than four million books, volume of external usage, and staffing levels place it behind only Oxford and Cambridge, according to the most recent derived figures (SCONUL, 2007–2008: 36). Tangible recognition of the library's value to the wider academic community was recently made by the Higher Education Funding Council for England (HEFCE) who designated it as one of its five National Research Libraries based on the following four criteria:

- a unique collection or a critical mass of rare material;
- a significant and essential contribution to the national research base;
- associated costs beyond what the host higher education institution (HEI) could be expected to bear; and
- a track record of high quality services and facilities to external users.

This designation secured the library a new funding stream (see HEFCE, 2008). The singularity of the John Rylands University Library was further underlined in the 2008 Review of HEFCE Funding for Research Libraries, where particular mention was made that a number of its user-respondents had emphasized the advantages to the research community outside the "golden triangle"—Oxford, Cambridge, and London—of having an outstanding research library located in the north of England (HEFCE, 2008: 22).

DISCIPLINARY PERSPECTIVE

The MA: DTCE's prime objective is "the use of digital technologies, the broadcast media, and/or interpersonal, group or organisational communications techniques to enhance practice and the professional and academic development of educators in technology-rich environments" (University of Manchester, 2010). The design of every course unit in the MA: DTCE, including M&IL, reflects this disciplinary interest in the professional development of educators. This section explains why such a perspective is considered important and how such a course could contribute to and integrate with the more generic, interdisciplinary work with postgraduate research students now being undertaken in Manchester by the JRUL.

Carr and Kemmis argue that it is the ability to apply knowledge to practice that represents true rationality and professionalism in the discipline of education:

> Practitioners tend not to experience their expertise as a set of techniques or as a "tool kit" for producing learning. They can identify some "tricks of the trade" and techniques, certainly, but these are employed in complex patterns, in overlapping sets, in combinations dictated as much by the mood or climate of the class, the particular set of aims being pursued, the kinds of subject matter being considered, the particular image which governs the teaching/learning exercise at hand … and by all sorts of other factors which shape the situation moment by moment. (Carr and Kemmis, 1986: 36–37)

Therefore, professionalism in the discipline of education ideally consists of an ongoing and self-reflective process of inquiry. Carr and Kemmis believe these processes of self- and group reflection to be the hallmark of the professional educator, as opposed to more functional definitions of professionalism, such as qualifications, licenses to teach, and so on (cf. Mezirow, 1990).

Therefore, the MA: DTCE does not provide technologies or practices to its student-practitioners and then expect them to be used in specific ways. Instead, practitioners are encouraged to self-reflect on their needs and then evaluate, and thus select from, a range of technological solutions that may meet those needs. Hence the equal emphasis placed on the C—communication—in the program title, alongside digital technologies themselves and the existence of courses like M&IL which do not investigate any specific technology directly. The MA: DTCE's student-educators are not just learning about technology: they are becoming more effective communicators and, through doing so, helping sustain their own and their workplace communities' informational environments and ecologies of resources (Luckin, 2008). As Whitworth notes:

> In order to be effective, teachers should ideally be constantly selecting these resources, based on the self-recognition of their needs and discussion with colleagues; analysis of the resources (theories, technologies, etc.) available; and the effective use of these resources once selected. In short, they should be information literate. (2009a: 113)

As a result of collaboration between the School of Education and the JRUL, these disciplinary objectives are now being extended to the interdisciplinary skills development of postgraduate research students. The course is being adapted to address their ongoing professional development, retaining the holistic approach and thus addressing how researchers work within all the frames of IL. Researchers need functional searching skills and an awareness of how to manage data and references, and avoid plagiarism; these constitute the content and competency frames in this general context. However, they must also reflect on what makes for effective practice, credibility, ethical considerations, and so on in their own specific research context, which will be distinguished from others both through working in a particular discipline and because of the essentially unique and original nature of a postgraduate research program. They must also consider the role of research in society, the way it is appropriated (and misappropriated) by the media, issues of intellectual property, enclosure of the information commons, open access, and so on.

DISCUSSION OF FACULTY AND LIBRARIAN COLLABORATION

The JRUL was only indirectly involved in setting up the original M&IL course; that is, it gave the same level of support as for any other course, for instance, help with compiling and accessing reading lists. However, in January 2010 the authors of this paper collaborated on a bid to the Higher Education Academy (HEA), the body responsible for professional development in the United Kingdom, to convert the course for use by postgraduate researchers both in the University of Manchester and, ultimately, across the sector. This revised version of the course addresses the issues raised in the previous paragraph. It is greatly shortened from the MA: DTCE version, intended to be followed in seven to ten hours of study time, but it has retained the same online learning model.

This development was provoked by a recent project which audited the provision of information literacy/information skills training delivered to all University of Manchester students, including undergraduate, postgraduate taught (master's level), and postgraduate research (PhD) students. JRUL staff members have been delivering such training for some time, with subject librarians tending to offer it within the departments with which they are associated, but up until now it has been a somewhat haphazard process, very much dependent on the skills and workload of individual librarians and thus offered inconsistently across the university. The audit has reviewed what is being delivered, at what stages of programs, whether the training is being done in collaboration with academics, and how it is supported within Blackboard, which is the institutional VLE (or virtual learning environment, often known in the United States as a course management system).

The audit also gathered data on what departments may have been doing on their own account. As a large academic institution, Manchester is "loosely coupled" (Weick, 1976), and a lot of creative activity takes place at departmental level, of which the more centralized structures, such as the library, are often unaware. It was through these enquiries that the connection was formed between the School of Education and the JRUL, which resulted in the coauthorship of this chapter.

The JRUL's existing IL and skills training is largely based around common definitions of IL such as those of the ACRL (2000). We are agreed that while these and similar approaches are essential elements of any IL skills development, they must be supplemented by attention to objective, intersubjective, and subjective schemes of value, as already noted. Hence the interest in adapting M&IL's innovative approach to the more generic needs of postgraduate research students.

The bid to the HEA was successful, and the subsequent project to convert the course along these lines commenced in February 2010, with the pilot implementation taking place in May and June and the final version released in November 2010 (see http://www.MAdigitaltechnologies.com/infoliteracy). Faculty–librarian collaboration has been undertaken through regular project meetings and attendance at the same academic conferences, such as the Librarians' Information Literacy Annual Conference (LILAC) 2010 and the HEA conference in August 2010. This has been relatively straightforward. However, we anticipate difficulty with the dissemination of knowledge about the course—and the collaboration which underpins it—to other faculty members who have not contributed to its creation and thus have no direct stake in it. This may apply both at Manchester and elsewhere following the materials' distribution as an open-access educational resource through the HEA. It is difficult to say in advance whether any strategies for alleviating these problems, and thus promoting faculty-library collaboration, will be successful. However, one approach we are taking is to try to make very clear which parts of the resource/course are intended to be generic and which could be adapted by different departments, disciplines, or academics to help personalize the resource. The resource will be released with a guidebook that will explain how to adapt it to different local contexts. This guidebook will include video- and audio-based material as well as written. Our intention is that this will make the resource more end-user friendly and thus more likely to be adopted outside the faculty–librarian team which created it.

Another option would be to integrate the new resource into staff development courses for research supervisors and academic staff more generally, along the lines suggested by Vedvik Tonning, Rullestad, and Skagen (2010). We will continue to develop this program through 2011.

PROGRAM PLANNING

As discussed, the online and on-campus versions of the course differ with respect to the level of program versus learner control, but they are otherwise the same. That is, syllabus, reading materials, discussion activities, and assessment are shared between the two modes. On-campus students therefore use the same VLE as online students, though they may access it according to different schedules.

The VLE in use is Moodle, which is of interest because Manchester is a Blackboard campus. Since its inception, the MA: DTCE has retained its own Moodle installation, hosted by an external agency. This has been done for two main reasons. First, because the MA: DTCE is an educational technology program with an emphasis on student-led explorations of their own needs, we feel obliged to offer them a range of technologies to explore rather than being restricted to the institution's central system. Also, access to Blackboard is tightly regulated. It is next to impossible to give students designer-level access to any Blackboard course, yet MA: DTCE students expect to be able to gain experience in manipulating a VLE as part of their learning. With a Moodle installation that is under the control of the teaching team, rather than centrally regulated by the institution, we can continue to offer them this opportunity. Bearing in mind our disciplinary perspective, Moodle is again more useful in this regard than Blackboard. Many of our students are working, or will go on to work, in small institutions which cannot afford a large, commercial VLE like Blackboard, but for which Moodle would be much better suited.

Setup costs for the initial offering of M&IL were minimal and incorporated in the typical annual budget of the MA: DTCE. The conversion of the materials for use in the library gave rise to further costs of approximately £5,000 (USD $8,000). Around half of this amount was covered by a grant from the Higher Education Academy, and we thank that organization for its support.

ONLINE LEARNING MODEL

The underlying ethos of the course has been explained, but to recap, it is based strongly around the integration of media and information literacy into the professional development of educators in the hope that they will both become more information literate in their own practice and can go on to teach M&IL to other learners. Thus, there is an emphasis on reflection and attention to the social impact of media and information as well as functional searching and evaluation skills.

The course is structured around nine key topics. Although there is some minor variation, in general each topic has the same format. There is a key reading, which all students should complete as their first activity in the topic. This is then complemented by an audio file (available for download as a podcast), supplementary reading where needed, and an activity with an accompanying discussion board. The course is entirely self-paced, apart from the setting of a final assessment deadline. Thus, there is no expectation that students will engage in group work, including group discussions, although the option is available to them if necessary.

The course begins with an introduction to multiliteracy, explaining how the basic idea of literacy has become associated with many fields, including media, information, visual, financial, environmental, and scientific literacy. All can be viewed within the framework proposed by Egan (1990) and explored with the help of Table 3.1 (see p. 49), which illustrates conventional, comprehensive, and critical literacies. Students are introduced to this idea early, as it drives the holism of the course. It is also an attempt to show how information literacy cannot be fully understood without an appreciation of these other literacies, which are *forms of value* that drive information searches and needs in the first place. IL is therefore not treated as a stand-alone set of functional skills: this encourages a perspective in which IL is decontextualized and removed from other systems of value. Instead, IL is placed within a broader context. Remember that the course aims to develop in students an understanding of the relational frame of IL. This requires both students and teacher to:

- explore and experience a variety of information searching strategies;
- expand IL into multiliteracies, gaining an understanding of the values (such as environmentalism and religion; refer to the activities that follow) which drive information needs and the strategies used to fulfill them;
- understand how all of these literacies can be expressed, and related activities evaluated, in objective, subjective, and intersubjective ways. (Whitworth, 2009b: 31)

As an illustration, an early course activity involves students defining a particular literacy, such as environmental, religious, or financial literacy, in conventional, emergent, and comprehensive terms (for a fuller description of this example, see Whitworth 2009b: 32–33). The objective is to illustrate the importance of the relational frame for the students and demonstrate that it is more than just a theoretical construct. This framework is then used in the remainder of the course to analyze the multiliteracies discussed therein (cf. Beetham, McGill, and Littlejohn, 2009), as well as the primary subjects, media literacy and IL.

For example, environmental literacy would be a driver of information searches and filtering strategies that inform environmental issues, but strategies used to conduct and evaluate the search would differ depending on whether environmentalism was viewed functionally, personally, or critically. Compare this with Lupton's work (2004; cited in Bruce, Edwards, and Lupton, 2007: 50–51). She investigated how students researched essays in environmental studies courses and found that IL could be applied to researching environmental problems without concern for the actual nature of environmentalism. From within the content and competency frames this would not be seen as a problem because, from this perspective, environmentalism simply produces an informational need which can be met in context-independent ways. Only through allying work in these frames with intersubjective and subjective schemes of value can the need be seen as stemming from wider ethical and moral considerations and thus *fully* meet the ACRL's (2000) requirements for information literacy practice. Lupton saw that this deeper kind of insight required students to "look beyond the topic to the field and discipline" (Bruce, Edwards, and Lupton, 2007: 51)—in this case, to understand the nature of environmentalism itself and how the information need emerged from it. Hence, the claim that the relational frame of IL must make explicit connections between IL and other multiliteracies as relevant—in this case, environmental literacy.

Once this framework has been outlined, students are then taken through first media and then information literacy in more detail but always with reference back to the underlying framework outlined in Table 3.1. Media literacy is first introduced in a general way, and then with a case study titled "Who writes the news?". Information literacy is presented first through the ACRL guidelines, but these are then critiqued using the arguments already outlined in this chapter. In these ways students are introduced to the holistic model of IL. Finally, bearing in mind that these are education students and thus are, or wish to become, practicing teachers, the course concludes by highlighting existing examples of information literacy teaching.

The version of the course being prepared with the JRUL contains seven topics rather than nine, including an introduction, then one topic covering each of Bruce, Edwards, and Lupton's six frames, and following the model outlined at the end of the Disciplinary Perspective section in this chapter.

IMPACT ON STUDENT LEARNING

The impact on student learning has been evaluated through analysis of students' assessed work and an e-mail survey (including more detailed focus group interviews with four participants), all using frameworks based on the six-frames model. This evaluation has included both the 2008–2009 and 2009–2010 cohorts. As no changes were made between the two offerings, the two cohorts have been combined in the data and no comparisons made between them.

Across the two groups, 35 students started the course, but three dropped out before submitting an assessment. Of the 32 full participants, 13 were on-campus students and 19 followed the course at a distance. All students were approached to complete a follow-up survey, and 16 replied (seven on-campus and nine online), a response rate of exactly 50 percent. Four students were also recruited for a focus group interview that more deeply investigated their portfolio activities.

Bruce, Edwards, and Lupton (2007: 40–42) include statements about the view of IL which has contributed to the frame and the kinds of activities and/or beliefs that would make up a curriculum based in each frame. In Table 3.2, the "view of IL" is taken directly from their work: the "relevant activities" are our own, based on their suggestions.

The sixth, relational frame is omitted because our analysis was intended to show how these five frames combined into the relational frame and not to treat that frame as a mode of teaching in its own right. Therefore, what we hoped to see was distribution of students' beliefs and practices across the five frames rather than there being overemphasis on one or another.

Students were therefore asked how they would rank the statements about IL suggested by Bruce, Edwards, and Lupton (2007). They were asked to pick their first and second choices from the list, without further prompting. Results were as follows:

	Table 3.2. The Frames of Information Literacy	
Frame	View of IL	Relevant Activities
1. Content	IL is knowledge about the world of information.	Tell students about the use of a tool or technique.
2. Competency	IL is a set of competencies or skills.	Help students use a tool or technique.
3. Learning to learn	IL is a way of learning.	Students solve a problem, without a tool or technique being prescribed in advance.
4. Personal relevance	IL is learned in context and is different for different people and groups.	Students reflect on prior experiences.
5. Social impact	IL issues are important to society.	Students work to transform policy or (their own or others') practice.

The following statements about IL were ranked *first* by respondents:

- Information literacy is knowledge about the world of information: 1
- Information literacy is a set of competencies or skills: 4
- Information literacy is a way of learning: 5
- Information literacy is dependent on context and is different for different people/groups: 3
- Information literacy is important to society: 3

The following were ranked *second*:

- Information literacy is knowledge about the world of information: 1
- Information literacy is a set of competencies or skills: 3
- Information literacy is a way of learning: 4
- Information literacy is dependent on context and is different for different people/groups: 3
- Information literacy is important to society: 5

This is a crude test, but it does suggest that the course has not swayed students toward any particular view of IL and thus any particular frame, though there is a tendency to move away from the "content" frame. However, it should be added that a chi-square test here does not show a statistically significant result, therefore this tendency could have occurred by chance, as the result of sampling.

The course's impact on students' professional and personal development was also surveyed. Again, space precludes deeper, more qualitative analysis of students' answers to these questions, but the positive impact can be briefly seen in two ways. Of the 16 students who replied to the questionnaire or answered this question in the focus group, 11 had used the portfolio resources they had created in a real teaching setting. This number included one student who had given the resources to a colleague to use. Of the five who said they had not used their portfolio resources, one student pointed out that she had not had the opportunity to do so, having moved on to PhD study since leaving the MA: DTCE.

In addition, 13 out of 16 respondent students said they had changed their practices or beliefs about media and information sources since finishing the course, including several who qualified this statement with words like "significantly so," "totally," and "definitely." Of the remaining three respondents, two gave ambiguous answers ("to an extent," "slightly") and the final student said she had not changed her practices or beliefs. Both of these answers suggest the course has had a positive impact on students' personal and professional practice. Its transformational objective has, on the surface, been fulfilled.

ASSESSMENT OF ONLINE LEARNING

Assessment takes place through students' compiling a portfolio of four teaching and learning activities which they have created to address literacy deficits within a specified target population. The portfolio can address media literacy, information literacy, or other multiliteracies such as health or environmental literacy. Activities are wrapped in a commentary with which the learner explains what deficits they have identified and how the four activities will address them at the objective, subjective, and intersubjective level. Portfolios are currently presented in the form of a simple Word-compatible document, but in 2010–2011 e-portfolios will be introduced. It is with this portfolio that the holistic ethos of the course is most obviously applied.

These portfolios were also analyzed as part of the evaluation of this course. This was not undertaken by means of the survey but through a content analysis of submissions. Hence, all 32 students who completed the course were included in this analysis.

Each portfolio contained four activities that were read by the researcher and then assigned to one or more of the five categories of activity given in Table 3.3 (see p. 60), one for each of the five frames. An activity could be assigned to more than one category. As an example, two activities from one student's portfolio will be presented in slightly abridged form (focusing on those elements which are important for the analysis).

The first activity is therefore coded as falling into the competency and personal relevance frames. The second is coded as the way of learning and—because they are publishing this student-created newspaper—the social impact frame.

The four focus group participants also undertook this task on their own and then in discussion with other students and the researcher. This was done as a form of member checking, judging the reliability of the researcher's overall allocation of activities to categories. Note that student DL13 was the student who created the media literacy activities outlined in Table 3.4 (see p. 61).

Though there are differences, these often occur with secondary categorizations rather than the whole. Students are also more likely to consider their activity to have been intended to transform practice. Indeed, this tendency is at 100 percent when it comes to describing their final activity. We interpret this as suggesting students have accepted the need to transform practice as the ultimate objective of any definition of IL and therefore had the intention of doing so in their portfolio, even if in the assessor's opinion they did not follow through on this intention. A wider sample is needed to be sure of this conclusion, however.

Where the member checking process revealed discrepancies, the data were adjusted to match the students' view of their work, even in cases where the researcher did not

Table 3.3. Part of a Student Portfolio for M&IL	
Activity Text	Coding
Title: How are young people represented in the news?	
Aims of session: The aim of this activity is to investigate how young people are represented in the news and look at reasons why they are presented in such a way.	
Task: The tutor shows various news headlines from the newspapers about young people and asks students to think about how the headlines make them feel and how readers might react to the stories.	Reflection on practice
Each student picks a headline and analyzes the corresponding news story, looking at how young people have been portrayed. What techniques has the newspaper used to get a certain point of view across and promote credibility? For example, quoting specialists or professionals, using statistics, imagery, language? Students should make notes of their findings.	Use of a tool or technique
Students are then asked to rewrite the article briefly and include the opinion or point of view of young people to demonstrate how different the story might be were young people able to give their account of events.	Use of a tool or technique
Title: Producing a newspaper	
Aims of session: To decide on roles within the team, agree on a plan and content, and begin work on the publication.	Solving a problem
Task: With the help of the tutor, students identify the roles and responsibilities required to get their newspaper published and decide who in their team would be best suited to each role. The tutor acts as a facilitator to encourage collaborative learning and encourage students to take ownership of the newspaper.	
Having decided on roles and responsibilities, students work as a group to plan the publication. Once the action plan has been created, students can then begin to work on their individual responsibilities. These may include researching topics, arranging interviews, proofreading articles, and acquiring images.	Transforming practice

agree with the students' characterization of their activities; this was done to ensure uniformity of practice. Across all submitted portfolios there were $32 \times 4 = 128$ activities. Each activity could be classified in more than one frame. The categories (frames) and the number of activities which fell into each were as follows (see also Figure 3.1):

- Telling students about a tool or technique (content frame): 46
- Teaching students how to use a tool or technique (competency frame): 60
- Setting a problem that learners have to solve (learning to learn frame): 24
- Getting the learners to reflect on prior experience (personal relevance frame): 61
- Transforming policy or practice (social impact frame): 27

In all, 10 of the 32 portfolios included at least one activity from each of the five frames, and these could therefore be considered truly relational. Seven more portfolios

Students	Activities			
	Table 3.4. Results of Member Checking Process			
	#1	#2	#3	#4
DL13	R: 1, 2 S: 1, 2	R: 2, 4, 5 S: 2, 4	R: 3, 4 S: 3, 5	R: 3, 6 S: 6
C16	R: 1, 2, 4 S: 1, 2	R: 2 S: 1, 2, 4	R: 2, 3, 5 S: 3, 5	R: 2, 3, 4 S: 6
C33	R: 1, 4 S: 1	R: 2 S: 2, 4	R: 3,4 S: 3, 4	R: 4 S: 6
C34	R: 1, 2 S: 1, 2	R: 2, 4 S: 4	R: 2, 4 S: 2, 4	R: 4 S: 6

Note: R = researcher's opinion; S = students' opinion; numbers follow the numbered frames given in Table 3.2.

did not include an activity from every frame but did include one which was considered transformational (though this number drops to four if only the assessor's original categorization was used, as noted in the description of the member checking process above). Around half of all portfolios, then, indicated that students had recognized the need to transform the literacy practices of themselves or of others.

M&IL is also encouraging its student educators to develop programs of education in multiliteracy, not just information and media literacy. The 32 portfolios dealt with the subjects shown in Figure 3.2 (the numbers add up to more than 32 due to some occasions where two literacies were clearly in use).

Where specific and clearly defined groups of learners were being targeted in a portfolio, these groups were as follows: English as a Foreign Language (EFL) teachers;

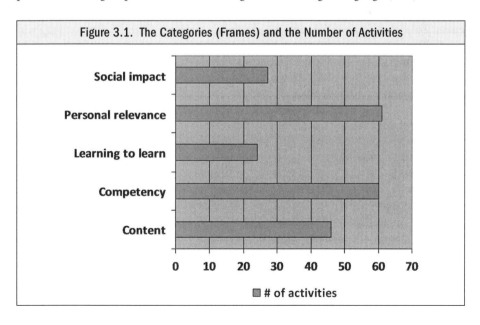

Figure 3.1. The Categories (Frames) and the Number of Activities

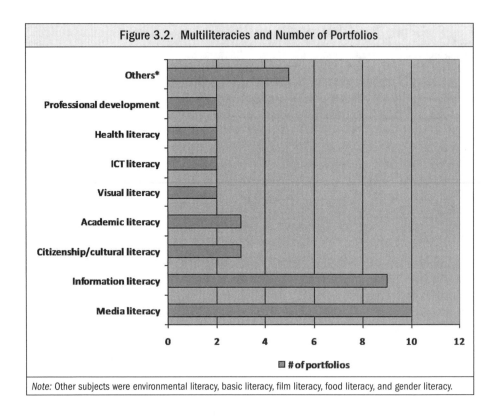

Figure 3.2. Multiliteracies and Number of Portfolios

Note: Other subjects were environmental literacy, basic literacy, film literacy, food literacy, and gender literacy.

EFL learners; computer science students; parents; volunteer teachers (Brazil); adult-education tutors; Middle Eastern women; Chinese secondary school students; fashion retailing students (United Kingdom); and Egyptian nationals. Though not every student clearly identified his or her context in this way, those that did were thinking about IL and other literacies not as something decontextualized but as skills which are integrated into particular contexts and which must therefore be explored in different ways depending on context.

CONCLUSION

Our conclusion is that M&IL has been successful so far in introducing students to the holistic approach to IL and that there is evidence they are continuing to use the approach after completing the course in their personal lives, in their later studies, and/or in their professional activity. The course has successfully taught its subjects within a framework of multiliteracy and thus encouraged students to see how IL cannot be understood and applied without reference to forms of value developed through the application of these other forms of literacy. We believe the course shows that it is possible to teach IL in ways that encourage learners to see how to apply it in their own individual context; but which also keep them apprised of objective forms of value (e.g., scientific method) and intersubjective (e.g., laws, ethics, economics, community standards) as well. Through teaching in such a way, practice can be transformed. We believe these principles can be incorporated into most IL instruction without significant impact on the workload of faculty, library staff, or students. The innovative blended format of this course allows its extension beyond the traditional academic semesters and also outside the faculty–librarian team that created it.

REFERENCES

Andrews, R., and C. Haythornthwaite. 2007. "Introduction to E-Learning Research." In *The Sage Handbook of E-Learning Research*, edited by R. Andrews and C. Haythornthwaite, 1–52. London: Sage.

Argyris, C. 1999. *On Organizational Learning*. Oxford, UK: Blackwell.

ARWU. 2010. "Academic Ranking of World Universities." Shanghai Ranking Consultancy. http://www.arwu.org.

Association of College and Research Libraries (ACRL). 2000. "Information Literacy Competency Standards for Higher Education." American Library Association. http://www.ala.org/ala/mgrps/divs/acrl/standards/informationliteracycompetency.cfm.

Beetham, H., L. McGill, and A. Littlejohn. 2009. *Thriving in the 21st Century: Learning Literacies for the Digital Age*. Glasgow: The Caledonian Academy. http://www.academy.gcal.ac.uk/llida/outputs.html.

Blaug, R. 2007. "Cognition in a Hierarchy." *Contemporary Political Theory* 6, no. 1: 24–44.

Bourdieu, P. 1977. *Outline of a Theory of Practice*. Cambridge, UK: Cambridge University Press.

Bowden, J., and F. Marton. 1998. *The University of Learning: Beyond Quality and Competence in Higher Education*. London: Kogan Page.

Bruce, C., S. Edwards, and M. Lupton. 2007. "Six Frames for Information Literacy Education: A Conceptual Framework for Interpreting the Relationship Between Theory and Practice." In *Change and Challenge: Information Literacy for the 21st Century*, edited by S. Andretta, 37–58. Adelaide, Australia: Auslib.

Carr, W., and S. Kemmis. 1986. *Becoming Critical: Knowing Through Action Research*. Geelong, Australia: Deakin University Press.

Clark, R., and R. Mayer. 2003. *E-learning and the Science of Instruction*. San Francisco: Wiley.

Egan, K. 1990. *Romantic Understanding: The Development of Rationality and Imagination, Ages 8–15*. London: Routledge.

HEFCE. 2008. "Review of HEFCE Funding for Research Libraries." Bristol, UK: Higher Education Funding Council of England. http://www.hefce.ac.uk/pubs/RDreports/2008/rd04_08/.

Hess, C., and E. Ostrom, eds. 2007. *Understanding Knowledge as a Commons*. Boston: MIT Press.

Janis, I.L. 1972. *Victims of Groupthink*. Boston: Houghton Mifflin.

Levine, P. 2007. "Collective Action, Civic Engagement, and the Knowledge Commons." In *Understanding Knowledge as a Commons: From Theory to Practice*, edited by C. Hess and E. Ostrom, 247–276. London: MIT Press.

Luckin, R. 2008. "The Learner Centric Ecology of Resources: A Framework for Using Technology to Scaffold Learning." *Computers and Education* 50, no. 2: 449–462.

Lupton, M. 2004. *The Learning Connection: Information Literacy and the Student Experience*. Adelaide, Australia: Auslib.

Mezirow, J., ed. 1990. *Fostering Critical Reflection in Adulthood: A Guide to Transformative and Emancipatory Learning*. San Francisco: Jossey-Bass.

SCONUL. 2007–2008. *Annual Library Statistics*. London, UK: Society of College, National, and University Libraries.

Thompson, D. 2008. *Counterknowledge*. London: Atlantic.

University of Manchester. 2010. "MA: Digital Technologies, Communication and Education Web Site." MA: DTCE portal. http://www.madigitaltechnologies.wordpress.com.

Vedvik Tonning, A.S., T. Rullestad, and T. Skagen. 2010. "Integrating Information Literacy within the University Curriculum: Cooperation between University of Bergen Library and the Centre for University Pedagogy." Paper presented at LILAC 2010. Limerick, Ireland: Librarians' Information Literacy Annual Conference.

Weick, K.E. 1976. "Educational Organizations as Loosely Coupled Systems." *Administrative Science Quarterly* 21, no. 1: 1–19.

Whitworth, A. 2007. "Communicative Competence in the Information Age: Towards a Critical Pedagogy." In *Change and Challenge: Information Literacy for the 21st Century*, edited by S. Andretta, 85–114. Adelaide, Australia: Auslib.

Whitworth, A. 2009a. *Information Obesity*. Oxford, UK: Chandos.

Whitworth, A. 2009b. "Teaching in the Relational Frame: The Media and Information Literacy Course at Manchester." *Journal of Information Literacy* 3, no. 2: 25–38.

4

Finding Your Fate
The Evolution of a Librarian–Faculty Collaboration to Bring History Online

Kristina DuRocher and Lisa Nichols

INTRODUCTION

A librarian and a history professor, inspired by an article in *Perspectives*, set out on a journey together, a collaborative project to breathe life into one unit of a survey history course at a regional eastern Kentucky university. Together, we developed an online component that offers a model for other librarians and faculty members in transitioning collaborative projects to the online environment. This chapter outlines the evolution of our collaborative unit as it changed from a face-to-face class with an online component into an entirely online project. This two-week project, as part of a global studies general education course, illustrates the challenges as well as the strengths of taking a joint project online. As our experience demonstrates, such collaboration requires flexibility and continuous assessment to create a successful shared model.

Kristina DuRocher, a historian, and Lisa Nichols, an instructional librarian, first met in August 2005 during new faculty orientation at Morehead State University (MSU) and found common ground in sharing an alma mater, the University of Illinois at Urbana-Champaign. At orientation, Nichols expressed her desire to increase faculty engagement with the library, and DuRocher noted that she wanted to find ways to include students in hands-on historical research. Shortly afterward, Nichols read an article, "Engaging Students in the Game of Research," by Theresa Mudrock and immediately sent it to DuRocher, who agreed the central premise offered an innovative way of bringing both their goals to fruition (Mudrock, 2005a: 15–17).

In the article, Mudrock discusses how she, as a history librarian, engages students in historical research through role-playing in what she termed a "game of research." Her technique was similar to an approach taken at the United States Holocaust Memorial Museum, where entrants are given an identity card of an actual person, which they use to trace the events of that person's life through the course of the war, thereby fostering a "direct identification with Holocaust victims" (Ochsner, 1995: 241). Similarly, students in Mudrock's course adopted a persona whose fate they researched in the library over the course of a semester. The idea was fascinating because it allowed students to make a personal connection with history. It was, however, impossible to implement a similar course at MSU as neither instructor had access to a semester-long class devoted to library research. However, we decided to try it on a smaller scale and met several times to discuss ways we might adapt Mudrock's approach into a single unit for History 201; thus, our collaborative project began.

Over the next four years, we created our own version of the "game of research" that has evolved in its scope, methods, and format. Within the course History 201, what began as a unit on World War I evolved as we shifted our topic to World War II and then to a focus on the Vietnam conflict. The methods of this unit progressed along with the topics, expanding to include both primary and secondary sources. The delivery mode changed as well from mostly face-to-face dissemination to an all-online format. This move required us to redesign our collaborative project to maintain the essential elements students most benefited from without losing the aspects of working together that we both enjoyed. Throughout our collaboration, we continually assessed our success both in terms of impact on students and in meeting our desired goals. The result is a progression that offers an innovative and inspiring model for information literacy instruction and librarian–faculty collaboration in an online environment.

When we began, our goals were to engage students in an interactive exercise that would allow them to participate in discipline-based research while gaining information literacy skills. As our collaboration evolved, we, in turn, noticed an increase in positive feedback from students, most of whom reported more engagement with the subject and more interest in the historical context of their research assignments. These results are despite the fact that the project required more critical thinking and use of evaluative skills than did other aspects of the course. Unit assessments also demonstrate that students met our discipline-specific goals while gaining greater self-assurance in their own library and research skills and made a meaningful and personal connection with the topic.

RELATED LITERATURE

When we read Theresa Mudrock's (2005a) article, "Engaging Students in the Game of Research," we each saw different strengths in her approach of creating such a game. Mudrock, a history librarian at the University of Washington, offered Nichols an innovative way to approach information literacy at both the student and faculty level. Mudrock's article described a unique approach to student-centered research, one that created a portal for students to find and use information in new ways and encouraged the use of a variety of library resources for research. DuRocher enjoyed the idea of personalizing past events for students who often felt history had little impact on their daily lives.

Mudrock was not our only influence in creating and modifying our own collaborative research activity. Samuel Wineburg's (2001) assertion that each generation must seek for itself its own historical meanings and importance called for historians, as educators, to focus on connecting the past to students' futures. Wineburg shifted DuRocher's perspective on instruction, and she agreed with his stance that teaching history as if it were a static set of facts discourages students from an awareness of how the past has shaped our world today. Wineburg notes that historical thought is not natural to students; it is a learned skill. Professors must teach students the art of questioning and interpreting sources.

The use of primary sources to engage students is accepted and used in many history classrooms but, along with Samuel Wineburg, David Kobrin, in *Beyond the Textbook: Teaching History Using Documents and Primary Sources*, suggests that professors should encourage students to act as historians and follow their own paths to come to their own understandings of the past (Korbin, 1996). Thus, the idea of a smaller scale game of research appealed to DuRocher, as it would allow the opportunity for students to be active researchers in the college classroom.

For Nichols, her influences included authors such as Ann Grafstein, whose 2002 article, "A Discipline-Based Approach to Information Literacy," argues that success comes from discipline-based collaboration between faulty and librarians, not just through the library itself. Although Nichols sought to improve partnerships with faculty, as Patricia Durisin (2002) in *Information Literacy Programs: Successes and Challenges* notes, this collaboration is not the only hurdle librarians face in teaching information literacy. Kate Manuel's (2002) article, "Teaching Information Literacy to Generation Y," points out that especially among current students, self-confidence in their own computer skills led them to overestimate their ability to find and evaluate information. Nichols's experiences mirrored those of other instruction librarians. She witnessed firsthand how students repeatedly failed to evaluate the results of open web searching and, more often than not, neglected to consider their source for accuracy, currentness, or authority. In creating this unit, Nichols sought not just to normalize collaboration between librarians and faculty but also to embed the evaluative skills needed for students who utilize the Internet for information gathering.

Nichols was aware that this collaborative project would be a way to deal with library anxiety with this generation of students. Constance Mellon first defined the idea of "library anxiety" as both a fear of using the library and of the librarians themselves in her 1986 article, "Library Anxiety: A Grounded Theory and Its Development." This apprehension, Mellon proposed, stemmed from students' feelings of inadequacy and shame in asking for help. Library anxiety has a negative impact on information-seeking behaviors, but Mellon found that personal interaction with librarians in instructional settings helped lessen student concerns. This collaborative project offered Nichols the opportunity to work with large groups of students each semester multiple times, thereby allowing students the opportunity to get to know her as a person, see that she is neither aloof nor scary, and experience decreased trepidation about using the library.

As noted previously, we currently teach this unit completely online, but it began as a face-to-face class with an online component. As we modified the model for online use, we consulted John F. Lyons's (2004) article, "Teaching U.S. History Online: Problems and Prospects," which emphasized that online courses often reach a diverse mix of traditional and nontraditional students, complicating modes of delivery. In an online course, without a professor to present the material, students may feel alienated from the course, and Lyons encourages assignments that personalize a student's experience as much as possible. As this mirrored our collaborative goals, we kept in mind that our model, especially as we modified it into an entirely online format, needed to allow for student adaptation and be engaging and successful for students of varying abilities.

INSTITUTIONAL CONTEXT AT MOREHEAD STATE UNIVERSITY

At MSU, a small public institution in eastern Kentucky, our population includes many nontraditional and local students. We draw more than 67 percent of our students from the eastern Kentucky region. Our students are, in general, from underserved high schools. As such, some students struggle with academic success, as evidenced by high dropout and low graduation rates. Many nontraditional undergraduates struggle with the online environment, which for them is new and in every respect unlike their prior school experiences. Yet, over the past few years, enrollment has been declining at the main campus while increasing in the Instructional Televised courses and online environments.

We implemented our model in the undergraduate course History 201: Global Studies, which covers world history since 1500 and satisfies a general education requirement. In the on-campus course, the student population is composed primarily of freshmen and sophomores. Most students are not history majors, and the education requirements of Kentucky do not currently require a world history class be completed in the later high school years. As a result, many of our college students enter the classroom with little knowledge of world history. In the online environment, the student makeup is more diverse. The undergraduates taking this course tend to be nontraditional students in some way. Some students reside off campus and even out of state, and many work at full-time jobs and have families. This wide-ranging online population may have a better sense of current world matters, but generally have little memory of history from their secondary education experiences. Two sections of the survey class participated each semester, ranging from 30 to 60 students.

DISCIPLINARY AND INTERDISCIPLINARY PERSPECTIVE

As we have already suggested, our collaboration grew out of a desire to incorporate meaningful library-based historical research. Students often bypass the library portals in favor of the open web and then accept the materials they find as historical truth, regardless of the source. In all formats, we sought to offer students a contextual experience with the past that created a meaningful understanding of a historical reality and increased students' online skills for searching and evaluating information.

Although we desired an interdisciplinary collaboration, we each had our own perspectives and goals. Our library research objectives were to teach the students basic information literacy skills: finding, accessing, and using information efficiently and ethically. We wanted to ensure that students gained an understanding of how to develop search strategies in order to find precise results and to realize that not all resources are freely available online. Since students would be involved in historical research, we also wanted them to learn to use print indexes to find primary sources not indexed electronically, as well as how to access scholarly databases for online searches. An example Nichols used asked students what type of sources an open web search would elicit if they wanted to find scholarly information on breast cancer or spanking as a form of child discipline. Although students appreciate the humor in this example, it also helps them realize that scholarly databases, indexed by people and not word-matching algorithms by machines, can find the scholarly material they need in fewer steps, thereby saving them time and effort.

We also wanted to lessen library anxiety. Some students avoid using the library or fail to ask the librarians for assistance. In structuring the collaboration as we did, we not only gave students a mini tour of the library while pointing out specific locations to access the resources they would need for their projects but also met individually with students and cotaught the sessions on primary and secondary sources. This personal interaction, as well as assisting the students one on one, helped students perceive the librarians as helpful guides rather than authoritarian guardians of the stacks.

For a history professor, the struggle to engage students in the past can be frustrating. Although primary sources are the basis of all historical interpretation, many students do not have the skills to evaluate and engage with historical sources on their own and, unfortunately, when teaching 500 years of history in 15 weeks, the amount of time spent actively engaging in primary source analysis is limited. This emphasis on content resulted in a primarily lecture-based course, which not only failed to involve students in hands-on historical experiences but also was unsuccessful in giving them a sense of what historians do as researchers. This is vital to a liberal education, for students often feel that the past, as represented in textbooks, is uncontested and permanent. However, understanding the process of historical research allows them to recognize that creating historical meaning is a process of ongoing interpretation.

Our teaching goals for both the face-to-face and online components included guiding students in analyzing primary and secondary sources and evaluating them as constructed information. In addition, we desired to introduce students to searching within scholarly databases and to educate them on critically considering the sources found on the open web.

DISCUSSION OF FACULTY–LIBRARIAN COLLABORATION

As with any collaboration, we faced many time-related issues. Our constraints were both real and historical. Working on creating a unit that would meet our teaching and learning goals was challenging. First, we needed to determine how to situate the unit within the course. We chose a two-week window for the project, with a hybrid approach. During the first week, students met in the library and had a session on online searching, followed later in the week with a session on using print materials. Students were required to find a minimum of two online sources to complete their project. Other online components included a pre- and postsurvey and assistance through e-mail during their out-of-class research time.

As we began our first collaboration, the decision for the historical timing of the unit was to model Mudrock on a smaller scale. Her syllabus and course materials (Mudrock, 2005b), including her sample fates, are available on her website (http://www.lib .washington.edu/subject/History/perspectives/char.html) and offered us a starting point. Since Mudrock had focused on World War I, we also decided to center on this global conflict. This unit came at a convenient time in the semester, past the midway point, when students welcomed a break from the classroom routine but with enough time left in the semester to accommodate such a project.

We then developed our version of the game of research in which we created a set of historical "fates." Our fate cards, unlike Mudrock's, were not based on actual people, but rather on generic roles, such as an American Red Cross nurse or a British soldier in the trenches. One of our goals in generating fates was to decenter the United States and concentrate on international issues, so most fates focused on the European experience of both the Entente and Central powers. Each of our fate cards included an inspiring image and target questions to guide students as they researched historical events and persons. Our fate cards also provided more structure and context to assist the students, who had only two weeks to complete this assignment. In addition to a short description of the fate's character, we created between four and six focusing questions for students to explore in the historical context of their personae. For example, one of the fate cards explored the theme of chemical warfare, as illustrated in Figure 4.1.

We did not, however, simply hand the fates out and let the students explore. We decided that they needed to understand the historical sources and library research before we allowed them to delve into their fates. First, the unit took place after students learned about World War I in class. At the session in the library, Nichols gave a short presentation reminding students of the types of historical sources available and reiterating the differences in primary and secondary materials. We then had students choose their fates out of a bowl, with a short period for "trade-ins" if they desired. For the remainder of the class, Nichols led the students through the online component of the unit, modeling web database searches in order to demonstrate how to form the type of search strings they might use to find answers to questions about their fates. During the second library meeting, Nichols introduced students to the *Readers' Guide to Periodical Literature* and led them on a brief tour of the needed library locations to see where the magazines and newspapers were located. We then allowed class time for students to explore resources and their fates using online and print resources from the era of study, while we remained available to answer questions and offer point-of-need assistance.

After this, students had a brief amount of class time to troubleshoot any issues they encountered as they worked on creating a historically informed, primary-source-based document relevant to their fates. During this time, students could e-mail either instructor for additional help. Students also filled out a postunit survey online. For their assignment, students were required to locate at least four primary sources, two of which needed to be online. Based upon these sources, students would complete one of three possible assignment choices. First, they could compose letters home from the perspectives of the individuals represented by their fate cards that incorporated the answers to the questions on their cards. The second option allowed students to discuss in a diary entry or entries their experiences as the person on their fate card in that situation. The third alternative was less personal, suggesting the student create a hypothetical interview with the fate card persona, writing both the answers and the questions.

As with any new initiative, the project planning and development of materials was time-consuming. After we decided on a time frame, we split the workload, with DuRocher sketching out historical fates, creating the assignment for the project, and assessing student work. Nichols then took the fates and shaped them based on the materials available in the library and online, created the presentations and handouts for the classroom sessions, and led the library sessions.

Figure 4.1. Sample World War I Fate Card

Gas masks for man and horse demonstrated by American soldier, circa 1917–1918, 1918–1919. ARC Identifier 516483 / Local Identifier 52-S-2303.

You are a soldier fighting with the 370th U.S. Infantry. You are gassed as you're fighting under French command during the Meuse-Argonne campaign. Your task is to discover what it was like to suffer from a mustard gas attack. Some questions to explore include the following:

> What are the symptoms of mustard gas exposure?
> What sort of treatment was available to you?
> What kinds of gas masks were available?
> What was your prognosis likely to be?

Keep in mind that some of the information you need will be found through Health Sciences resources.

Our first iteration of the course components was successful in many ways. The students enjoyed the experience, evidenced by those wishing to repeat it with World War II and remarking positively on it in their evaluations; many noted that the activity was the highlight of the course. Although we spent a great deal of time before the unit fine-tuning the fates and presentations, a few issues developed that required revision. The issue of historical time was the primary problem that emerged for each discipline. Even though students had learned about World War I, they were much less familiar with it than with World War II, and sometimes students confused the two. World War I was a modern war, yet students live in a postmodern world so they had a difficult time imagining themselves in that era. This proved an issue in the outcomes for Nichols, as students often became frustrated when they could not find materials in online database searches because they were using postmodern terms, overlooking the historical context of the era. Searching for "African American" instead of "Negro" (the term used at the time) in online searches led to some student aggravation with the scholarly database searches. Those students expressed a desire to google their fates, thereby missing a central point of the assignment.

In our assessment of this unit, however, we were encouraged and impressed overall by the level of student engagement, so we decided to implement the unit again the following spring semester with some changes. These included adding historically appropriate search terms to the fate cards and creating a short presentation on keyword searches for online databases that highlighted locating World War I sources. During our second attempt, both of these modifications improved the students' experiences, although some still struggled to find appropriate online sources through databases.

After our second venture, we decided that the idea and collaboration were solid but that the implementation remained problematic. Although it meant altering the entire project, we felt that since the World War I fates were not leading students to good primary sources and positive searching experiences, we needed to shift our focus to the World War II era. This modification included other changes, primarily expanding the scope of the assignment to include both primary and secondary sources in order to help students distinguish between the two and to offer them exposure to other scholars' viewpoints.

Although the time needed to research new fates was an issue, creating new scenarios offered DuRocher an opportunity to have students explore some of the less-told experiences of World War II from a variety of perspectives, such as a Nazi soldier under the command of General Rommel or the American soldier held as a prisoner of war by the Japanese. Having access to more and varied sources on World War II, including popular magazines of the time period, allowed us to add some interesting cultural fates.

After the first implementation of the new model in the fall semester of 2007, we felt the changes improved students' experiences. We found that students were eager to learn about other facets of the war and that most had a basic level of background knowledge about the war itself. The library resources of this era, especially those available online, were also richer, more varied, and easier to access than those for World War I. Interestingly, though, we found that as we revised and taught the unit over the next three semesters, these initial strengths eventually became weaknesses. Students' familiarity with the war, especially from a U.S.-centered point of view, resulted in a lack of personal perspective. Students repeatedly were unwilling to go beyond the one-dimensional readings of history influenced by current culture, viewing all Germans or Japanese as universally bad, and the Americans and their allies as unquestioningly good. Although we were meeting our goals with regard to information literacy, the level of engagement and critical analysis of historical sources was less than we had hoped to see. After much thought, we decided to reconceptualize the unit one more time, this time focusing on the Vietnam conflict.

DuRocher suggested Vietnam as the next topic because so few students in secondary schools learn history beyond World War II, and this generation of students always seemed fascinated by the subject in class. Vietnam's contested history and cultural baggage allowed us to create fates that dealt with ethical dilemmas, many of which still exist today. With Vietnam being the first televised and media-saturated war, it offered an exponential increase in the sources and materials for students to explore. In addition, it allowed students to expand their understanding of primary sources beyond newspapers and magazines to include videos, interviews, and photographs.

By Vietnam, our fate cards had undergone a complete evolution from our World War I unit. In the first component, we focused primarily on events and people who embodied the general concepts of the war itself. For Vietnam, our concentration was on people and their choices, which we felt offered students the opportunity to make a personal connection with the past and consider the controversies of the time. In designing our fate cards, we sought to create products that looked at the conflict from a variety of perspectives, selecting experiences that were both supportive and combative. We also included viewpoints from both an American and a global perspective. International opinions were often unknown to students, sparking their curiosity, and encouraging many to consider outsider perspectives, even those with which they admittedly disagreed. Because the topics were inherently complex and often controversial, students gained an understanding about what motivated people to behave in certain ways and how the Vietnam experience contributed to our current global politics. Our controversial fates for this era included being a member of the Silent Majority, a member of a radical student organization, an evacuee at the fall of Saigon, a U.S. Army wife living on base, a nurse stationed in Da Nang, a draft dodger, or one of the Winter Soldiers, among others (see Figure 4.2). These fates forced students to put themselves into historical events as they grappled with difficult, real-life issues of the late 1960s and early 1970s.

In the beginning of our collaboration, the combined online and face-to-face model we had developed offered us a comfortable balance, as it allowed us to observe firsthand what students understood as well as their struggles. Our observations and student feedback led us to tailor our future sessions and materials. It also demonstrated for us how students relied on the online components for research, confirming to us that undergraduates felt more comfortable doing research as they did much of everything else: online.

In moving to an all-online format, we sought to embrace students' previous knowledge in a student-centered learning model and encourage them to relate their previous skills to library-based historical research. In creating the online unit, we already had the smaller pieces necessary, created from our hybrid sessions and evaluations. We just needed to reconsider the most effective approaches for online collaboration.

Once DuRocher decided to teach the global studies class online, we began to consider how to transition this unit to accommodate online learners. We started by reimagining the fates based on available online resources and modified the unit to include handout options to post online to replace our face-to-face presentations. With the online course, the collaboration is also less personal for both of us. Instead of team teaching and assisting the students together, most of our collaboration takes place before the semester begins. Once we reach the Vietnam unit, Nichols is then available to students as a research guide, embedded in Blackboard and via e-mail.

CHALLENGES OF THE ONLINE COLLABORATION

We faced two major and discipline-specific challenges during the online evolution phase of our partnership. For Nichols, the primary issue that emerged was student overconfidence in their ability to find information. Just as the University of California–Berkeley

---

Figure 4.2. Sample Vietnam Fate Card

Lieutenant Commander Dorothy Ryan checks the medical chart of Marine Corporal Roy Hadaway of Ca-lera, Alabama, aboard the hospital ship *USS Repose* off South Vietnam. Miss Ryan, from Bronx, New York, is one of 29 nurses aboard the hospital ship selected from 500 volunteers of the Navy Nurse Corps.

Image: ARC Identifier: 532500: Navy Nurses. 04/22/1966; General Photograph File of the U.S. Marine Corps, compiled 1927–1981, documenting the period 1775– 198; Record Group 127: Records of the U.S. Marine Corps, 1775– 999; Still Picture Records Section, Special Media Archives Services Division (NWCS-S), National Archives and Records Administration at College Park.

You are a Navy nurse working on a hospital ship, the *USS Repose* off South Vietnam. Your task is to discover what it was like to work in a war zone surrounded by the wounded and the dying.

> Describe your daily experiences and reactions to them.
> Describe your working and living conditions.
> Describe your typical day.
> Discuss the stress of your job and how you deal with it.
> Discuss any personal safety issues or fears.

Teaching Library surveys found that "students think they know more about accessing information and conducting library research than they are able to demonstrate when put to the test" (Maughan, 2001: 83), we too found that our students were no different. After the first semester, we developed a preunit and postunit survey to help us understand students' previous research experiences and found, for example, that most students claimed to know how to use the *Readers' Guide to Periodical Literature* already, only to find during class that they were unfamiliar with this resource. (In one class, despite affirmative preunit survey responses, students verbally admitted that none of them knew how to use the *Readers' Guide*.) Our students also overestimated their ability to perform library research. Many entered the classroom with what Stephen J. Bell calls IAKT (I Already Know That) Syndrome, in which they are convinced that the librarian has nothing new to offer them (Bell, 2007). On the preunit survey, students indicated they were "moderately comfortable" or "very comfortable" finding items needed for research, both online and in print. Students clearly based their answers on their perceived abilities, not actual practice. For example, 30 to 55 percent of students rated their ability for using the *Readers' Guide*, their ability to do subject heading searching, and their skills at online database searching as "very comfortable," the highest level for completing these tasks.

This student perception proved a challenging issue for Nichols, as one of her major goals of the collaboration was to promote sufficiency in areas that many students claimed to have already achieved. We alleviated this disconnect between what students believed and what we were seeing in class by changing the preunit survey format from a Likert scale to an open-ended question. We asked students to explain what the *Readers' Guide to Periodical Literature* was, an approach similar to our face-to-face verbal queries. Most students, when asked for a specific answer, realized that they might not fully understand the topic, opening them up to the new learning experience. Indeed, when we surveyed our spring 2008 sections with this open-ended question, only 1 in 32 students attempted to explain the *Readers' Guide*. The second way we sought to resolve this issue was to stress the difference between academic sources and searches and those on the open web. Nichols's approach and tone focused not on disregarding the open web but on demonstrating that using scholarly databases and good searching skills would result in finding better and more accurate information in a shorter time period. We wanted students to realize that we all use the open web, but in order to be responsible users of the information we find on the web we need to take an extra step to critically evaluate what we find there.

Another major challenge we faced in engaging students in historical research, especially the online components, was plagiarism. Although the issue of plagiarism can occur in any student writing, in our experience it appeared to be more prevalent in the all-online environment. Despite having an ethics and plagiarism clause in the syllabus, and even with reminders that the assignment must be in their own words, students in the online class were much more likely to plagiarize content than those who met with us face to face. The urge to cut and paste from a source, or several sources, often appeared to be too overwhelming to resist. When addressed, the student response often centered on the idea that the source answered the questions on their fate card better than they felt they could. This desire to use someone else's words may come from a student's inexperience with doing research, as well as a failure to understand the directions of the assignment. Another possible reason may be that in an online format, students are more comfortable relegating the authority to another voice. This is perhaps a side effect of the online course, in which fewer students develop a personal connection and rapport with the professor and librarian. Without that comfort zone created from personal interaction, students may be less at ease writing their answers in their own voice, especially since there is an element of creativity involved in each of the essay options.

After the first semester, plagiarism became a central issue within the course. DuRocher implemented several changes in an attempt to educate students and maintain academic integrity. These included having students sign an honor statement and posting a handout on what constitutes plagiarism. In the directions, DuRocher clarified to explicitly direct students to write their essays in their own words and voice and, finally, made it clear that the penalty for plagiarism was steep, including but not limited to failure of the assignment with academic reports filed. We wanted to be sure students understood that cutting and pasting without giving credit was not an acceptable academic practice and to instead teach them proper citation methods.

Other students found that the relative anonymity of an online class offered them the opportunity to engage in new ideas or ethical choices without fear of personal embarrassment, peer criticism, or regional or cultural pressure. Some students discovered that the format more easily allowed them to adopt the personae of their fate fully and without risk, as they were not attempting to conform to their own personal identity. As we will discuss in the evaluation section, the online format, in essence, made the role-play aspect of the fates more engaging for students, with many remarking that they had a personal connection to the conflict in living family members. Overall, students were more willing to discuss in detail their personal connections with these historical experiences in the online courses than in the face-to-face format.

2 PROGRAM PLANNING

The program plan for this collaboration in an online environment began with an increased demand for courses online to serve a growing population in our region that was either pursuing a job full time or regionally isolated from campus. The early positive response to online courses at MSU resulted in a request for additional courses, especially those that would satisfy a general education requirement. Currently, MSU offers 300 courses online each semester, with that number increasing by 30 percent each year. DuRocher first offered History 201 online in the fall of 2008, and this shift in format required an entire reconceptualization of the course and some changes to our collaborative unit.

It has taken three semesters for the online course to evolve into a model that satisfied the needs of everyone involved: the students, the librarian, and the professor. DuRocher developed the online course using Blackboard Academic version 7.3, which is the recommended format for online courses at MSU. The vast majority of instructors, approximately 99 percent, utilize this format, as training and assistance are readily available from the dedicated support staff. In addition, MSU employs an instructional designer to assist professors in creating course models in Blackboard. The format of the overall course is one of weekly units, with some exceptions such as the Vietnam activity, which, as a research project, requires multiple weeks. Before the due date, students choose their fates and download the supporting documents and directions for the assignment. While this allows students ample time to engage in research and the professor to troubleshoot with students having difficulties, students start researching before the content on Vietnam is covered. Most students, however, do not seem to struggle with a lack of historical knowledge about the war. This is due to the online sources that we steer students toward, most of which have an introductory page to contextualize the source.

The online format required a reconceptualization of how to approach this collaboration. As noted earlier, we needed to have our conceptualization and preparation done before the semester began. Although the transition to an online format presented both of us with a learning curve, we felt it went smoothly for two reasons. First, we had already worked together for several years and had developed a clear understanding of each other's overall goals, strengths, and approaches. Secondly, we had already implemented and modified the unit, twice overhauling it completely. In addition, we had years of feedback that guided our understanding of what students gained from the experience.

With the online format, we learned how to use the features of Blackboard to offer students an interdisciplinary experience online. This included a discussion board for questions, which allowed for student centered learning as their peers could provide assistance. Another challenge was to create a folder that archived all the materials directly into Blackboard, so that the students had their own repository of information. The online format also allowed us to insert links directly into the folder of the assignment. For the library component, the course included a button on the menu that took students directly to the library portal. In addition, we also used the library's live chat function. We were lucky in that there were no extra costs associated with this, other than our time learning to use the interface and re-creating our unit. We were also fortunate to have advice from the designer in the Instructional Technology department. One of the pluses of moving to the online format was that relying on the Internet solved many of the access issues we had experienced within the physical library. With the Internet, students were able to use, post, and interact with these materials at any time.

ONLINE LEARNING MODEL

Our focus on creating an innovative online model for information literacy was to maintain the same goals as our previous blended sessions: giving students the tools to become familiar with both library-based methods of scholarly research and thinking critically about historical sources. For an online class, we knew one of the greatest difficulties would be the information literacy aspect, as it is difficult to convince students who feel they have a high level of understanding of online searching to engage with a specific library resource. During our exchanges on this issue, we concluded that more of our emphasis needed to be on teaching evaluation methods for online sources, and that while we would continue to utilize the library portal we would expand our definition of viable resources beyond those of the library and into the larger scholarship available on the web.

Although we continued to identify scholarly databases students could access on campus, we expanded our definition of acceptable sources to include approved online scholarly collections, linked and listed for students to explore. Nichols created a pathfinder (soon to be a LibGuide) listing scholarly materials on Vietnam available through MSU's library, such as EBSCO's Military & Government Collection. In addition, DuRocher located historical databases for students to use in their research such as the

Vietnam Center and Archive, hosted by Texas Tech University (2010), which includes more than 3 million digitized primary sources (http://www.vietnam.ttu.edu/). The decision to give students a list of approved sites and resources, instead of allowing them to find the materials on their own, was recognition that by using an online format students had access to an array of sources unavailable in the library holdings.

We also allowed students to use one source that did not appear on the lists of approved links as long as they could demonstrate that the source was credible. The directions explicitly forbade the use of Wikipedia (except for the references sections), and we created a handout to help students evaluate websites to determine if they were scholarly in nature, valid, and unbiased. Adding the web evaluation component to the class integrated a necessary skill for students accustomed to unfettered open web searching. The other major modification was assigning fates. After discarding the idea of giving students fates based on last name groupings, we decided to allow students to pick their fates themselves. Ideally, we dreamed about creating a website that students could go to which would choose their fate randomly, perhaps from "The Wheel of Fate"; however, that programming feat has yet to be accomplished. We had concerns about students picking their own fates, primarily that they would choose the first experience they read, which could limit their ability to immerse themselves into or even care about that character. We also worried that all the students might choose the same one or two fates, leaving many interesting areas unexplored.

Our worries about the fates were unfounded. Students picked from a wide range of fates, likely based on their gender, age, and personal knowledge of the conflict. Some noted that they picked the fate they knew the least about, while some chose based on previous knowledge or personal interest. In part, this diversity is likely due to the nature of online courses, which encompass students from more varied backgrounds than does a campus face-to-face general education course.

We were both new to teaching in an all-online format. Although DuRocher conferred with MSU's instructional designer for Blackboard in constructing the course, and students had access to help with technical issues within Blackboard, we otherwise learned on our own. After consulting with literature about online teaching and discussing our own goals, just as we created our first set of fates on our own, we also delved into the online experience on our own. Although online teaching offered a different experience from more traditional forms of instruction, we found the change invigorated us. Teaching online encourages instructors to determine exactly what they hope to communicate to students and how to develop the most effective pedagogical strategies.

IMPACT ON STUDENT LEARNING

Our objectives were to engage students in active learning, problem solving, and higher-order thinking. The game of research approach was appealing to us because it encouraged students to engage with the material rather than memorize historical facts. First, students practiced the skills of finding and evaluating information by locating primary and secondary sources applicable to their fates. Second, they analyzed their resources to create a historically informed primary source. In writing a response from the viewpoint of their fates, students gained both empathy by placing themselves in a historical moment and an understanding of how primary sources function for the scholar, as snapshots of events and emotions.

Assessment: Our Hybrid Experience on World War II

After our first attempt, we gauged student learning with a variety of evaluative methods, beginning with an anonymous preunit and postunit survey using a Likert scale. DuRocher embedded this study into the participation grade, with a bonus question at the end of the survey that students turned in for credit. Using the Likert scale, our survey instrument measured student comfort level for using online databases. It focused on how students conduct subject-heading searches in the library catalog and when using the *Readers' Guide to Periodical Literature*. On the postunit survey, we also included several open-ended questions, including "What did you like about this activity?"; "What did you learn from this activity?"; and "What changes would you suggest for next time?" The entire list of postunit survey questions can be found in Appendix 4.1.

In the spring of 2007, our second semester of the World War II unit, students showed growth in several areas, especially in terms of library skills and online searching (see Table 4.1). This demonstrates that students believed they had learned something about online searching, most likely better search techniques, from our sessions. The most striking increase was in subject-heading searches, with 53 percent of students concluding that after instruction and practice they were "very comfortable" performing this task.

Survey Results from 2007

In the open-ended questions, we generally found that students reported more engagement with the materials and enjoyed being active agents in their own learning process. In the spring of 2007, we found a variety of responses to the question, "What did you like

Table 4.1. World War II Unit (FtF) Survey Results			
Preunit Survey	How comfortable do you feel doing these tasks on your own?		
	Very Comfortable	**Somewhat Comfortable**	**I Have No Idea How to Do This**
Locating primary sources?	30%	48%	22%
Searching for information using the online databases (EBSCO, etc.)?	45%	41%	16%
Doing subject heading searches in the library's catalog?	20%	59%	23%
Postunit Survey	How comfortable do you feel doing these tasks on your own?		
	Very comfortable	**Somewhat comfortable**	**I Have No Idea How to Do This**
Locating primary sources?	49%	47%	4%
Searching for information using the online databases (EBSCO, etc.)?	64%	34%	2%
Doing subject heading searches in the library's catalog?	53%	38%	9%

about this activity?" Many noted the issue we were attempting to resolve, with one student writing, "I like that it made me use the library sources because I haven't had to in the past and need to learn." Another student addressed the other information literacy aspect we sought to integrate, noting, "It allowed everyone to learn about the library's resources, regardless of the [sic] previous experience, and it was also a refresher on basic research techniques." Another remarked on their previous lack of knowledge, exclaiming, "I learned that there are a bunch more databases thatn [sic] EBSCO! Also, I had never used Net Library before this activity. Net Library was a great resource for me and is useful for other classes as well." Students gaining and practicing skills in this class that they could utilize for the entirety of their career fulfilled Nichols's goals of information literacy.

Other student responses focused on the historical aspect of the unit: "I liked 'choosing our fate.' I thought it was pretty cool seeing at random what we could have been back in the time of World War II." A few students commented on how interesting they found their fates to be and eagerly joined in the role-playing aspect of the "game." This assessment of the World War II unit confirmed our judgment, based on student interactions, that students enjoyed tracking down the possible experiences for their fates and that they benefited from the unit both in historical knowledge and in research skills.

Assessment: Our Hybrid Experience on Vietnam

In our assessment a year later, during the spring semester of 2008, the last one in which we used the hybrid format, with the unit now focused on Vietnam, our modifications showed further improvement in student skills. Our assessment format expanded to include scaled answers, open-ended questions, and true/false statements. Most students in the preunit survey chose the middle answers, with 63 percent of the students ranking their ability as "good" when searching online databases (see Table 4.2). In searching for information on the Internet, 52 percent felt their skill was "good," with another 38 percent rating their ability as "excellent." Not a single student described his or her online searching proficiency as "limited."

Despite their high preunit survey self-assessments, there was still an incredible upward shift in most categories of the postunit survey for the spring of 2008 Vietnam unit. In addition, the true/false questions demonstrated that students felt they had

Table 4.2. Vietnam (Hybrid) Preunit Survey Results				
	Rate your ability to accomplish each of these tasks on your own:			
	Excellent	Good	So-So	Limited
Searching for information using the library's online catalog (Find Books and More)?	30%	47%	20%	3%
Searching for information using the online databases (EBSCO, etc.)?	27%	63%	7%	3%
Searching for information on the Internet?	38%	52%	10%	0.0%

gained skills and confidence from their library research experience. In answering the question, "I feel more confident in my ability to find materials in the library," student response was 100 percent "true." As one student noted, "I always think that I know how to use the resources the library has to offer, but every time I participate in one of these 'activities' I seem to learn something I definitely did not know before."

Results of 2008 Survey

Students' open responses focused primarily on the historical aspect of the class. One student wrote that he or she learned, "How to better find sources, plus a little bit extra about the Vietnam War." Another found the hands-on approach exciting: "I liked how we got to review how to find certain print sources. I had forgotten part of that. The microfilms are fun to look at, seeing how the old newspapers and magazines were." The only negative feedback we received had to do with issues of time. First, students desired more time to research and complete the project; second, the timing of the Vietnam unit placed it near the end of the semester. As one student noted, "Maybe do it earlier in the semester: around exams everyone has too much work to be doing." Another student wanted the unit to take place earlier, suggesting, "I would do this activity at the begining [*sic*] of the year so that it could help us all semester." This feedback supports our belief that we were meeting our goals.

ASSESSMENT OF ONLINE LEARNING

When we moved to an online format, we also needed a new method of student assessment. The first semester found the Vietnam assignment due right before finals week, and so we had limited feedback from students. In the following semesters, we broke the unit down and began it earlier. Despite not having much formal feedback in our first semester, many students attached notes or comments to their assignments about their personal interest or reaction to the assignment. Some students recalled having relatives in the conflict, and several had asked permission to interview family and friends for their papers. One student commented, "I am probably closer to that era than most of your students. I am 47 years old, the war was in its climax when I was growing up. I hae [*sic*] worked with several Vets who served there. It must have been a horrible thing to serve your Country and be hated by some of their countrymen. What I liked was I read a couple stories from individuals who served and talked about it. They were human. They felt. They were trying to survive." Our analysis of student responses led to the development of an anonymous survey embedded within the participation grade of the course with open-ended questions, such as, "What did you like/dislike about the Vietnam exercise and why?" The assessment also included several general questions about the course itself, in which students prominently mentioned the Vietnam exercise.

Many students began noting that they lacked prior knowledge about the Vietnam Era, such as the student who noted, "It is a war that we do not learn about or study in school," and "I liked learning about Vietnam, because most of my history classes in the past just brush past it acting like it didn't happen." In addition to being an interesting topic, many found the role-playing aspect to be their favorite part. Statements like "I liked getting to research specific characters involved in or affected by Vietnam" and "I liked that I could imagine that I was the person and try to write about my made up experiences at the time" summarize student reactions.

The other theme prevalent in the feedback is the format of the assignment. Students valued critical and creative thinking, as evidenced in remarks by one student, who wrote, "I found it interesting to learn about the subject matters [*sic*] and to not write a paper like we do in most History classes. Instead we were able to write what we had learned in a different format." Another more succinctly noted, "I liked that the assignment was not simply a report on Vietnam." One student elaborated: "I especially liked the fact that we could choice [*sic*] a letter home as the assignment. It made you think about what the person felt when leaving and what their family must have went through when they left." This personal reaction is ubiquitous in the feedback, and most students ended with a discussion of their personal connection to this era. As one student observed, "I learned a lot about the treatment of POWs in North Vietnamese prisons that I didn't know before. I was fascinated as well as appalled." Another stated, "I liked the exercise, because it gave me the perspective of how people felt and lived as an American durind [*sic*] the war." Wrote another student, "I liked researching a person and trying to figure out what that person felt like during the Vietnam War. It was fun taking the role of a person from that period of time and understanding how they survived and felt during that time." These responses suggest that we met one of our objects for students to make a personal connection with history.

While most students discussed their enjoyment of the approach and the format of the assignment, they were less satisfied with their limited search options. Most would rather have searched the open web and not relied on the library databases: "What I didn't like about the Vietnam exercise was the list of Websites we were given to use." Others felt frustrated that they could not easily find the materials they wanted, noting, "I disliked the sources provided because I had trouble getting them to pull up the information" and "I felt that it was hard finding the right type of sources needed." This discomfort with using databases and finding scholarly information on the web is an issue that we continue to improve in the online environment. Students and faculty have grown accustomed to open web searching to find information, but full access to scholarly resources is not freely available on the web. For students, the requirement to use online databases appears to have been a source of contention, likely because they did not have the skills to search them successfully and found the experience frustrating. In our earlier units, the face-to-face interaction helped us assist students having these same difficulties at point of need. Due to the asynchronous nature of the online class, those students did not have the advantage of receiving immediate help when problems arose. Although we supplied materials designed to help in their research, the students did not always understand how to apply them.

The answers on the online student assessment instrument reflect an interesting shift from the face-to-face hybrid class experiences. In these earlier units, DuRocher observed that students did not successfully imagine themselves within the role-play and often failed to engage with the fate fully, while Nichols was pleased by the students' increased comfort level and ability to find information through the library resources. In the online environment, however, the opposite perspective appears to prevail. The negative comments from most students address their frustrations with the search process, finding materials, or being uncertain in their evaluation of the materials they encountered. The majority of responses noted that most students felt they knew little about the Vietnam conflict before the assignment but had learned and viewed history differently after the unit, which was exactly what DuRocher wanted to see.

It is our consensus that the online format offers pedagogical challenges in teaching skill-based activities. Unlike our earlier face-to-face efforts, the librarian cannot easily model narrowing a topic or performing precise searches and cannot demonstrate skills directly with each student. While we have discussed making greater use of web tutorials and LibGuides, we suspect that the online students may ignore them, assuming that they already possess the necessary proficiency. The information literacy skills that students successfully gained in earlier units appear to be missing from the Internet component, and that is disconcerting. Online students, however, embraced the material and its personal aspects beyond that of a traditional, face-to-face, general education class. They recall the unit as the high point of the semester and appreciated that the assignment allowed them to intersect their own personal interests with the larger historical record. As we continue to collaborate in the online environment, we will examine new approaches as they surface and modify our efforts to increase students' acquisition of information literacy skills. If we decide to strengthen our web tutorials and add LibGuide pages, then we will need to find a way to ensure that students make use of them, either by including questions on the final exam or by building in another assessment such as bibliography analysis.

CONCLUSION

The journey of our partnership led to many avenues for engaging students in online learning, problem solving, and research skills. What began as a cooperative unit on World War I has evolved as we created multifaceted fates for historical events and taught students how to research these personae through searching online databases. We recognized that such collaboration takes time, and we constantly sought feedback in order to improve and further engage students.

Our earlier hybrid format, combining face to face and online, allowed us to develop a fully online approach to teaching information literacy. We see this as an evolving model for helping other faculty and librarians create their own interdisciplinary collaboration. Through this liaison, we offered students a contextual experience with the past that created a meaningful understanding of a historical reality and increased students' online skills for searching for and evaluating information. This model is innovative because it offers diverse undergraduate populations the opportunity to, quite literally, choose their own fates. Students have the chance to follow their own interests, to find new and different sources, and to combine these efforts with their own personal views, which results in varied responses. In addition, educators can use this online model for any instructional unit that encourages students to take on roles or consider multiple perspectives of a topic, an era, or an event. For instance, this approach could be used for examining art movements or artists, literature and writers, or to expand on themes in cultural studies and education.

We based our collaboration on a shared inspiration to revise the manner in which university students learned in just one component. We focused on creating a partnership that allowed us to strengthen a student-centered learning module. Our approaches, topics, and implementation methods evolved, but our goals remained hands-on, engaged learning. We hope that our success encourages others to collaborate, utilizing all of the online resources currently available in order to continue to educate students to gain online literacy in a world that requires it on a daily basis. Online collaboration requires ongoing reevaluation, and while our current learning module functions well, we continue to consider the future possibilities of emerging resources such as that of wikis, tags, and Skype.

REFERENCES

Bell, Stephen J. 2007. "Stop IAKT Syndrome with Student Live Search Demos." *Reference Services Review* 35, no. 1: 98–108.

Durisin, Patricia, ed. 2002. *Information Literacy Programs: Successes and Challenges*. Binghamton, NY: The Haworth Information Press.

Grafstein, Ann. 2002. "A Discipline-Based Approach to Information Literacy." *Journal of Academic Librarianship* 28, no. 4: 197. Academic Search Premier, EBSCOhost.

Kobrin, David. 1996. *Beyond the Textbook: Teaching History Using Documents and Primary Sources*. Portsmouth, NH: Heinemann.

Lyons, John F. 2004. "Teaching U.S. History Online: Problems and Prospects." *The History Teacher* 37, no. 4 (August). http://www.historycooperative.org/journals/ht/37.4/lyons.html.

Manuel, Kate. 2002. "Teaching Information Literacy to Generation Y." In *Information Literacy Programs: Successes and Challenges*, edited by Patricia Durisin, 195–218. Binghamton, NY: The Haworth Information Press.

Maughan, Patricia Davitt. 2001. "Assessing Information Literacy among Undergraduates: A Discussion of the Literature and the University of California–Berkeley Assessment Experience." *College and Research Libraries* 62, no. 1: 71–85.

Mellon, Constance A. 1986. "Library Anxiety: A Grounded Theory and Its Development." College & Research Libraries 47, no. 2: 160–165. *Library, Information Science & Technology Abstracts*, EBSCOhost.

Mudrock, Theresa. 2005a. "Engaging Students in the Game of Research." *Perspectives* (December): 15–17.

Mudrock, Theresa. 2005b. "Engaging Students in the Game of Research: Syllabus and Course Materials." University of Washington Libraries. http://www.lib.washington.edu/subject/History/perspectives/.

Ochsner, Jeffrey Karl. 1995. "Understanding the Holocaust through the U.S. Holocaust Memorial Museum." *Journal of Architectural Education* 48, no. 4: 240–249.

Texas Tech University. 2010. The Vietnam Center and Archive. Texas Tech University. Accessed February 8. http://www.vietnam.ttu.edu/.

Wineburg, Samuel S. 2001. *Historical Thinking and Other Unnatural Acts: Charting the Future of Teaching the Past*. Philadelphia: Temple University Press.

Appendix 4.1. Vietnam Unit: Pre- and Postunit Survey Questions

	Rate your ability to accomplish each of these tasks on your own:			
	Excellent	Good	So-So	Limited
Searching for information using the library's online catalog (Find Books and More)?				
Searching for information using the online databases (EBSCO, etc.)?				
Searching for information on the Internet?				
Locating primary sources?				
Evaluating websites (for validity, currency, accuracy, etc.)?				
Doing subject heading searches in the library's catalog?				
Citing sources correctly and avoiding plagiarism?				
Using the *Readers' Guide to Periodical Literature* to find information on a topic?*				

*This question was asked only on the postunit survey for the Vietnam Unit. An open-ended question (What is the *Readers' Guide to Periodical Literature* and how do you use it?) was asked on the preunit survey.

Questions from the Postunit Survey only:

True or False?

I now have a better idea of what kinds of materials the library has for me to use.

I feel more confident in my ability to find materials in the library.

I have a better understanding of how to find information using print indexes and bibliographies.

Open-Ended Questions

What did you like about this activity in the library?

What did you learn from the "Game of Research" activity?

How would you improve this activity?

Open and Online Learning

SECTION INTRODUCTION

In this second part of the book, the author teams explore open and fully online learning initiatives. According to the United Nations Educational Scientific and Cultural Organization (UNESCO, 2010), open learning is defined as "instructional systems in which many facets of the learning process are under the control of the learner." The term *open* in this context means more than open access and emphasizes teaching practices that place the learner at the center. According to UNESCO (2010), open learning "attempts to deliver learning opportunities where, when, and how the learner needs them." While open learning does not necessarily require online initiatives, the terms are related, especially with the development of distance-learning programs at open universities, such as Athabasca University and The Open University. The ongoing expansion of distance learning worldwide and developments in Web 2.0 technologies such as blogs, wikis, and social networking have also contributed to the advance of open learning in higher education.

This section features information literacy collaborations in fully online courses taught at a distance. UNESCO (2010) defines distance learning as "a system and a process that connects learners to distributed learning resources." This format is characterized by a "separation/distance of place and/or time between instructor and learner, amongst learners, and/or between learners and learning resources." Increasingly, the term *online learning* is used in place of, or interchangeably with, distance or distributed learning to describe a wide range of technology-mediated environments. For example, I. Elaine Allen and Jeff Seaman (2009) define online learning as "a course where most or all of the content is delivered online" and, in this context, online courses "typically have no face-to-face meetings." Open and online learning methodologies are having a significant impact on higher education globally. According to the International Council for Open and Distance Education (ICDE) (2009), "the open and distance university movement is removing barriers of geography, time and cost while maintaining quality of education." This focus on learner-centered practices, often mediated by technology, continues to expand in influence. The ICDE suggests that "in some countries open and distance education now serves more than one third of the student population and this is growing rapidly."

For this section, the author teams describe open and online learning efforts to teach information literacy at the undergraduate and graduate levels. This work takes place in interdisciplinary contexts and in specific disciplines such as social work, computer science, business and accounting, and education. This section describes courses and programs that are fully online using many different technologies to engage learners.

The first chapter in this section, "Supported Open Learning: Developing an Integrated Information Literacy Strategy Online," is coauthored by Clarissa Gosling and Ingrid Nix from The Open University, United Kingdom. This team examines a faculty-librarian partnership to integrate information literacy as well as information communication and technology (ICT) skills in an online social work program. This model is designed for work-based students who are actively engaged in careers while seeking professional certifications and qualifications through distance learning. The Open University provides a "supported open learning" methodology in which students work toward their degree at their own pace, working individually and in collaboration with peers, while receiving support from tutors, staff, and librarians. The online component increases collaborative opportunities among learners and with instructors, while expanding the technologies utilized, such as a modules-based learning environment, advanced search tools, and electronic library resources. This chapter illustrates the relationship between information literacy and ICT skills and the importance of this combined knowledge set in work settings. It also demonstrates the value of faculty-librarian collaboration, from planning through assessment, in the design of interactive online learning environments.

In the next chapter "Information-Literate Avatars: Resource-Based Learning in Second Life," Jenna Kammer and Tracey Thompson from New Mexico State University (NMSU) discuss the virtual world of Second Life as a distance-learning medium. The authors describe a resource-based learning approach to information literacy that prepares students to be active researchers using the Aggie Island Information Commons, which is NMSU's virtual library in Second Life. The authors expand upon an introductory course at the university, initially designed to deliver technical skills for navigating virtual environments in different disciplines, to include advanced information literacy skills and service learning within Second Life itself. This innovative methodology challenges learners to apply information literacy while working with community or academic organizations that have a virtual presence. This team faced many challenges including limited access to computing resources for Second Life, difficulty in locating relevant community organizations in this environment, and lack of funding. Through their collaboration, however, faculty and librarians overcame the roadblocks and demonstrated how an emerging virtual environment can be effectively developed to support information literacy.

The last two chapters in the book shift to online learning initiatives in graduate programs. In the first of these two chapters, David Lavoie, Andrew Rosman, and Shikha Sharma from The University of Connecticut (UConn) present a constructivist model for online pedagogy in "Information Literacy by Design: Recalibrating Graduate Professional Asynchronous Online Programs." This partnership extended beyond a faculty and librarian team to include a curriculum and instructional designer, media specialist, and students in clearly defined roles that shaped the ongoing evolution of asynchronous online courses. Through its instructional design center and faculty-librarian partnerships,

UConn developed a Resource-Enriched Learning Model (RELM) that supported faculty development and promoted a constructivist approach to online course design. This novel approach informed the design of UConn's first fully online asynchronous graduate program, the master of science in accounting (MSA). The authors describe a holistic approach to teaching information literacy online, in which learning outcomes are embedded throughout the curriculum and the program is designed collaboratively among all stakeholders representing multiple perspectives.

We close the book with another graduate model in "Working Outside the Org Chart: A Faculty–Librarian Partnership to Design an Online Graduate Course" by Susan M. Frey and Rebecca L. Fiedler from the Bayh College of Education at Indiana State University (ISU). The authors describe the development of a fully online information literacy course at the graduate level within the context of an open-access institution. This chapter explores collaboration as a matter of trust which allows faculty and librarians to share professional identities in a way that challenges traditional roles within an institution. Through an equal partnership, a faculty-librarian team at ISU designed a fully online, three-credit graduate course Accessing Information with Technology for the Department of Curriculum, Instruction, and Media Technology (CIMT). The asynchronous online format allows the instructors to reach learners who are working professionals and completing the course from locations around the world. The success of this initiative is defined by the willingness of the faculty and librarian team to build trust and to defy assumptions about established professional roles.

In all four chapters, faculty–librarian teams emphasize the importance of collaboration in the design of open and fully online courses and programs at the undergraduate and graduate levels. While the needs of your student population may differ somewhat from the learners discussed in this section, several key recommendations emerge from the practices offered here:

- Locate connections between information literacy and related literacy types such as information, communication, and technology (ICT).
- Consider the needs of working professionals in the design of online learning strategies and incorporate this perspective in open and online initiatives.
- Recognize the application of information literacy in real-world practice and work settings and develop connections between theory and application as well as actual and virtual contexts.
- Build peer support and collaboration into online learning initiatives.
- Provide a network of support for online learners that includes faculty, librarians, instructional designers, and advanced online resources.
- Transition relevant information literacy initiatives into the virtual world of Second Life and use Web 2.0 technologies such as blogs and wikis to advance learning.
- Develop a virtual pedagogy that moves beyond technical skills to include critical thinking, interactivity, research, and service learning in virtual environments.
- Leverage partnerships to overcome technical, institutional, and budgetary challenges.
- Expand faculty-librarian teams to include other stakeholders such as curriculum and instructional designers, media specialists, and students.

- Create faculty development programs concomitantly with online learning initiatives.
- Match the needs of learners with the design of programs such as the use of asynchronous online learning for working professionals and adult learners at a distance.
- Build trust in the design of faculty-librarian partnerships and challenge traditional assumptions about institutional roles.

As this section demonstrates, teaching information literacy in open and online learning environments extends beyond technology considerations to also include an emphasis on learning outcomes, pedagogical theory, and collaborative practice. While each institutional context may vary somewhat from your own academic or library setting, the lessons learned from each partnership will generate ideas about the revision of existing courses or the development of new open and online curriculum.

REFERENCES

Allen, I. Elaine, and Jeff Seaman. 2009. *Learning on Demand: Online Education in the United States*, 2009. The Sloan Consortium. http://www.sloan-c.org/publications/survey/pdf/learningondemand.pdf.

ICDE Executive Committee and EADTU Executive Committee. 2009. "Maastricht Message—Open Universiteit." From the M-2009 World Conference (23rd ICDE World Conference and the 2009 EADTU Annual Conference), June 10. http://www.ou.nl/eCache/DEF/2/11/255.html.

United Nations Educational Scientific and Cultural Organization (UNESCO). 2010. Technology and Learning—Definitions." UNESCO. http://www.unesco.org/education/educprog/lwf/doc/portfolio/definitions.htm

Supported Open Learning
Developing an Integrated Information Literacy Strategy Online

Clarissa Gosling and Ingrid Nix

INTRODUCTION

This chapter explores some of the challenges met by library staff working on a distance learning degree program for work-based learners, specifically the social work degree at The Open University (OU), in the United Kingdom (UK). We reveal how close collaboration with the academic team writing the degree enabled library staff to integrate information literacy (IL) alongside information and communication technology (ICT) skills throughout that program, including integrated assessment. We consider how the collaborative process influenced the design of this program. Examples of activities are provided along with insights into how students value the development of IL skills within their social work practice. We conclude with lessons learned and implications for practice within distance learning and, more broadly, technology-enhanced learning environments.

Information literacy skills, such as online search skills, are fast becoming essential for study, and are increasingly found in the workplace. This is especially true within the field of social work, as the development of IL skills by practitioners enables their use of evidence to inform their decision making and to develop their ability to engage in evidence-based practice.

A series of activities to develop students' IL skills within the degree program was developed based on the requirements of the relevant professional bodies and the institution. As a distance-learning program it was key to design these activities so that they support students with low confidence using ICT or working online. Furthermore, based on our experience of work-based learners, they are often highly discerning about the relevance of skills activities—another challenge to the author-designer. Finally, a key desired outcome is to support learners to develop confidence in their preparedness for practice, including practice-related skills.

The task of building such skills development into modules is not always straightforward. It requires recognition by module leaders of the value of the activities. Support at the module planning stage can then result in integrated, well-designed activities to fit the learner's study context rather than activities that seem tagged on to the main study materials. Further formal recognition and reward via assessment can bring added benefit, motivating learners to engage rather than skip the activities, ensuring the opportunities to develop the skills are utilized. Through this program we were able to help the students develop these skills, and the survey results discussed at the end of the chapter demonstrate the benefit this approach had on the service users with whom they worked.

RELATED LITERATURE

Information Literacy

Information literacy is defined by the United Kingdom's Chartered Institute of Library and Information Professionals (CILIP) as "knowing when and why you need information, where to find it, and how to evaluate, use and communicate it in an ethical manner" (CILIP, 2004). It is seen as a key skill within academic study and is included in the OU's levels framework which clarifies what students should be expected to study at each level of their qualification (Centre for Outcomes-Based Education [COBE], 2005). As described by Badke (2009), IL, ICT, and media literacy are overlapping skills sets that have developed over time from different drivers and seem to be converging. This shows that there is synergy between IL and ICT, that the rapid increase in computing and especially the Internet has led to an exponential growth in readily available information, and so the importance of IL to combat information overload has increased (Taha, 2007).

The OU uses Moodle as a virtual learning environment (VLE) to enable online delivery of modules on a standard platform that easily allows the use of a range of online tools within the learning materials. This move to online delivery of learning materials has meant that there is a growing opportunity for the inclusion of electronic library resources as well as an understanding of the need for students to develop their information literacy skills. The use of a VLE to successfully deliver integrated IL skills material to distance learners has been demonstrated at a range of different institutions (Patalong, 2003; Joint, 2003).

One issue with integrated IL activities is that if they are not tied into assessment, students may skip them because they concentrate their efforts on those parts of the module that contribute toward their assessment, as described by Kirkwood: "For materials and activities in any medium to be valued, they must be integrated within the pedagogy and aligned with the assessment strategy in order for students to engage fully with the range of learning opportunities offered" (2006: 328). So for IL to be seen by students as an important part of their studies it must be integrated into the pedagogy of their study material, and their developing IL skills must be assessed. A study in the OU's Faculty of Health and Social Care (Thomas, 2005) showed a low level of student engagement with nonassessed IL material, although this study indicated that those students who engaged with the IL activities valued them. These findings mirror what Laurillard (1979) described when looking at the different learning styles which suggested that students' learning is deeper the more actively they are required to engage with the material.

Thomas (2005) also shows the importance of library staff working with academics and their ability to act as agents of change by encouraging the adoption of online learning and a new way of thinking about the delivery of material to students. This view is shared by Laverty and Stockley (2007) in their discussion of the multidisciplinary team approach that they have adopted. Owens and Bozeman (2009) also highlight effective librarian–faculty collaboration and share ways in which they have encouraged this approach and the impact this had on the learner experience.

Social Work

The use of ICT in social work has been increasing due to the computerization of many tasks and also a number of U.K. government directives (Cabinet Office, 1999, 2000; Rafferty and Steyaert, 2009) which required that all services be accessible electronically by 2005 to improve public access. Furthermore, technologies are increasingly being used to interact with service users in more effective ways. These developments have inevitably had an impact on social work education. To fully prepare students for their social work practice, their studies must include the most common ICT skills that they are likely to need once they start working (Miller-Cribbs, 2001; Ayala, 2008; Nix, 2010).

The importance of IL within the practice of social work is increasing as the idea of evidence-based social work practice becomes more important (Thyer and Kazi, 2004; Bilson, 2005; Smith, 2004). *Evidence-based practice* is a common term discussed within decision making in health and medicine, but it is also a key concept within social work. Sheldon and colleagues (2005) conducted two large-scale studies of social workers and their attitudes toward evidence-based practice and showed that, although there was enthusiasm for the idea of this way of working, there were a number of obstacles to it actually happening. The most significant obstacles according to this study were lack of time, lack of access, and the cost of materials. The United Kingdom's National Health Service has made a core collection of electronic resources available nationally for all health workers to enable them to access the evidence on which to make decisions; however, no such similar collection has been bought for social workers. This means that each agency must purchase electronic content separately and therefore many social workers have little or no way to view these materials. Without access to evidence to inform their practice they are unable to engage in evidence-based practice.

INSTITUTIONAL CONTEXT

The Open University is the only university in the United Kingdom dedicated to distance learning. It offers a range of qualifications in different subjects, including professional programs aimed at work-based learning students. This means that the students are already working as practitioners within the fields of their studies and are studying to gain their professional qualifications while continuing to work. Frequently, they are sponsored by their employers to do this. Because of this, students are actively required to bring to bear their working experience while they study and to apply and reflect on the theoretical learning from their studies, relating it back to their work context and work practices. Between 2004 and 2008 a new OU social work degree was developed to meet the changing requirements of social work education in the United Kingdom, reflecting the emerging social work practice needs.

The OU's model of teaching and learning is known as "supported open learning." In the "open learning" model, students learn in their own time, reading module materials, working through learning activities, writing assignments, and, increasingly, working collaboratively with other students. Depending on the module, the student may learn from module textbooks provided in print, also available online through the VLE, in addition to a range of supporting material, including broadcast material, made available in a number of formats. The OU, like many universities, is moving toward electronic delivery of learning and support and is exploring practices to engage students in technology-enhanced learning (Littlejohn and Pegler, 2007). Although OU students previously studied mainly alone, in dialogue with their tutor only during occasional tutor group meetings, through the move to online learning students are now increasingly able to communicate and collaborate together. The "supported" aspect of the model includes support from a tutor and staff in one of the 13 regional and national centers, as well as from centralized areas, for example, the library.

The OU has a large electronic library and works with the academic teams to embed resources into OU modules and to develop the students' IL skills. Although IL activities had previously been embedded into some OU modules, the new social work degree was the first undergraduate degree program in the university to fully integrate and assess IL skills across the award. This approach had not been used previously, because for most modules offered by the OU library staff had to work with each module team independently. This involved selling the benefits of IL to them and persuading them to include IL activities within the study materials when often there was already too much material planned for inclusion. The social work degree offered us the unusual opportunity to include IL at the start of the award-level planning process.

The OU's social inclusion policy means that it offers a great deal of flexibility for students to choose their pathway through the modules available. In undergraduate programs, although students are advised to start with the introductory, first-level modules, not all of them take that advice and may start with modules at a higher level. This makes skills development through the different levels difficult as students may not complete the modules in the order expected.

In contrast, the OU social work degree requires students to complete a sequence of three core practice learning modules in a set order. Alongside these modules they complete other theory modules, some of which are optional. By concentrating on the defined pathway through the three practice learning modules, we were able to map an approach for IL skills development across three levels for the first time. This meant that we were able to build on, and consolidate, what had been done in previous modules and so develop students' higher-level IL skills in a more comprehensive way.

DISCIPLINARY PERSPECTIVE

In 2001, the U.K. Department of Health introduced a social work degree as part of the reforms to social work training (Department of Health, 2001). The OU took this opportunity to update and increase the social work diploma modules already offered in order to create a full degree program. Three degrees were produced to meet the Care Council requirements and the different legislation governing social work in each of three different nations: Scotland, Wales, and England. The first graduates, totaling 346, completed their degrees in 2008.

One of the Care Council requirements was for students to engage for set periods in work experience during their studies so that they are able to apply their learning in practice. OU students differ from other U.K. social work degree students because they are mature students (not straight from high school) and they are usually already employed in social work settings, and therefore bring considerable experience of work-based practice. The combination of real work pressures and demands on study time mean these students are likely to be highly selective about which activities they engage in, being critically aware of context-specific details and requiring learning to be relevant and of practical value.

Another Care Council requirement that would impact on the approach taken to skills development was that by the end of their degree programs students were required to demonstrate ICT skills of a level equivalent to the European Computer Driving Licence (ECDL) (General Social Care Council [GSCC], 2002). This syllabus covers a range of computing skills, from word processing to working with spreadsheets and databases, to communicating online and finding and retrieving information, the latter relating closely to information literacy, requiring skills in using online search facilities.

During the planning stages for the degree a proposal was put forward to integrate IL and ICT throughout the program. The case to integrate IL was based on both external (U.K.) requirements for the social work degree and internal OU policy. The external requirements were those of the Quality Assurance Agency (QAA) Benchmark Statement for Social Work (The Quality Assurance Agency for Higher Education, 2008) and National Occupational Standards (TOPSS England, 2002), which together set out the requirements for achievement of the degree in social work. Although not explicitly stated as IL skills, they are clearly IL skills as per CILIP's (2004) definition, and both of these documents identify IL skills as core to the program.

Within the OU, the integration of IL is increasingly seen as an important part of OU study to improve the employability of OU students. As a result of this, the university's *Learning and Teaching Strategy* (The Open University, 2002) and the *Undergraduate Levels Frameworks* document (COBE, 2005) both have statements that require information literacy within all OU learning materials.

Based on these requirements the inclusion of IL was agreed on by the social work team and was written into the degree documentation that was agreed to by the university. Furthermore, there was a clear alignment between some of the ICT skills competencies required for the degree, which included skills for working online and for finding and retrieving information, and the development of IL activities in the course.

DISCUSSION OF FACULTY–LIBRARIAN COLLABORATION

The strict external requirements for the degree allowed us to start working with the academic team during the early stages of the planning process. This led to us being able to devise an approach which, once approved, was a firm commitment to the integration of IL across the program. The benefit of our involvement from the early stages meant that the IL strategy was planned from the start rather than tacked on later. This highlights the importance of the timing of the first contact between the library staff and the academic team developing the modules.

Having established the essential presence of IL and ICT within the program, the next step was to examine how the links and interdependency between IL and ICT might be explored and used to their best advantage. It became apparent that a collaborative approach and interwoven strategy of skills development would strengthen our proposal and therefore offer an improved student learning experience. We could build on the differences between IL and ICT by combining the two skills sets, as well as reinforce what had been covered in previous skills activities. To implement this agreement we developed a plan showing possible sequences of learning for ICT and IL, specifically how to create logical skills development and progression across three levels of study, and presented this to the program team.

To implement the plan, we worked closely with each module team in turn to guide them on how they could incorporate skills development activities into their course material. This built on the experience we had gained from work with other module teams. Since the practice learning courses were to be developed and launched iteratively, the first collaboration took place on the Level One module, enabling a working method to be devised. We subsequently faced the challenge that each module was developed by a different group of academics, and they were not always aware of what had been covered in the previous module. Despite this challenge, consistency was achieved by minimizing changes in the staff involved in writing the IL and ICT activities.

This consistency of staffing meant that we could ensure there was coherence within the skills activities and that a clear pathway for progression existed, with the activities in one module building on and developing what had been practiced previously. The activities could also be written in a consistent style and approach, including a consistent author voice. More generally, we were able to take a holistic viewpoint over the learning approaches and terminology used within the program, helping to establish a consistent learner experience. This was important in the development of the assessment strategies for the different modules, where we were not only able to integrate IL and ICT into the assessment but also advise on the strategy overall so that it was aligned to students' skills. The way in which IL was assessed within the degree will be discussed in this chapter.

The benefits of our collaboration with the module teams meant that we could embed the IL activities within the course material, where they were not only an essential part of the student study material but they were also assessed, as recommended by Kirkwood (2006), ensuring students engage in this part of the program.

PROGRAM PLANNING

Plan for Skills Development

All OU students have in common the need to get up and running using OU systems and services as part of their experience with distance learning. This includes skills in getting online and navigating resources, and other skills in relation to creating and organizing work and communicating online. The process of engaging in such technology-enhanced learning therefore in and of itself requires a baseline of computing skills. In 2006, when the degree was to be launched, such skills were expected to be new to many students, especially social work students whose primary focus was to work with people, not computers. An approach for skills development therefore needed to be designed which recognized the level of support and guidance this student group might need as well as the specific skills they might be interested in based on their work-based settings. Included within the suite of skills used for distance learning were many of the ICT skills required for the degree. It therefore became logical to use the introduction to technology-enhanced learning as a means to develop a range of skills. Once introduced on the first-level module, the students could then develop these further during the second- and third-level modules and also ideally apply the skills in their work-based settings.

For both ICT and IL skills we decided to mirror the core program strategy for the main social work teaching, namely to develop skills on the first core module through *awareness* raising, on the second module through *applying*, and then on the third module through *critically evaluating* those skills. This would be done by introducing skills in the context of the students' study requirements, using technologies as part of their learning experiences. These skills at the second level would be extended and students asked to apply them in their practice settings. For this purpose the skills would relate to work-based practice scenarios. By the third level students were expected to critically evaluate their use of skills, contextualized by their work-based practice requirements.

The next step was to map OU's *Levels Framework* document onto this structure to create a clear and systematic progression in the information literacy skills development through the degree. To demonstrate skills progression through the three modules, an outline was created based on how we would differentiate between the levels, which is shown with the IL learning outcomes from OU's *Levels Framework* (COBE, 2005) in Table 5.1.

Within each of the three levels, activities were developed to cover the different IL skills:

- Be aware of the key information resources in the particular subject area.
- Identify a need for (more) information on a topic.
- Plan and carry out a search for information on a topic using the most appropriate sources.
- Critically evaluate information.
- Organize information so that it can be retrieved and presented.

Table 5.1. Plan to Implement IL Learning Outcomes		
Level	IL Learning Outcomes (COBE, 2005)	Plan for IL Skills Development through the Program
1	You will begin to **recognize** and **use**, with guidance, **skills in finding and choosing information** for a specific purpose.	**Develop skills:** specific subject search; predefined list of resources; apply given criteria to given resources
2	You will learn how to **apply** these skills to identify, **search for, and use information accurately and critically** in the context of specific tasks.	**Apply skills:** choice of topics; select resources from list; apply criteria to own resources
3	You should be able to **use and develop** your skills to **identify, search for, and critically evaluate** information in **complex contexts**.	**Critically evaluate:** own topic; select own resources; develop own criteria for evaluation

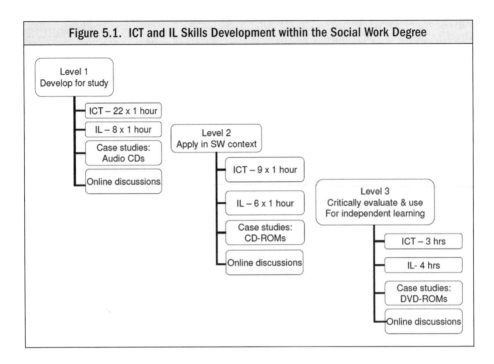

Figure 5.1. ICT and IL Skills Development within the Social Work Degree

This approach meant that students would cover each of these skills at least three times over the course of their degrees and would reinforce their previous application of these skills. Although some academics might have preferred the skills work to have been designated to limited parts of the program and gotten "out of the way," the pedagogical consideration—that skills development is facilitated by regular opportunities for practice, as described by Dewald et al. (2000)—strongly influenced the approach taken. Based on this principle we designed activities spread evenly across the three modules and the program.

The resulting mapping of study time showing ICT and IL, alongside other e-learning components, is shown in Figure 5.1.

Presentation of Material

The online nature of supported open learning and growing availability of online library resources meant that the IL activities would take place online, but for two of the three modules the majority of teaching material was in fact print based. However, instead of placing the detailed instructions within the core module texts (printed books), it was more appropriate to provide printable Adobe Acrobat Reader documents in PDF format to download from the module website. From the downloadable instructions we directed students to links to online search tools, tutorials, and other materials, such as online databases. Since we anticipated that these would be subject to frequent change, our approach enabled increased flexibility and cost effectiveness by being able to swiftly replace out-of-date instructions on the module websites during the life of the degree.

One consideration that affected how we presented the skills activities to students was their probable level of ICT skills and confidence working online. Being able to develop IL skills depends on students having a certain base level of ICT knowledge and being fairly confident using the Internet. Faculty experience on similar courses in the past had shown that many of the students lacked ICT confidence. So we designed a "belts and braces" approach for guidance and support building on our work with previous modules and how they delivered similar material. We aimed to provide comprehensive support using screenshots and step-by-step instructions, especially in the first-level course, where the bulk of the skills were introduced.

ONLINE LEARNING MODEL

IL Activities

For each module a series of IL skills activities was introduced within the printed study material. These activities directed students to undertake searches relevant to the subject area currently being studied. Students were referred from the printed text to their module website for more detailed downloadable instructions. The ICT and IL activities used the same template, to ensure that they were presented consistently and to aid the students in following the instructions. Different parts of the activity were separated into different boxes with clear guidance for any actions that students were expected to take or questions they were meant to consider. Each activity then ended with a feedback section where the module team gave some general comments on the activity and what the students should have achieved.

The IL activities were flagged within the study calendar, as shown in Table 5.2. This study calendar showed students the resources they needed for each week of study to help them plan their time.

We designed the first-level activities so that they gave very detailed instructions accompanied by numerous screenshots. This method provides less confident students with as much support as possible, albeit this is a fairly directive method and may not necessarily encourage students to learn independently. This approach was aimed at students with low confidence who were working on their own (as distance-learning students) and might easily be put off if the guidance made too many assumptions about what they were familiar with. As students developed their confidence with the early activities, we designed the IL activities to become more open-ended through the program. This then allowed the students to investigate areas that interested them personally whilst still maintaining a structured approach to their learning. Because the social work degree had a set pathway, it enabled us to develop students' skills across the modules and to refer back to IL activities studied on previous modules to make explicit the fact that these activities were building on one another.

To demonstrate how we developed the students' searching skills across the three different levels, an example of an activity from each of the modules, developing students' skills in searching for information, is shown in Table 5.2.

As these examples show, at the first level we present a step-by-step approach for students to find a specific resource that we had previously identified. Then, at the second level, students are given an initial search term and are then asked to think of

Table 5.2. Sample Searching Activities at Each Level on the OU Social Work Degree

Activity Level	Activity Task	Activity Steps
1st Level	Find a journal article in Social Care Online.	• Type "fully engaged" in the KEYWORDS field and click on the button that says Exact Phrase. • To narrow the search to the date on which the article was published, type "13/11/2003" in the PUBLISHED DATE FROM field and "13/11/2003" in the PUBLISHED DATE TO field. (Later in the course we will look in more detail at other search techniques.) • Click on the button that says ARTICLES ONLY.
2nd Level	Find newspaper articles in NexisUK.	• Type "poverty" into the first search box, then click on the SEARCH button. • Think of other terms that could be used to describe the poor and try searching for these terms. Does the way they're portrayed change when you use a different term? Is one of them seen in a more positive light than the others? • Try searching for words associated with the poor, for example, "benefits," "scroungers," "homeless," "gypsies." How are these portrayed in tabloids and broadsheets?
3rd Level	Find articles in Web of Science to improve students' understanding of an article they have previously read.	• Note one issue, argument, or concept that Garrett referred to that you did not understand or want to find out more about. You will search Web of Science to identify an article which might tell you more. • Begin your search to find two abstracts of articles that answer your search question from the Garrett article. Don't forget that searching is an iterative process, so you will amend the string based on the results it produces.

other terms to search for so they can compare the results when using different terms. Although they are given some ideas to look for, they are also free to use their own search terms, too. Finally, at the third level, students are asked to identify a search topic based on a journal article that they had previously read and are then free to search for articles which help them to improve their understanding of the issues raised.

Accessing Resources

At the time of setting up the degree the library offered a service to module teams by which content and services could be introduced in a supportive framework, called MyOpenLibrary. This personalizable miniportal provides students with a core list of library resources selected for them by the module team and library staff. Given the vast and growing range of library resources and how intimidating this might appear to new undergraduate students, it was felt appropriate to build students' confidence and guide them to relevant materials through a gradual and managed introduction to the wealth of different materials available.

It was decided to use MyOpenLibrary on all three modules, gradually extending the links to be included. Students are able to personalize it by adding other items (Ramsden, 2003) and thus develop their own selection of material to support their studies. The interface for MyOpenLibrary is split into different sections for different types of content. Each section holds a set of links to key items selected for their relevance to the module. For the second- and third-level modules, additional materials were included. Students can access MyOpenLibrary during their study of other modules and can continue to develop their collection of resources.

Students were also expected to use RefWorks, an online bibliography management tool, to manage references and create bibliographies for assignments. Their use of RefWorks was introduced within the ICT activities in the level-one module and was then developed throughout the degree. The rationale behind the introduction of RefWorks so early in the degree was to enable students both to understand how a database works (as part of their ICT skills development) and also how to reference material in their written work.

Student Support

Students who had queries about any of the IL activities were directed to contact the Library Helpdesk. The Library Helpdesk offers support to students in using electronic resources and with their skills development. We were able to use the queries received from students to refine and improve the IL activities for each subsequent year. One example of this process resulted in a reduction of the number of enquiries received about RefWorks (which students found particularly challenging) the following year.

IMPACT ON STUDENT LEARNING

A small-scale study called "Prepared for Practice?" was conducted as part of the Practice-Based Professional Learning Centre for Excellence in Teaching and Learning to look at how well graduates of the OU social work degree felt that it had prepared them for a career in social work. As part of the study graduates were asked about their views on IL aspects of their degree. Thirty-three graduates were sent an online survey six months after graduation, resulting in 19 responses. The first section looked at their social work skills and in the second section they were asked to answer a series of questions about either IL or ICT, and 10 students answered the questions about IL. The survey was part quantitative and part qualitative; Figure 5.2 shows the quantitative data from part of this survey.

These responses reveal that six months after graduation the majority of former students continue to perceive that the learned IL skills bring value to their practice. Furthermore, the majority agree that the skills are being used in their practice and that the degree prepared them well for this. The majority agreed that they have extended the IL skills learned during the degree to other areas of their practice. We can conclude that the IL activities on the degree program were understandable and realistic for the students to undertake, as none indicated that they needed help from colleagues to use these skills in their practice.

For the qualitative section the questions were designed to call to mind specific occurrences where they had used either their IL or ICT skills by encouraging recall of feelings

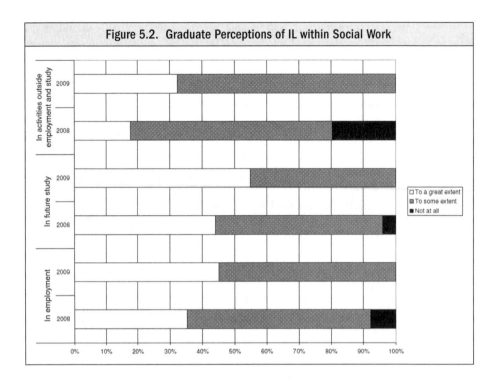

Figure 5.2. Graduate Perceptions of IL within Social Work

and motivations. This provides us with evidence of how they developed their IL skills and use in their practice and the impact on service users. For social work students the link to the possible benefit to service users is arguably one of their key motivators and is the rationale behind evidence-based practice.

In answer to questions asking them how they had used their IL skills, what they had achieved and the impact this had on service users all ten responses mentioned being able to search for, or find, relevant information for a particular situation. Eight of them mentioned the use of this as evidence for their practice and how it informed what they did, three of them mentioned the importance of keeping up to date with new information in a particular area, and one mentioned being able to evaluate what he or she had found. This shows the importance of evidence-based practice to graduates and how their use of research literature has made an impact on the service users with whom they work. One of them explained exactly how the research of an issue had impacted his or her work and the benefit of this to the service users with whom the individual was working:

> The research I used recently helped to inform the decisions that were made regarding placing siblings together in a long-term foster placement. It benefited them in that they were placed together rather than in separate placements. (Respondent 14)

Another response talked about the importance of evidence-based practice more generally and how important it is to develop this within social work as a subject compared to other health professions:

Through the use of research during my placement in mental health and my studies of K315 I gained an appreciation of the need for social work to assert itself in a field where social work is said to have a theoretical hole at the centre of the enterprise and that this causes it to leave social work and social work values at the mercy of more powerful empirically informed professions such as psychiatry. (Respondent 16)

Other questions asked whether these skills were ones that they had learnt during their studies, or whether they already had them, and eight of them said that they had developed these skills during their studies while two said they already had some skills in this area. This shows the importance of developing IL skills within the program as they are skills that the students didn't have prior to entering the program.

This is a small-scale study of 33 individuals, 10 of whom chose to answer about IL, so these results can only be seen as indicative. But they present a strong picture of the importance of IL within social work and how evidence-based practice in social work can improve the services provided.

ASSESSMENT OF ONLINE LEARNING

Students were expected to demonstrate their commitment to ICT and IL skills development through their assessment in the degree. Regular assignments with a small percentage allocated to skills work were designed so that students would not be intimidated and could see their skills work as a regular feature in which they could gradually increase in competence and confidence.

Formative

The assessment of IL was influenced by the assessment which needed to take place for ICT skills. One of the considerations was that skills development needed to take place over time, to maintain "fluency" and to keep current with emerging related skills (for instance, as interface updates are introduced). In addition, since students had different levels of familiarity with the skills, it would be beneficial to offer opportunities for self-directed learning and practice. We therefore introduced online interactive quizzes which would provide immediate feedback and could therefore be used as diagnostic or self-assessment tools. Due to the intensive occurrence of ICT activities on the level-one module, it was decided that there were already sufficient practice opportunities and additional online quizzes were not necessary. However, since on levels two and three learners were expected to engage increasingly in independent study, formative online quizzes were introduced. IL questions were included in these, integrated alongside ICT, to practice new and review existing skills.

Use of Online Quizzes

In addition to the need for formative practice, another key factor played a part. To demonstrate that the ICT skills had been achieved before graduation, ICT skills were assessed directly and marks awarded for them (creating summative assessment). This would thereby provide an audit trail for the ICT skills achieved. Students submitted several assignments per module in which they demonstrated computing work they had completed. However, it was necessary to provide sufficient summative assessment points to cover the range of ICT skills required to be demonstrated. It was therefore decided that as well as formative online quizzes on levels two and three we would use them summatively on all three modules. And since IL had been included in the formative online quizzes, it was also included in the summative online quizzes for those courses on levels two and three.

Each module has three summative quizzes, spaced equally throughout each module. Each quiz assessed skills and knowledge which had been introduced in activities during that study period or occasionally reviewed items studied in earlier modules. The quizzes (and their formative equivalents on levels two and three) provided sequences of 10 to 15 questions. The questions were divided into clusters around different topics, such as IL, ICT, and ethical terminology. Within a topic the questions might include some sequences building on on another. The IL questions in the quizzes covered a range of skills, including identifying functions within a database interface screen; selecting what Boolean operators should be used to combine specified keywords into an effective search string for a given scenario; what to think about when evaluating information; picking the most relevant reference from a list for a situation; referencing; copyright; and plagiarism. In addition, different question types (such as multiple choice, drag and drop, text input) could be used to develop a variety of demonstrations of a skill.

For instance, the two questions in Figures 5.3 and 5.4 show progression from developing the student's ability to construct a reference through sequencing its component parts in the correct order to later inputting text to enter the actual reference details.

The drag-and-drop activity in Figure 5.3 requires recognition and then sequencing—a simple task compared to the text input question shown in Figure 5.4. This places demands on the learner, needing to actively identify information based on contextual

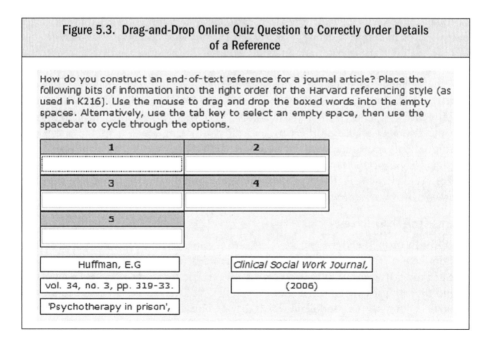

Figure 5.3. Drag-and-Drop Online Quiz Question to Correctly Order Details of a Reference

How do you construct an end-of-text reference for a journal article? Place the following bits of information into the right order for the Harvard referencing style (as used in K216). Use the mouse to drag and drop the boxed words into the empty spaces. Alternatively, use the tab key to select an empty space, then use the spacebar to cycle through the options.

1	2
3	**4**
5	

Huffman, E.G

Clinical Social Work Journal,

vol. 34, no. 3, pp. 319-33.

(2006)

'Psychotherapy in prison',

Figure 5.4. Text Input Online Quiz Question on Referencing

You are a K216 student writing an assignment and are in the process of inserting your end of text references. Type in the missing details so that the references are correct, according to the course Assessment Guide. You may need to look up some of the information required. Type the text into the spaces provided and pay attention to spacing, capitals and punctuation. (Since the CMA system is **not able to let you format text in italic** you may skip this referencing requirement when inputting your answer.)

This is echoed in an audio case study (K113, Audio 1, section 2). The legal requirements are also relevant (HSC Resource Bank). This was discussed using another approach (Howe, K113, Offprints, pp. 18-19).

References

A. [_____] (2003) 'Psychosocial work' in K113 *Foundations for Social Work Practice*, Offprints, Milton Keynes, The Open University, pp. 15-24.

B. [_____] (2008) *HSC Resource Bank: Law*, Discrimination due to disability in England and Wales: Disability Discrimination Acts 1995 and 2005, The Open University, http://learn.open.ac.uk/mod/oucontent/view.php?id=77254 [Accessed 21 May 2008].

Open University (2006) K113 *Foundations for Social Work Practice*, Audio 1, **C.** [_____], 'Untitled', **D.** [_____] The Open University.

---

information, requiring exact knowledge and accurate input. We found that many students find it exceptionally difficult to reference accurately, and it therefore became a priority to break down the skills required into manageable and incremental steps, to enable them to improve their proficiency to a level that was acceptable. The online quizzes gave instant feedback to students and so proved to be an excellent means by which to provide practice opportunities in a variety of ways for a skill which would otherwise be difficult and unrewarding to practice.

Written Assignments

The skills of searching for and identifying relevant information to support discussion, and practice decisions, as well as the ability to reference correctly, were also assessed in written assignments where marks would be given according to the quality demonstrated. As they progressed through the degree students would be expected increasingly to draw on resources outside of the module material. To further motivate students to develop their referencing skills, in the final module the *technical* skills of referencing were awarded discrete marks in addition to discrete marks for the *presentation* of references, that is, appropriately drawing upon and citing references within the written text. Finally, in the final module End of Course Assessment (ECA)—the examinable component—students were given a research task to inform the main assessment. They were asked to plan and evaluate a search and to include in their ECA details of what they searched for and what results they found, as well as a summary of how well their results met their expectations. They also received marks for their technical and presentation skills in referencing.

As a result of these various approaches, the formative assessment encouraged practice through engaging interactive online quizzes, which provided instant feedback. Students were encouraged to develop their referencing skills in the knowledge that at the end of the degree they would be assessed directly on this skill in their ECAs. The net result was that students engaged in IL proactively and noted improvements in their skills and benefits in their practice.

CONCLUSION

As educators we owe it to our students to prepare them for the work contexts in which they practice. The interconnectedness of ICT and IL skills means these skills become key enablers for technology-enhanced learning and technology-enhanced work practices. This chapter has shown that recognizing this synergy inspired a collaborative approach on a practice-based learning degree and informed an integrated program of skills development. Furthermore, external drivers from professional bodies convinced the wider team to accept this into the assessment strategy, spanning each level of the degree in recognition of the need to enable skills development over time and building a clearly identified sequence of skills.

Traditionally, part of the challenge has been convincing academics at the planning stage, and students at the learning stage, that engaging in IL activities is worth the effort. Having the facility to identify outcomes, such as learner perceptions of where IL brings most value, in this case their accounts of its benefits to service users in their social work practice, helps library staff make a case to academics for specific IL activities. This can then inform study time allocation, and how activity designers create motivating activities for learners. The online nature of the activity delivery makes it possible to close the feedback loop by editing the activities swiftly and reusing activities across the institution.

We have highlighted the importance of library involvement from an early stage in order to ensure that IL skills development fits cohesively with the overall approach of the program, allowing meaningful opportunities for practice and development of the skills, rather than being added on at a later stage. This also conveys to the students the intrinsic value of this activity as part of academic (and work) practices. To support students in the early stages, tensions exist between very specific instructions versus more generic and open-ended instructions, which are less supportive. By taking a program view and designing increasing flexibility of choice, a developmental approach can be taken, enabling students to access support when they need it, whether within guidance documents, from online webpages, or via a help desk.

It was further made possible by the affordances of the online delivery of the modules. This enabled the introduction and development of skills using interactive online activities, a range of powerful search tools, and facilities for skills development with rapid feedback and support. Our evaluation shows the importance of IL within social work and how its development enables evidence-based social work practice. This means that the relevant information can be found and passed on to service users and colleagues so they can make informed decisions. This is increasingly important to students wanting to engage with evidence-based practice, needing to find reliable evidence on which to make decisions or offer advice to colleagues and service users.

This approach to IL integration has been achieved by ensuring a close collaboration between the academic staff developing the teaching materials and specialists in skills development, both library staff for IL and dedicated ICT teaching staff. All members of the team were able to draw on their differing experience and knowledge to improve the quality of the finished degree course. The knowledge gained from the experience of colleagues and students is now informing practice, and forging and strengthening links across modules and teams within both the Faculty of Health and Social Care and the library.

REFERENCES

Ayala, Jessica. 2008. *Blended Education in Social Work: A Case Study in Teaching, Learning and Technology*. Saarbrücken, Germany: VDM Verlag.

Badke, William. 2009. "Media, ICT, and Information Literacy." *Online* 33, no. 5 (September/October): 47–49.

Bilson, Andy, ed. 2005. *Evidence-Based Practice in Social Work*. London: Whiting and Birch Ltd.

Cabinet Office. 1999. *Modernising Government (Cm 4310)*. London: Cabinet Office.

Cabinet Office. 2000. *E-government: A Strategic Framework for Public Services in the Information Age*. London: Cabinet Office.

Centre for Outcomes-Based Education (COBE). 2005. *Undergraduate Levels Framework*. Milton Keynes, UK: The Open University.

Chartered Institute of Library and Information Professionals (CILIP). 2004. "Information Literacy: Definition." London: CILIP, December. http://www.cilip.org.uk/get-involved/advocacy/learning/information-literacy/Pages/definition.aspx.

Department of Health. 2001. "Radical Reforms to Social Work Training to Raise Social Care Standards." Department of Health, March 27. http://www.dh.gov.uk/en/Publicationsandstatistics/Pressreleases/DH_4010557.

Dewald, N., A. Scholz-Crane, A. Booth, and C. Levine, C. 2000. "Information Literacy at a Distance: Instructional Design Issues." *The Journal of Academic Librarianship* 26, no. 1 (January): 33–44.

General Social Care Council. 2002. "Accreditation of Universities to Grant Degrees in Social Work." General Social Care Council, May. http://www.gscc.org.uk/NR/rdonlyres/F889F154-ADD1-4A14-9D3B-4771D5ECC576/0/Accreditation.pdf.

Joint, N. 2003. "Information Literacy Evaluation: Moving Towards Virtual Learning Environments." *The Electronic Library* 21, no. 4: 322–334.

Kirkwood, A. 2006. "Going Outside the Box: Skills Development, Cultural Change and the Use of On-Line Resources." *Computers & Education* 47, no. 3 (November): 316–331.

Laurillard, D. 1979. "The Processes of Student Learning." *Higher Education* 8, no. 4 (July): 395–409.

Laverty, C., and D. Stockley. 2007. "How Librarians Shape Online Courses." *Journal of Library & Information Services in Distance Learning* 2, no. 4 (April): 41–55.

Littlejohn, A., and C. Pegler. 2007. *Preparing for Blended Elearning*. London: Routledge.

Miller-Cribbs, Julie, ed. 2001. *New Advances in Technology for Social Work Education and Practice*. New York: CRC Press.

Nix, Ingrid. 2010. "Technology-Enhanced Learning for Social Work Education and Practice." In *Professional Development in Social Work: Complex Issues in Practice*, edited by Janet Seden, Sarah Matthews, Mick McCormick, and Alun Morgan, 150–156. New York: Routledge.

The Open University. 2002. *Learning and Teaching Strategy 2002–2006*. Milton Keynes, UK: The Open University.

Owens, R., and D. Bozeman. 2009, "Toward a Faculty-Librarian Collaboration: Enhancement of Online Teaching and Learning." *Journal of Library & Information Services in Distance Learning* 3, no. 1 (January): 31–38.

Patalong, S. 2003. "Using the Virtual Learning Environment WebCT to Enhance Information Skills Teaching at Coventry University." *Library Review* 52, no. 3: 103–110.

Quality Assurance Agency for Higher Education (QAA). 2000. *QAA Subject Benchmark Statement for Social Policy and Administration and Social Work*. Mansfield, England: The Quality Assurance Agency for Higher Education.

Quality Assurance Agency for Higher Education. 2008. "QAA Subject Benchmark Statement for Social Work." Quality Assurance Agency for Higher Education, February. http://www.qaa.ac .uk/academicinfrastructure/benchmark/statements/socialwork08.asp.

Rafferty, J., and J. Steyaert. 2009. "Social Work and the Digital Age." *British Journal of Social Work* 39, no. 4 (June): 589–598.

Ramsden, A. 2003. "The OU Goes Digital." *Library and Information Update* 2, no. 2 (February): 34–35.

Sheldon B., R. Chilvers, A. Ellis, A. Moseley, and S. Tierney. 2005. "A Pre-Post Empirical Study of Obstacles to, and Opportunities for, Evidence-Based Practice in Social Care." In *Evidence-Based Practice in Social Work*, edited by A. Bilson, 11–51. London: Whiting and Birch Ltd.

Smith, D. 2004. *Social Work and Evidence-Based Practice*. London: Jessica Kingsley Publishers.

Taha, A. 2007. "Knowledge Maps for E-literacy in ICT-Rich Learning Environments." *Journal of Library and Information Services in Distance Learning* 2, no. 4 (April): 67–78.

Thomas, J. 2005. "Integrating Knowledge Management Skills into a Critical Health Practice Course Using eLearning: A Case Study at the UK's Open University." European Association of Distance Learning Universities Working Conference 2005, Rome, November 10–11. http://www.eadtu.nl/proceedings/2005/papers/Judy%20Thomas.pdf.

Thyer, B., and M.A.F. Kazi. 2004. *International Perspectives on Evidence-Based Practice in Social Work*. Birmingham: Venture Press.

TOPSS England. 2002. "The National Occupational Standards for Social Work." Skills for Care, May. http://www.skillsforcare.org.uk/developing_skills/National_Occupational_Standards/ social_work.aspx.

6

Information-Literate Avatars

Resource-Based Learning in Second Life

Jenna Kammer and Tracey Thompson

INTRODUCTION

When faculty at New Mexico State University (NMSU) began to use Second Life as a distance-education platform, the Professional Occupations, Technologies, and Fine Arts division at NMSU's campus in Alamogordo supported the endeavor by creating a fully online, special topics course to introduce students to basic Second Life skills. This course, Introduction to Second Life, is designed to prepare an NMSU student for taking one of the many subject-specific courses, such as Intercultural Communications, that are offered in Second Life on NMSU's virtual campus, Aggie Island.

Student evaluations of the pilot session of Introduction to Second Life showed that they learned technical skills in the course but did not learn the skills necessary to research in Second Life. The course instructor teamed up with a librarian to determine what information literacy skills a student in this virtual environment needs by mapping the outcomes in the Association of College and Research Libraries (ACRL) Information Literacy Competency Standards (ACRL, 2000) with the Second Life experience. The result was the design of a service-learning project that allows students to apply and be assessed on all five of the ACRL standards. This interdisciplinary assignment asks students to volunteer with a nonprofit or academic institution in Second Life and gives students a chance to develop relationships in other areas of this virtual world beyond the NMSU classroom.

Introduction to Second Life is designed using the theory of "resource-based learning," which embraces information literacy and teaches students how to use electronic resources, such as virtual world resources, websites, and multimedia for academic purposes. To provide the resource support for the class, Kammer and Thompson collaborated to construct the Aggie Island Information Commons, a virtual library with a collection that supports the research needs of Second Life students. The Information

Commons has since been funded for research and development based on its collaborative potential.

Second Life

Second Life (http://www.secondlife.com) is a free, online virtual world created by Linden Lab. In this environment, users create an avatar or character that interacts with objects and other avatars in the virtual space. Second Life has a fully functional economy and a three-dimensional modeling tool that allows users to create objects. Everything in this environment, including buildings, landscape, and information resources, is created by Second Life users.

Second Life provides a three-dimensional virtual environment for personalized learning experiences (see Figure 6.1). Teachers are able to customize the virtual classroom and interact synchronously with students using voice, text, and movement. For example, in a course such as Intercultural Communications, students go on field trips within Second Life to watch a Kabuki play or visit a French resort. Students can then discuss the experience as a group using a combination of audio or instant messaging tools. At NMSU, teachers have used Second Life to host online classes, hybrid courses, study groups, single class sessions, and office hours.

A resident in Second Life needs to use information access systems and search strategies to find answers to daily questions in this environment, such as how to buy land, collect objects, meet people, or learn new skills. Once information has been found it must be

Figure 6.1. Home of OECS 255 Intro to Second Life

evaluated for accuracy, timeliness, currency, and authority. Second Life users also need to be fluent in intellectual property laws and follow the same approach to information ethics as is expected in real life. This is a special concern as this virtual world is based upon users retaining intellectual rights to any items they create.

RELATED LITERATURE

This review of literature provides a foundation for integrating information literacy into Introduction to Second Life and examines the need to teach information literacy in this virtual environment. Explored are several integral facets of the course, including information literacy, resource-based learning, and service learning. While many resources discussed here are not directly related to Second Life, we analyze how resource-based learning and service learning can be applied in this virtual environment.

Information in Second Life

Students in a traditional face-to-face college course use a variety of familiar formats for conducting research such as books, magazines, maps, or websites. Students in Second Life face unique challenges when using information resources. They are confronted with a new interface, technology, and information access system. They learn how to walk and dress for the first time in a virtual land, while also learning how to access, retrieve, evaluate, synthesize, and create information in unfamiliar formats, such as the Second Life "notecard" (an item that can hold text or hyperlinks). Many educators who use this virtual world for teaching acknowledge that there is a high learning curve for students when using this platform for distance education. Sanchez (2009a) explains that the learning curve is related to the difficulties using the Second Life interface and software, as well as expecting this virtual world to be more like a video game than it is. Because of these challenges, only 10 percent of users who register with Second Life return to this environment (Sanchez, 2009b).

Grassian and Trueman (2007) describe virtual worlds as the "next virtual step beyond the Web" (p. 84) in that it advances online communication, collaboration, and connectedness. For libraries, the virtual world becomes another space in which to deliver library services, programs, and instruction. Grassian explains that virtual worlds provide librarians with new opportunities to design information literacy into curricula. For example, one idea Grassian and Kaplowitz (2009) present is to have students evaluate the historical accuracy of a replica, such as a model of the Globe Theatre located on the virtual space known as Renaissance Island. Davis and Smith (2009) also explored the idea of embedding librarians into courses held in virtual worlds. Their research found that embedding librarians into a Second Life course using traditional pedagogy did not necessarily improve students' information literacy, but they recommended repeating the study using experiential learning techniques, such as a pedagogy based on active learning.

Resource-Based Learning Environments

Resource-based learning is an active learning technique that focuses on preparing students to access and evaluate information. In Second Life, a resource can consist of a notecard, object, media, texture, scripts, landmarks, calling cards, or even word of mouth. It can be three-dimensional, interactive, or text based. There is also a large network of traditional digital resources, like blogs, search engines, digital serials, books, and journals about the environment itself. A resource-based learning design in Second Life has the potential to support student learning using a wide variety of "virtual objects and human resources" (Schmeil and Eppler, 2009: 668). This teaching method also has the potential to reduce cognitive overload as students learn where to find and access information, rather than memorizing facts.

Resource-based learning is a neutral pedagogy that involves self-directed learning through a variety of resources (Beswick, 1977) and is recognized as a model that can develop information literacy. When combined with a problem-based approach, the model becomes one of a constructivist nature that asks students to use resources to support investigation and problem solving (Hill and Hannafin, 2001). In doing so, students are inadvertently learning to access, evaluate, and manage information to support learning goals. Learning in a resource environment can be scaffolded in the instructional design by adding formative assessment, reflection, tutorials and research consultations with the instructor or librarian. A resource-based learning environment provides students in the digital age with guided opportunities for investigation, discovery, and engagement in the learning process (Hill, 2007).

Jeong and Hmelo-Silver (2010) found that computer science students engaged in problem-based learning would choose to consult knowledge resources to solve problems in a technology-mediated learning environment. However, their research also stated that more learning happened when the students already had familiarity with the resources and sufficient guidance to use them effectively. This implies that teaching students about virtual world resources before asking them to research in this environment could be a successful teaching strategy. For example, an instructor could introduce the Second Life "notecard" (a simple text file within the Second Life interface) to students in an activity that demonstrates notecard construction, intellectual property considerations, and evaluation before students begin collecting and organizing notecards that will support their research. Scaffolding efforts such as this could improve literacy and awareness as students work with virtual world resources.

There are other challenges for students doing resource-based learning projects. Students can feel overwhelmed with too much information (Bransford, Brown, and Cocking, 1999). Also, managing information on different servers and platforms, such as Second Life, Blackboard, the Internet, and remote computer files, can create overly complex information management scenerios (Tergan, Gräber, and Neumann, 2006). A Second Life student could have thousands of virtual items stored in inventory that he or she has collected as resources for a research project. In addition, students may not have the skills to evaluate the information they encounter at early stages in the learning process (Hill and Hannafin, 2001). In Second Life, it is important to remember that the challenges of resource-based learning are in addition to technical challenges students might already be feeling as they learn the interface and software.

Service Learning Projects

Service learning is a common undergraduate learning pedagogy that provides students with the opportunity to apply what they have learned in class to a real-life situation

(Simons and Cleary, 2006). In Second Life, opportunities for service learning are similar to real-life service learning projects as students find an organization that meets their learning goals and act as volunteers for the duration of the project. Sanchez (2009b) describes the virtual world as a new space for service learning projects and notes that service learning experiences in virtual worlds can be as authentic and instructional as they are in real life.

Lambright and Lu (2009) describe factors that influence the learning outcomes in a service project. Assignments that include instructor support, are integrated with the course material, and require reflection have the ability to meet learning objectives more successfully than projects that do not. Sanchez (2009b) also supports the value of blogging project reflections as a method for building community in an online environment. From these two perspectives, it can be interpreted that a good design for a service project in Second Life should include instructor support, mentor support, and opportunities for reflecting on the Second Life volunteer experience.

INSTITUTIONAL CONTEXT

New Mexico State University (NMSU) is a land-grant institution of higher learning. Founded in 1888, NMSU serves the diverse community of New Mexico with five campuses and extension offices in each of its 33 counties. It is the only university that is classified as both a Carnegie Research Institution and Hispanic-serving institution, and it is home to the only honors college in New Mexico. The university has a strong agriculture program with cooperative extension service offices across the state. Another research focus is the engineering program, which has strong ties to the National Aeronautics and Space Administration (NASA) and the White Sands Test Facility.

NMSU in Second Life

NMSU purchased virtual space in Second Life to be used as a platform for teaching and learning. This space was named Aggie Island and is an interdepartmental partnership between the College of Distance Learning and the Information and Communication Technologies department. Aggie Island supports NMSU's vision of "one university," which is a term that refers its relationship between NMSU and its five statewide campuses, departments, and organizations. Using this model, the five campuses function as one university rather than disparate campuses. For students, this enables them to take classes on multiple campuses with seamless transfer of credits to their home campus. Aggie Island provides one virtual campus on which all of these sectors can learn, share, and collaborate.

NMSU students and teachers access Aggie Island from across the state and from a variety of departments, including Geographic Information Systems, Library Science, Computer Science, Communications, Anthropology, and Sociology. A grassroots governing body of teachers, staff, and students known as the Aggie Island Architects formed to organize and support the needs of this diverse learning community. The group is responsible for land management, development of the island, and promotion of Second Life on campus.

Aggie Island is divided into public and private space. The public space is open to all users in Second Life and can attract visitors from around the world. The private space is reserved for NMSU students and teachers. Students gain access to the private area of the island through invitations from their instructors. This restriction allows the instructors to hold classes with minimal interruption. The Aggie Island Information Commons is built in the public space and is open to all.

OECS 255: Introduction to Second Life

Introduction to Second Life is a special topics, one-credit, elective course offered by the NMSU campus in Alamogordo. This course was developed to teach Second Life skills to students taking other courses that incorporate this environment, such as Historic Preservation or Intercultural Communication.

After the first semester of working with students on Aggie Island, it became clear that students with Second Life technical skills performed better in the environment. Introduction to Second Life is designed to prepare students to take other classes in Second Life, while also preparing students to use this virtual world in business, play, or to pursue other learning endeavors. The course emulates a hybrid course in that it meets both in the Blackboard Learning Management System and also synchronously in Second Life. Blackboard is used for assignment information, assignment drop box, grade books, and to provide a forum for asynchronous discussions and student reflection (see Figure 6.2). Class instruction is performed via weekly meetings in Second Life.

Introduction to Second Life has been offered three times since Aggie Island began in 2007. While this class was originally created to teach introductory Second Life skills, it was redesigned in 2009 to prepare an NMSU student for using Second Life in an academic

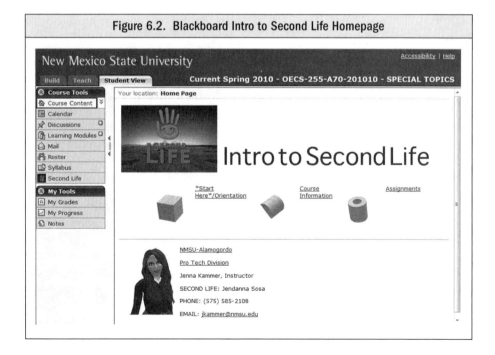

Figure 6.2. Blackboard Intro to Second Life Homepage

situation. The redesign is mapped from the ACRL (2000) Information Literacy Standards for Higher Education and requires students to perform a service project that demonstrates evidence of Second Life skills which would be useful in other virtual classroom situations. The standards provide a defined model that can be used as a guide to teach information literacy, and it gives measurable criteria against which the students can be evaluated. The rubric is useful to the students by clearly defining their learning expectations. The instructional goals of this course are that students will become comfortable, competent, and successful in Second Life so that they may continue to use this virtual world in their academic or professional lives.

INTERDISCIPLINARY PERSPECTIVE

Introduction to Second Life is a computer technology course offered in the Occupational Education in Computer Science (OECS) department at NMSU's campus in Alamogordo. OECS courses prepare students with technology skills that can be useful in the workplace or academic setting. Other OECS courses include Introduction to PowerPoint, Creating a Web Page, Internet Applications, and Database Design. Some OECS instructors, like Kammer who has a background in library science, choose to integrate critical thinking and information literacy into the skill-based curricula to provide a wider perspective of how the software fits into the workplace.

OECS attracts students from different disciplines, ranging from computer science to criminal justice. Introduction to Second Life is one credit, which also means many students will take this course as an elective or to maintain full-time status. Many students who take Introduction to Second Life are doing so out of curiosity about virtual worlds or to learn how to make money in this environment. Some students are already Second Life residents but are trying to improve their skills. The service learning project in this course is flexible enough to provide learning experiences for students with multiple learning objectives.

FACULTY–LIBRARIAN COLLABORATION

NMSU–Alamogordo instructor Jenna Kammer and NMSU–Las Cruces librarian Tracey Thompson formed a partnership to explore the growing potential of Second Life. Kammer contacted Thompson after hearing of a presentation given by Thompson on Second Life at the annual conference of the New Mexico Library Association. The original goal of the partnership was to collaborate to build a virtual library space, the Information Commons, that would support self-directed information literacy instruction and provide help resources for new Second Life students, including those taking Introduction to Second Life.

At the time of this faculty–librarian partnership, Aggie Island was already created and partitioned for the interaction of faculty, staff, and students. Despite real-life physical distances, Kammer and Thompson are able to meet both synchronously and asynchronously in Second Life using voice chat and text chat. The Second Life interface also easily records transcripts of chat sessions and keeps a history of previous chats, making it easy to document meetings. Because of the visual representation of the avatar, there is a sense of physical presence that is lacking in chat rooms and Voice Over Internet Protocol (VOIP) communications, such as Skype. Kammer and Thompson met in Second Life nearly a year before they finally met in person.

Securing funding for the project was a challenge for this interdepartmental, inter-campus, faculty–librarian partnership. While both libraries from the home campuses were willing to contribute funds to the project, the accounting aspect of moving the funds from real life into Second Life was rather complicated. Initial financial support for the Information Commons came from the College of Extended Learning funds that were already in Second Life. The faculty–librarian team also pursued outside financial support through a grant from Amigos Library Services. The grant was awarded to Thompson "to explore how traditional library services may need to be redefined to meet the needs of the virtual student and instructor" (Thompson, 2009). Designing information literacy into Introduction to Second Life fit within the para-meters of the grant and was a natural project for collaboration between faculty and a librarian.

PROJECT PLANNING

Introduction to Second Life had been offered one time before the faculty–librarian team formed. Simultaneously, courses from other disciplines emerged on Aggie Island as more instructors from the NMSU network began to explore the educational possibilities of this environment. After an informal needs assessment demonstrated that faculty would like students to have a foundation in Second Life technology before taking their virtual courses, the faculty–librarian team began redesigning Introduction to Second Life so that it would support the academic skills a student would need to succeed. The foundation of the redesign was based on the ACRL (2000) Information Literacy Competency Standards for Higher Education, as information literacy skills are transcendent across disciplines and can be applied to any aspect of their education. It was expected that students who learned information literacy skills in Second Life would have the ability to think more critically about the virtual environment.

The faculty and librarian team needed to organize the project possibilities and goals in preparation to seek funding. Kammer had used logic modeling to plan a pre-vious project and designed a logic model that would help in the planning, implemen-tation, and evaluation of the course and its components based on a course from the University of Wisconsin Extension (http://www.uwex.edu/ces/lmcourse/). Different factors of the project were paired with expectations to answer the questions, "What are we trying to do? How do we want to accomplish it? How will we know we have accomplished it?" The logic model in Figure 6.3 shows the relationship between the inputs (investment), outputs (activities), and outcomes (results) that were expected from the project.

Using the logic model, it became clear that the faculty and librarian team would need to collaborate to secure funding for the project, volunteer time and skills, evaluate technology availability on campus, and map the ACRL (2000) Information Literacy Standards to Second Life skills. With these investments, the team would be able to design the Introduction to Second Life curriculum, build an Information

Figure 6.3. Logic Model

SITUATION
Resource-Based Learning Design to Support Virtual World Information Needs

INPUTS	OUTPUTS		OUTCOMES
What we invest...	*What we do...*		*What will happen...*
Money	Information Commons		Readiness
People	Collection Development		Retention
Technology	Virtual Reference		Support
Instructional Design	Support Services		
	Website		
	Workshops		
	Curriculum Mapping		

EVALUATION
How will we know...
Needs assessment (survey, interviews), usage statistics, field observations, UbD framework

Commons that would hold resource materials for students and instructors, and provide adequate technical and resource support. The logic model also demonstrated that the goals of the project extended beyond the course objectives. The complete project would aim to:

1. Prepare students with the information and technical literacy necessary for taking a course in Second Life.

2. Provide students with peer, institutional, and community connections.

3. Support students' research and technical needs.

Curriculum Planning

Introduction to Second Life was designed around the essential questions, ideas, and authentic activities of the curriculum mapping technique from the Understanding by Design (UbD) theory (Wiggins and McTighe, 2005). The backward design of UbD requires that curriculum is designed around performance indicators rather than assessment or textbooks. Using the backward approach, all content, activities, resources, and assessments are developed to support learning the outcomes of the ACRL (2000) Information Literacy Competency Standards for Higher Education and answering the essential questions of the curriculum (see Appendix 6.1).

The team used the resource-based learning approach to develop a service learning project that is central to meeting the outcomes. The service learning project requires students to choose a research topic and a Second Life organization where they can volunteer or observe as part of the research process. The service learning project is resource based and supported by the collection and reference support at the Aggie Island Information Commons. Students use electronic resources to find an organization in Second Life, collect background information, and make contact with a project leader in that organization. Then, students apply technical skills learned from the course as a volunteer for this organization.

Resource-Based Learning Environment Planning

Supporting the resource-based design of the service learning project required a structure that could house the different support materials students would need for their research. The team met in Second Life with the Aggie Island Architects management group to design a virtual library that had the look and feel of an authentic New Mexican structure, complete with arches, stucco, and Saltillo tile. Using initial funds from the College of Extended Learning, the team hired a professional builder to create a structure that had all of the physical components of an information commons: versatile social space, collections space, and technology space. The result is a two-story, three-wing, U-shaped building with a central courtyard for socializing and a presentation/classroom space in the back (see Figure 6.4).

The Aggie Island Information Commons is modeled after the national trend in physical libraries where the library expands beyond the traditional library model to include reference, instructional and technical services, media, culture, and interpersonal social and learning spaces. Inspired by the bricks-and-mortar examples set by Loyola University Chicago, University of Arizona, Indiana University, and the University of

Figure 6.4. Aggie Island Information Commons

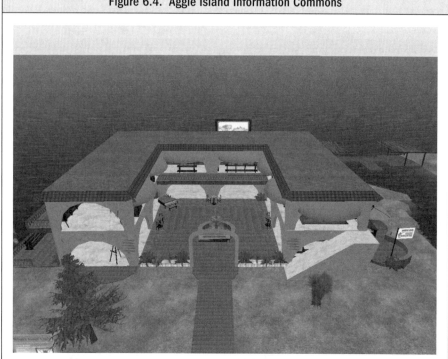

Pennsylvania, the Aggie Island Information Commons executes the C3-learning framework for distance education: collaborative, contextual, and connected learning spaces (Sims, 2008).The mission is to expand the virtual reference services of the five NMSU libraries and support Second Life learning activity.

Planning for the collection development of the Information Commons involved researching the resource preferences of Second Life users. The faculty–librarian team distributed a survey to Second Life educators and librarians on information habits and needs in this virtual environment (see Figure 6.5). Results indicated that Second Life users would like information presented in textual, visual, and multimedia formats. The resources grew to include collections of notecards, landmarks, and links to NMSU online subject guides. To support the interdisciplinary Aggie Island student population, the collections were divided into the major departments at NMSU and linked to NMSU subject course guides.

Technology Planning

The technology required to run Second Life successfully is quite substantial and has been known to prevent students with older computer systems or slow bandwidth from participating in this space. Also, the learning curve for using Second Life is often high, as virtual worlds are a new concept for many people. Even creating an account can be a daunting process.

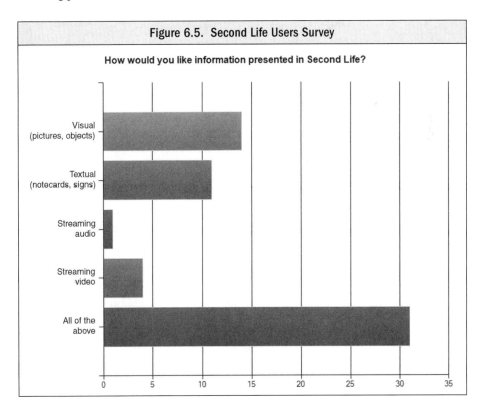

Figure 6.5. Second Life Users Survey

Supporting the technical aspect of Second Life was a major factor in planning for this project. Several efforts were made to create access points on each of the five NMSU campuses so that students could use Second Life from the libraries and lab computers. Training programs were also offered to librarians at each campus to be able to provide in-person support of Second Life resources.

The faculty–librarian team created a website on the NMSU-Alamogordo Web server (http://secondlife.nmsua.edu) that could act as an online service point for housing Second Life support documents, Aggie Island events, and easy access to the Second Life Uniform Resource Location (SLURL) of Aggie Island. Technical documents for logging in and getting started in Second Life pointed to this website as a starting point for accessing the SLURL which would transport one directly to Aggie Island once Second Life was properly installed (see Figure 6.6).

RESOURCE-BASED LEARNING IN A BLENDED ENVIRONMENT

At NMSU, instructors are encouraged to create online learning spaces that will maximize the potential for socialization, collaboration, and active learning. For Introduction to Second Life, the learning space includes the virtual world, Aggie Isand in Second Life, the Information Commons on Aggie Island, and the Blackboard Learning Management

Figure 6.6. Second Life Uniform Resource Location (SLURL) of Aggie Island

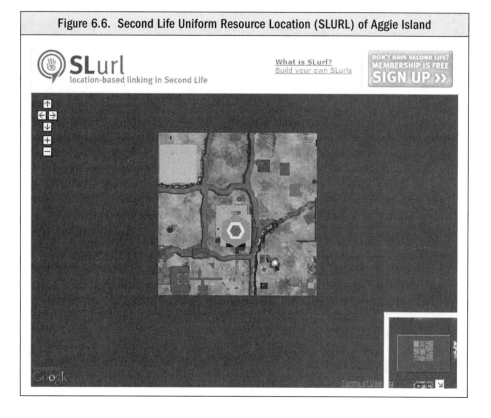

System. The course requires careful planning for integrating these different learning spaces.

Blended Learning

The definition of blended learning usually implies a combination of face-to-face and online learning spaces, but can include the combination of one or more learning systems (Bonk and Graham, 2006). Introduction to Second Life utilizes both the Second Life platform and the Blackboard Learning Manangement System to support both asynchronous and synchronous learning. The course meets weekly in Second Life while housing discussions, blogs, assignment instructions, and some resources in the Blackboard Learning Management System (see Figure 6.7).

To reduce the cognitive overload of learning to use these different spaces at once, it is a prerequisite for students in Introduction to Second Life to either have taken an online course in Blackboard before or to attend a Blackboard workshop prior to beginning the course. Support materials, including videos, step-by-step technical guides, and a "tech prep" session are also provided to students in the first week of class. In addition, the first week of class is devoted to setting up the technical components of the course, which include the installation of Second Life, navigating the online course, and creating an avatar in Second Life.

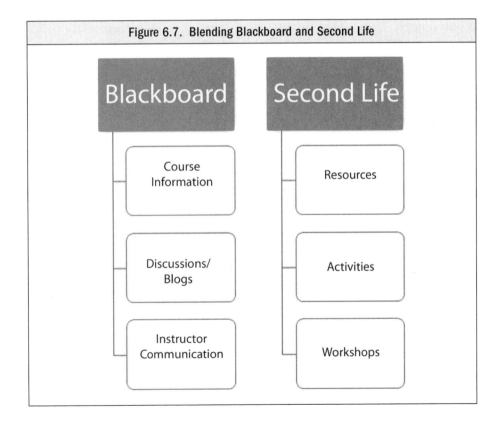

Figure 6.7. Blending Blackboard and Second Life

The Resource-Based Learning Environment Model

Introduction to Second Life is divided into three levels of learning: skills, application, and presentation. Each of these levels lasts approximately three weeks and prepares students for the next level of learning. For example, in *Level 1: Skills*, students learn the basic skills for using Second Life, beginning with communication, appearance, and movement. The instructor meets weekly with students to present workshops and facilitate field trips. In *Level 2: Application*, students begin researching an area of Second Life that they would like to learn more about, such as learning to build a house, running a business, or exploring the different Second Life cultures. They will choose a nonprofit organization for their service project that needs volunteers. Many students choose service learning projects related to their academic or professional interests. For example, a student studying art might choose to work with a nonprofit organization that needs volunteers to set up an art exhibit. In *Level 3: Presentation*, students work with evaluation, citation, and information ethics as they prepare a poster session to describe their service experiences. In preparing their presentation, students must make decisions about intellectual property and ownership as they create freebies, distribute notecards, and apply textures for their poster display.

Each of the levels in this course offers different opportunities for resource learning. In Level 1, the instructor provides resources for students as they learn to communicate, navigate, build, and script (scripting is the term for giving behavior to Second Life objects using the LSL scripting language). These resources include the course textbook, machinima (videos taken inside Second Life), and in-world Second Life toolkits (collections of objects). For example, in a Level 1 workshop on "Communication, Appearance, and Movement," each student is given a kit with information that describe how to use communication tools, clothes for altering appearance, landmarks for visiting other islands, and a notecard with the weekly active learning assignments. The activities in Level 1 expose students to Second Life resources, like notecards and search tools, in instructor-guided and activity-based workshops.

In Level 2, the students begin collecting their own resources or working with the resource collections in the Information Commons. At this point in the course, the students should understand which type of resources are available and have a modest understanding of how to use them. Activities in Level 2, such as information management workshops and collecting research for the service learning project, provide an opportunity for students to apply Level 1 skills to their own authentic scenerio.

Service Learning Project

At the heart of Introduction to Second Life is a service learning project that encompasses all of the outcomes for the course. The project begins halfway through the course in Level 2 after students have learned core Second Life skills, such as communicating, navigating, basic building, and basic scripting. The service learning project begins by asking students to choose a research question or problem that they want to answer within Second Life (such as, "What are the cultural norms in the land of Gor?"). To answer the question, students work with an organization in Second Life related to their topic and document all resources that were consulted to find the answer to their question.

To document learning, students prepare a poster display within Second Life of their findings. The poster display also provides an opportunity for students to use their Second Life skills such as building, texturing, and scripting.

For students, the hardest part of the project can be finding an organization with which to volunteer. To start the project, Kammer puts out a call to various groups in Second Life asking for service opportunities. Kammer keeps a running list of the organizations who need volunteers in Blackboard so that students can get ideas for the different volunteer activities in Second Life. Simultaneously, Thompson is introduced to the class as an embedded librarian who can assist students in making connections with nonprofit organizations in Second Life. Thompson participates in the synchronous lab sessions and also has access to a discussion forum on the service project in Blackboard. Students then make contact with the organization in Second Life and begin work by meeting with a mentor to get instructions for their task. Usually tasks are simple and include helping build exhibit spaces or constructing kits for events in Second Life. Almost all of these nonprofit organizations are run strictly by volunteers and are eager to have extra help setting up new virtual spaces.

The objectives for the service learning project are:

1. Given a collection of resources, students will choose an organization for whom they will perform four hours of volunteer service.

2. Students will complete the service project of their choice using skills learned in Level 1, items from the resource collection, and consultations with the instructor, librarian, and mentor.

3. Using the class blog, students will document the service project experience by writing on their experiences and documenting resources in each post.

4. Using Second Life building, scripting, and communicating techniques, students will present a textual and visual description of the service project with a rubric rating of at least 70 percent (http://www.jendanna.com/teaching/SLP_rubric.pdf).

Garrison and Kanuka (2004) discussed the potential for blended learning spaces to provide a transformative experience for students. In Introduction to Second Life, this theory was applied to the service learning project where students are asked to blog about their experiences in Second Life. The goal of this aspect of the project is to build a more meaningful learning experience as students reflect on their project. The instructor creates blogs within the Blackboard Course Management system. Each blog post requires students not only to reflect weekly on their experiences but also provide citations to resources that were consulted in the process. These blogs are networked so that students can easily read and comment on on another's posts. Notifications of new blog posts also feed to their homepage in Blackboard so that students can keep up with the latest activity.

IMPACT ON STUDENT LEARNING

The outcomes of this project are to prepare students for taking online classes in Second Life while improving their information literacy (readiness), fostering real-life connections in Second Life world (retention), and assisting students with technical and resource needs (support). Using a combination of assessment and feedback, the project appears to have a positive impact on the Aggie Island learning community.

Readiness

Introduction to Second Life was redesigned to teach students information literacy skills necessary for using Second Life as a student or professional. Students are evaluated on their information literacy skills in this virtual environment using a pre- and postproject self-assessment, before and after the completion of the service learning project. The results of the self-assessments indicate that there is a conceptual change between the beginning and the end of the project as students spend more time working with Second Life resources. Blogging about the research process also seems to positively affect resource learning as students share links, tips, and tricks for gathering resources.

The service learning project provided several students with connections that then turned into business partnerships within Second Life. For example, one student worked as a volunteer for a cultural organization and helped manage the free gift area for a festival. He described the service learning project as an opportunity to learn about running a Second Life business:

> The service learning project gave me an opportunity to learn how to open and run a Second Life business. I now own my own shop and land and make items to sell like shirts and rugs and other nifty things. Introduction to Second Life was a great learning experience that continues to help me today.

Retention

One of the project goals for the redesign of Introduction to Second Life was to provide motivation for students to return to Second Life to take other courses, start a business, or just for fun. The initial results show that 100 percent of students who successfully completed all components of the service learning project visited the virtual world after the class was over. Comments made from returning students indicate they return to Second Life after the course is over because they are comfortable with the interface and are engaged in communities outside of Aggie Island.

Instructor feedback about Introduction to Second Life and its usefulness has been favorable. In one interview, a Second Life Communications instructor describes Introduction to Second Life students as being prepared and skilled when they take her Second Life course:

> My experience as a Second Life instructor is that students who have completed Introduction to Second Life are very prepared for my class. One student who previously completed Introduction to Second Life is even helping other students who are brand new to Second Life. Ideally, I'd like to have it set up so students interested in Second Life classes would be able to (or even required to) take it first. That would allow me to use the first several weeks of class to be focused on the subject matter versus orientation to Second Life, which is necessary but is being met by having them attend OECS 255: Introduction to Second Life.

Support

Tools that track the traffic and usage in the Information Commons show the facilities are not simply used for resources. Students use the Information Commons as a home base, and several students marked this resource as "home" in their Second Life preferences. The presentation space in the Information Commons is often used for other classes from NMSU and other universities looking for a Second Life classroom. Informal interviews with other subject instructors indicate that they often send students to the Information Commons to explore and use the resources. One Second Life instructor describes this virtual environment as a resource for geography students:

> The Information Commons is a valuable resource for both students and faculty in Second Life, and it has the potential to redefine library services in a virtual environment. My Geography students have already commented on the existing facilities the Commons has provided.

It also became clear that students who had more interaction with the mentor, instructor, and librarian performed better with the service learning project. Students who blogged about positive interactions with their mentors were more likely to produce a complete project. Several students had to either switch projects midway because of unresponsive mentors or failed to produce a project because the mentor did not follow through. These results indicate that it is crucial to have a mentor who will be responsive, supportive, and cooperative. In Second Life, this means that mentors should respond quickly to instant messages, log in regularly, and provide students with tasks that can be done asynchronously. Also, mentors who were selected by the instructor tended to be more active in the project than were mentors chosen by the students. Either way, instructor communication with mentors proved to be as important to student success as communication with the students themselves.

ASSESSMENT OF ONLINE LEARNING

Teaching in Second Life enhances the opportunities for assessment beyond what can be done solely in the online classroom. In addition to traditional online assessment tools, like discussion, tracking, and electronic quizzes/assignments, students in Second Life can demonstrate learning through three-dimensional and dynamic presentations, like scripted posters or replicas of real-life objects. In addition, the interactive nature of Second Life allows instructors and students to meet in synchronous situations that include voice, text, and interpersonal communication.

In Introduction to Second Life, students collect and submit assignments in Second Life, while reflecting in Blackboard. In Level 1, students are asked to create learning artifacts that show knowledge of basic Second Life skills. For example, one artifact is to create a notecard with an embedded landmark and information about where to find freebies in Second Life and share it with the class as a group notice. Performing this task combines the skills of notecard creation, landmark navigation, and group communication.

The service learning project in Introduction to Second Life requires students to apply skills learned from Level 1 to an authentic task as a volunteer with an organization in Second Life. In the presentation phase of the class, student mastery of Second Life skills is fairly clear as they build and present a visual display of their experience. Students are given a checklist of each item that must be included in their three-dimensional display. Displays are required to include notecards, landmarks, and any other multimedia that would depict their experience. Evidence of information literacy skills are also included on this checklist as students are required to cite resources, follow intellectual property laws, and create Second Life bibliographies of resources from their project.

The faculty–librarian team developed a pre- and postproject self-assessment for students to evaluate their information skills before and after the service learning project (see Appendix 6.2). The pre- and postproject self-assessment is delivered in the Blackboard Learning Management system and permits students to compose the assessment in a word processing program or the default text editor. The self-assessment was designed around each of the ACRL (2000) Information Literacy Standards. Each question in the assessment correlates directly to a performance indicator from the standards.

CONCLUSION

Each of the three times Introduction to Second Life has been offered, a new action plan is prepared to improve the course. With each new section, it becomes clear what the information needs are and how best to prepare support resources for students in this environment. The first section did not include information literacy components. The second section included information literacy components but did not include reflection. The final section now includes an information literacy framework, blogging as a tool for transformative learning, and a breadth of information resources that support students new to Second Life.

Challenges

While the project is very rewarding and has fostered new relationships between NMSU branch campus and main campus librarians and instructors, it has not been without challenges. Not all campus computer labs are equipped with the technology to run Second Life. Also, questions about access have emerged during presentations and workshops about the project, such as, "Is it fair to put resources in the Second Life library that students can only use in Second Life? What if they can't access Second Life on their computers?"

While the service learning project is a great opportunity for students to make connections and develop technical skills and information literacy in Second Life, it can be difficult to find community organizations in Second Life that match the research interests of the students. The instructor needs to spend a large amount of time scaffolding the project as a guide for choosing organizations and preparing students with the skills necessary to complete their volunteer tasks.

In Introduction to Second Life, other instructors feared that adding the information literacy component to the course would make it less fun and engaging as students worked to meet standards in addition to learning Second Life skills. However, the results of the project indicate that information-literate Second Life students are more likely to continue using this virtual world for fun, business, or to take other courses in this environment.

The role of the librarian in Introduction to Second Life is also dependent on NMSU libraries and their support for sending a librarian to work in Second Life. At the time of this writing, there is only one librarian from NMSU interested in working as an embedded librarian or participating in the Information Commons. There has not been strong support from library administration to explore Web 2.0 technologies or the library as a virtual place. There has been a high turnover in both university positions and library positions, and while there is a grassroots movement on campus to explore emerging technologies, it has yet to receive widespread support. As a result there has not been much funding for Second Life, and most of the work on Aggie Island has been done on a volunteer basis. For the project to continue to succeed, more librarians from the NMSU libraries need to be committed to maintaining the resource collection in the Information Commons and supporting students in this environment.

Future Possibilities

The Information Commons has proven to be a resource-based learning environment that is useful to students and instructors using Second Life. The Information Commons now offers the venue for conference presentations, classes from other universities, and workshop space for New Mexico librarians. In the future, considerations about what resources best serve students in Second Life should be revisited. For example, are collections of landmarks useful to students? Are they too hard to maintain? Also, perhaps the Information Commons could house other resources, such as presentation tools for students to borrow for projects. Any other developments like this would require further investment of time and money from NMSU libraries.

Other future possibilities include offering Introduction to Second Life as a one-week, one-credit course that students could take before or during the first week of another course in this virtual world. This condensed version of the course could focus specifically on the information skills a student would need in Second Life: navigation, resource creation, and information management. Another possibility is to eliminate Introduction to Second Life and offer regular technical workshops at the Information Commons at the beginning of each semester. The service learning project could also be altered to an "internship" to allow students more freedom in the organizations or people with whom they choose to work. An internship could be evaluated using the same rubric that the self-assessments were used for the current service learning project.

The faculty–librarian team is also interested in doing more research on how well information literacy skills learned in Second Life transfer to real life. For example, if a computer technology student becomes a competent information seeker in Second Life, will he or she also be competent at finding information in another computer technology course, such as Introduction to HTML? Will research skills learned in Second Life transfer to researching for other subject areas, such as history or English?

Second Life has demonstrated its potential as an innovative distance-learning platform. It is well worth investigating as immersive virtual worlds continue to develop and expand.

REFERENCES

Association of College and Research Librarians (ACRL). 2000. "Information Literacy Competency Standards for Higher Education." American Library Association. http://www.ala.org/ala/mgrps/divs/acrl/standards/informationliteracycompetency.cfm.

Beswick, Norman. 1977. *Resource-Base Learning*. London: Heinemann.

Bonk, Curtis, and Charles Graham. 2006. *The Handbook of Blended Learning: Global Perspectives, Local Designs*. San Francisco: Pfeiffer Publishing.

Bransford, John, Ann Brown, and Rodney Cocking. 1999. *How People Learn: Brain, Mind, Experience, and School*. Washington, DC: National Academy Press.

Davis, Marian, and Carol Smith. 2009. "Virtually Embedded: Library Instruction within Second Life." *Journal of Library and Information Services in Distance Learning* 3, 3/4 (July): 120–137.

Garrison, Randy, and Heather Kanuka. 2004. "Blended Learning: Uncovering Its Transformative Potential in Higher Education." *The Internet and Higher Education* 7, no. 2 (2nd Quarter): 95–105.

Grassian, Esther, and Joan Kaplowitz. 2009. *Information Literacy Instruction: Theory and Practice*. New York: Neal-Schuman.

Grassian, Esther, and Rhonda Trueman. 2007. "Stumbling, Bumbling, Teleporting and Flying… Librarian Avatars in Second Life." *Reference Services Review* 35, no. 1 (June): 84–89.

Hill, Janette. 2007. "Reflections on Resource-Based Learning Environments: Continuing the Exploration of Opportunities and Obstacles." *International Journal of Knowledge and Learning* 3, no. 1 (February): 12–29.

Hill, Janette, and Micheal Hannafin. 2001. "Teaching and Learning in Digital Environments: The Resurgence of Resource-Based Learning." *Educational Technology Research and Development* 49, no. 3 (September): 37–52.

Jeong, Heisawn, and Cindy Hmelo-Silver. 2010. "Productive Use of Learning Resources in an Online Problem-Based Learning Environment." *Computers in Human Behavior* 26, no. 1 (January): 86–99.

Lambright, Kristina, and Yi Lu. 2009. "What Impacts the Learning in Service Learning? An Examination of Project Structure and Student Characteristics." *Journal of Public Affairs Education* 15, no. 4 (Fall): 425–444.

Sanchez, Joe. 2009a. "Barriers to Student Learning in Second Life." *Library Technology Reports* 45, no. 2 (February/March): 29–34.

Sanchez, Joe. 2009b. "Virtual Worlds: New Spaces for Service Learning." In *Service Learning: Linking Library Education and Practice*, edited by Loriene Roy, Kelly Jensen, and Alex Hershey Meyers, 169–178. Chicago, IL: ALA Editions.

Schmeil, Andreas, and Martin Eppler. 2009. "Knowledge Sharing and Collaborative Learning in Second Life: A Classification of Virtual 3D Group Interaction Scripts." *Journal of Universal Computer Science* 14, no. 3 (February): 665–677.

Simons, Lori, and Beverly Cleary. 2006. "The Influence of Service Learning on Students' Personal and Social Development." *College Teaching* 54, no. 4 (September): 307–319.

Sims, Roderick. 2008. "Rethinking (e)Learning: A Manifesto for Connected Generations." *Distance Education* 29, no. 2 (August): 153–164.

Tergan, Sigmar-Olaf, Wolfgang Gräber, and Anja Neumann. 2006. "Mapping and Managing Knowledge and Information in Resource–Based Learning." *Innovations in Education & Teaching International* 43, no. 4 (November): 327–336.

Thompson, Tracey. 2009. "Building an Information Commons in Second Life." Second Life. http://www.secondlife.nmsua.edu/info-commons.

Wiggins, Grant, and Jay McTighe. 2005. *Understanding by Design*. Alexandria, VA: Prentice Hall.

Appendix 6.1. OECS 255 Curriculum Framework		
ACRL Information Literacy Competency Standards for Higher Education	Enduring Understandings	Assessments
I. The information-literate student determines the nature and extent of the information needed. II. The information-literate student accesses needed information effectively and efficiently. III. The information-literate student evaluates information and its sources critically and incorporates selected information into his or her knowledge base and value system. IV. The information-literate student, individually or as a member of a group, uses information effectively to accomplish a specific purpose. V. The information-literate student understands many of the economic, legal, and social issues surrounding the use of information and accesses and uses information ethically and legally	• Information in Second Life is conveyed visually (textures), textually (notecards, textures), socially (voice and text communication), and spatially (interactive scripts). • Search tools in Second Life consist of search within the Second Life viewer (search, maps, profiles, inventory) and external websites that connect with the viewer (Secondlife.com search, XStreetSL, and other search engines/directories). • Information needs in Second Life include everyday life research (term coined by Head and Eisenberg, 2009) (buying land, collecting objects, learning skills), technical research (how to build, script, or do other SL tasks), geospatial research (maps, teleporting, finding locations), and resources (materials providing information on Second Life events, skills, tips, locations). • Evaluation of information in Second Life includes reviewing profiles of other avatars and viewing land and object ownership information. • Information management in Second Life includes inventory organization techniques, exporting photos, collecting SLURLs and managing chat logs. • Intellectual property laws from real life translate equally into Second Life.	Artifacts (object creation) Blogs (experience log) Discussions (comments on others' blogs) Posters Self-assessment

(Continued)

Appendix 6.1. OECS 255 Curriculum Framework *(Continued)*		
Essential Questions	**Content Topics**	**Connected Cocurricular Support Resources**
1. What aspects of Second Life are different from our first life? 2. What is "ownership" in Second Life? 3. How do information sources differ in Second Life? 4. How do information needs differ in Second Life? 5. What aspects of the Second Life experience translate to the real-life experience? 6. Do out of world search strategies work the same in Second Life?	**Level 1: Skills** (3 weeks) • Exploring • Basic skills • Creating *Key skills:* communicating, movement, appearance, inventory, objects, notecards, building, scripting, texturing **Level 2: Experiential** (3 weeks; 1 meeting with instructor, 1 meeting with librarian, 4 hours community service) • Determine topic • Choose mentor • Perform service • Document research • Manage resources *Key skills:* collaboration, application, writing, research, management **Level 3: Presentation** (2 weeks) • Present service project in visual form *Key skills:* visual/graphic formatting, building and/or scripting, oral presentation	Textbook Second Life website Collections of notecards Collections of landmarks Pathfinders of Internet resources Pathfinders of Second Life resources Subject guides Field trips Toolkits Machinima

Appendix 6.2. Self-Assessment	
Standard	**Questions**
Determining the need and extent for information	
1.1	Based on your experience using Second Life in the first few weeks of this class, what is a research question that you would like to further explore in Second Life? This question should be specific, able to be answered in the duration of this assignment, and related to your interests in Second Life. (For example, how does one build a house in Second Life?)
1.2	What resources will you use for the project? Remember that in Second Life, we have in-world resources (notecards, groups, maps, etc.) and out-of-world resources (websites, blogs, etc.). Please name some specific sources.
1.3	What are the costs and benefits that you need to consider in this project? For example, what skills will you need to learn to complete it? What other challenges will you face into answering this research question? Remember that costs can be time, money, or stress.
1.4	Please state your plan for collecting information for this project. (For example, "First, I will do a search in Google on my topic to collect background information. Next, I will . . .")
Accessing information	
2.1	What search engines, websites, or other Second Life resources will be the best for you to find information on your topic?
2.2	List five to ten keywords that you will use to search in and out of world for information about your topic.
2.3	What are the different systems and networks you can use to find information on your topic? (For example, if you think a group in Second Life will be helpful for you, please list that group name.)
2.4	Where will you look for new resources to use in your research?
2.5	How will you organize the different landmarks, objects, tools, and notecards that you collect in Second Life?
Evaluation	
3.1	What is the mission, location (SLURL), and who owns the organization that you are studying for your service project?
3.2	Describe how you will determine if you are working for a legitimate organization in Second Life.
3.3	What methods will you use to document your experiences?
3.4	Is researching in Second Life similar to researching in real life? What will you do differently in Second Life?
3.5	Will your personal value system affect choices you make in this project?
3.6	Who will you work with on this project to help you understand and learn new concepts?
3.7	How will you evaluate the quality of the information you collected?

(Continued)

Appendix 6.2. Self-Assessment *(Continued)*	
Standard	Questions
Information use	
4.1	How will you present your experience and the results of your research?
4.2	How will you plan and edit your presentation before uploading the materials to Second Life?
4.3	Which communication medium (text, animation, voice, etc.) do you think is the best way to convey the results of this research project in Second Life?
Information ethics	
5.1	How will you give credit to the owners and creators of different objects that you use in Second Life?
5.2	How will you make sure that you follow the Linden Labs Terms of Service when completing your project?
5.3	How will you set the permissions on objects at your project display? (For example, will you make your project copyable?)

7

Information Literacy by Design

Recalibrating Graduate Professional Asynchronous Online Programs

David Lavoie, Andrew Rosman, and Shikha Sharma

INTRODUCTION

The model for information literacy that we examine in this chapter is both conventional and novel. It is conventional in the sense that it is consistent with the well-established objectives and standards for information literacy as identified by the Association of College and Research Libraries (ACRL). Yet the model is novel in two ways. First, information literacy is practiced as a component of a constructivist course design engaged in by a team that includes the faculty member as content expert; the instructional designer as education and curriculum specialist; the librarian as the information literacy and resource specialist; media specialist to assist with technology and course design solutions involving software; and students to provide feedback to help continue to evolve and refine the course.

Second, information literacy is designed into constructivist-based courses for engaged, motivated, and independent learning. Students engage information literacy holistically by first determining the information need and then critically questioning the reliability, bias, and accuracy of resources. The process culminates with students communicating their findings in the form of a report, memo, paper, or other artifact. Information literacy in a constructivist-designed course sets out to produce students who are skeptical (i.e., have a questioning mind) and metacognitive (i.e., are self-reflective) and who consequently can approach tasks critically with "purposeful, self-regulatory judgment" (American Philosophical Association, 1990: 2). Ultimately, students develop the skills to be able to act independently with respect to information literacy (e.g., to be able to determine the information need, develop and implement an appropriate search strategy, and evaluate resources for bias and other limitations), rather than relying on the instructor to specify the information need and direct the students toward resources without considering reliability and bias of the sources.

RELATED LITERATURE

The literature reviewed in this section provides background on the motivation for considering information literacy in online environments, the way that current information literacy standards map into graduate online education, and the institutional setting of business education including accreditation as it relates to information literacy.

Impetus for a New Perspective on Information Literacy in the Online Classroom

The 2008 Sloan Survey of Online Learning (Allen and Seaman, 2008) reported that over 3.9 million (20 percent) of all U.S. higher education students were taking at least one online course in fall 2007.[1] This marked a 12.9 percent increase in online enrollments over the previous year, which far exceeded the 1.2 percent growth of the overall higher education student population. The survey defines online courses as those in which at least 80 percent of the course is delivered online. Among all institutions offering business degree programs, 33 percent have a fully online business program. The penetration rates were even higher among public institutions for all disciplines, including business with 43 percent of public institutions and approximately 22 percent for both private for-profit and private not-for-profit institutions. The report predicts further increases in online enrollments in light of the current economic downturn, unemployment, and fuel costs.

The flexibility and convenience offered by online programs has attracted older students who are often lifelong learners (Dutton, Dutton, and Perry, 2002). The global economy favors workers who can acquire and leverage new knowledge and skills. Online programs allow workers to stay current on the latest research in their respective fields, emerging technologies, and best practices. Full-time working professionals have become the fastest-growing segment of online education as they not only often have support from their employers but also the incentive of career advancement and promotion.

Prior to the Internet, technology was used to assist teaching by addressing the problem of how to provide access to education to those who were not in close proximity to the university, usually in the form of streamed video to an offsite location that resulted in a largely passive learning environment. Students could see lectures from another campus and might be able to participate in a minimal way, for example, to ask a question.

With the introduction of the Internet, the dialogue changed from merely providing access to education to providing access to a highly interactive form of learning. Although some might consider online learning to be a form of distance learning, its Internet-based delivery makes it very different because students can become much more actively involved. Online learning changes the approach to include significant active involvement by students. Stated differently, distance learning through streamed video was still lecture based whereas online learning, which is a derivative of distance learning, can include lectures but is not limited to that format. In particular, learning can occur without any lecture by leaving the acquisition of basic knowledge to reading texts and other resources that set up socially constructed engagement through activities such as threaded discussions.

Online courses have become popular even among traditional students who are on campus because of the convenience they offer (Parry, 2009). Regardless of the reason or whether students are taking courses at a distance or on campus, online classes offer students greater autonomy and in turn create meaningful opportunities for information literacy. The online learning environment nurtures and challenges students' cognitive skills as they encounter unstructured problems, make decisions, and construct new knowledge, which are information literacy–related activities often associated with the tasks performed by research librarians.

Information Literacy in the Asynchronous Online Graduate Classroom

ACRL standards (American Library Association, 2000: 2–3) delineate the characteristics of an information-literate person as someone who does the following:

1. Determines the extent of information needed
2. Accesses the needed information effectively and efficiently
3. Evaluates information and its sources critically and incorporates selected information into one's knowledge base
4. Uses information effectively to accomplish a specific purpose
5. Understands the economic, legal, and social issues surrounding the use of information, and access and use information ethically and legally

Challenging students to think critically is consistent with the learning objectives of many graduate students who have a sharpened focus on a professional field and subject matter and are likely to be mature, motivated, and independent learners who take responsibility for their own learning (Kerns, 2006). Students enrolled in professional programs are not just interested in getting good grades but instead expect to be able to learn and apply new knowledge and skills at work (Huang and Chuan, 2005).

Given the independent nature of learning in graduate education, a constructivist model that creates a learning environment in which students take charge of their own learning through problem solving, case studies, scenarios, discussions, and debates is well suited for comprehensive information literacy skills at the graduate level. A constructivist model allows students to bring past knowledge and experiences to bear in new situations and construct new meaning and knowledge that is relevant to their everyday life. It also changes the role of faculty from "sage on the stage" to "guide on the side" (King, 1993). Constructivist-based learning requires higher levels of critical thinking including conceptualization, analysis, synthesis, and evaluation (Allen, 2008). Critical thinking is an important lens through which information literacy in graduate curricula is considered.

If graduate education can be conceptualized this way, then how information literacy is integrated, taught, and assessed in the graduate online environment must consider the motivation of students and the level of cognition at which they operate. Many articles and case studies illustrate ACRL Standards 1 through 3, which deal with defining, gathering, evaluating, and using information. A study on credit-bearing library skills courses analyzed 100 online syllabi and found that skills associated with information seeking and evaluation of information sources were given more emphasis, while critical thinking and synthesis did not receive as much attention (Hrycaj, 2006). However, the study acknowledged several caveats, including the fact that it relied solely on course syllabi which are usually brief and, therefore, it could not assess the amount of class time that might have been devoted to each standard, as not all associated assignments, activities, and tasks may have been reflected in the syllabi. This study cautions against overgeneralizing its findings, citing the growing literature on faculty–librarian collaboration in disciplinary contexts where all five standards might be applied more comprehensively.

Even if there is a heavier focus on lower-level information literacy skills in credit-bearing courses, the importance of such skills cannot be overlooked. There is a general perception that graduate students are skilled researchers, but they often do not have the requisite skills (Donaldson, 2004). Graduate students come from diverse backgrounds, schools, and even countries with very different library systems and services (Liao, Finn, and Lu, 2007). A research study at Carnegie Mellon University Libraries (George et al., 2006) explored graduate students' information-seeking behavior related to their process of inquiry and scholarly activities and found that students had varying abilities and experiences related to finding and using resources. They reported feeling overwhelmed with information and resources available. Students admitted choosing resources and services based on familiarity and ease of access rather than on the basis of what was most relevant. Therefore, skills related to selecting sources and finding information are critical even at the graduate level as they lay the foundation for higher-level cognitive and evaluative skills.

To provide students an opportunity to learn, practice, and leverage all relevant skills requires an integrated model with clearer delineation of teaching roles. Some have proposed that generic skills that apply to all disciplines be taught by librarians, as they specialize in retrieval, structure, and organization of information (Orr, Appleton, and Wallin, 2001; Grafstein, 2002). Conversely, discipline-specific information literacy skills should be taught by faculty as they require evaluating the content of arguments, assessing the validity of evidence, and proposing original solutions. Information literacy skills taught and leveraged within a disciplinary context hone students' critical thinking skills and inhibit isolation of information from knowledge and process from content (Grafstein, 2002).

The success of online education particularly at the graduate level requires active, deliberate, and sustained collaboration among all stakeholders: administrators, faculty, instructional designers, librarians, technology specialists, and students. It requires a team approach where each member brings a set of skills that complements and contributes to the overall educational goals and objectives. Faculty bring subject knowledge and articulate course objectives; instructional designers facilitate pedagogy; librarians lend their knowledge of research process and information resources; technologists address hardware, software, and networking-related issues; and students as ultimate users of online education provide the necessary feedback for program improvement.

Following this team approach does not ensure that a course would engage all five ACRL standards for information literacy. Rather, the team approach needs to be combined with a constructivist course design or else the course is not likely to engage students beyond the third ACRL standard. Stated differently, the challenge to comprehensively incorporate information literacy as a learning objective is more likely achieved through courses that are student centered and when the design process involves a team of experts that includes the faculty member, instructional designer, librarian, and media specialist, while also providing a role for student input in course redesign.

Accreditation and Information Literacy

The Association to Advance Collegiate Schools of Business (AACSB) is the accrediting agency for collegiate business schools and accounting programs worldwide. The AACSB standards stipulate that undergraduate and graduate business programs should provide students with learning experiences that would develop their discipline-specific knowledge and skills as well as their communication abilities, analytical, technical, and reflective thinking skills (AACSB International, 2009). The goal is to enable business students to have the capacity to lead in organizational situations, apply knowledge in new and unfamiliar circumstances, adapt and innovate to solve problems, cope with unforeseen events, manage in unpredictable environments, and understand management issues from a global perspective (AACSB International, 2009).

AACSB standards recommend that faculty engage in instructional innovation, set high expectations for courses through clearly defined goals and objectives, and provide an interactive learning environment for students. The preamble to the standards emphasizes conceptual reasoning, problem-solving skills, and preparation for lifelong learning (AACSB International, 2009). As such, AACSB standards fit naturally with the information literacy standards set by the ACRL, which also stress lifelong learning.

INSTITUTIONAL CONTEXT

The University of Connecticut (UConn) is classified as a Carnegie Doctoral/Research University–Extensive (a category previously known as Research I) institution of higher education that serves a diverse student body of more than 29,000. There are 14 schools and colleges on the main campus and five regional campuses that offer graduate, under-graduate, and professional degree programs. UConn is committed to providing all students with the foundations for lifelong learning and has incorporated information literacy into its General Education guidelines. An information-literate student at UConn must exhibit an understanding of and competency in three integrally related processes (General Education Oversight Committee, 2003):

1. Information development and structure—an understanding of how information is created, disseminated and organized
2. Information access—an understanding of information communication processes and a facility with the tools required to tap into these processes
3. Information evaluation and integration—an ability to evaluate, synthesize, and incorporate information into written, oral, or media presentations

These competencies are based on ACRL's Information Literacy Competency Standards for Higher Education. To facilitate the development of these skills and traits in students, the UConn Libraries offer a multifaceted instruction program that includes classroom instruction, stand-alone credit courses, e-mail, and face-to-face consultations, work-shops, and self-paced information literacy tutorials.

Basic information literacy concepts are taught to all freshmen as an integral part of a required academic writing course in collaboration with the undergraduate instruction librarians. These skills are further developed and reinforced in upper years within the students' major fields of study. Each major program is required to work with library liaisons within their areas of study to identify and incorporate discipline-specific outcomes into upper-level research and writing courses.

Assessment efforts have included pre- and postproject tests, portfolios, and standardized tests. In 2004 and 2007, the university participated in Project SAILS (Standardized Assessment of Information Literacy Skills) developed by Kent State University. A paper version of SAILS was administered to a sample of students enrolled in freshman courses. The average freshman at UConn scored higher on all standards in comparison to the average for all institutions.

The master of science in accounting (MSA) is UConn's first completely asynchronous online graduate degree program. Its two core missions regarding skill development are to support and nurture information literacy and student-centered learning (http://www .business.uconn.edu/msaccounting). Although it started in 1999 as a traditional face-to-face program, it evolved into an asynchronous online program by 2003 as faculty sought an approach to address two concerns. First, students were all part time and often their work responsibilities conflicted with class, which was held once per week in the evenings. Second, faculty questioned the effectiveness of classroom learning in three-hour blocks that were passive almost by necessity at the end of a workday for both faculty and students. This confluence of events occurred at the time UConn had begun building its instructional design center with a designer who had embraced a constructivist approach to design, named the Resource-Enriched Learning Model, or RELM, in which the focus was primarily on faculty development and secondarily on the course (Lavoie, 2001; Lavoie and Rosman, 2007). This instructional designer has various degrees, including an MLIS.

It was as if a "perfect storm" of sorts occurred. We had a severe need for a different approach for course delivery and learning at the same time that the university hired a librarian/instructional designer who advocated a constructivist model of learning. In contrast to the book and movie, we reached a happy ending in which a learning community was formed with over a dozen faculty members who have been trained to be their own instructional designers and can discuss learning issues using the same terminology and perspective. It created a team approach to course development that involves faculty members, instructional designers, librarians, and media specialists when necessary. After seven years following this model, the MSA program has received recognition from the United States Distance Learning Association for best practices, continues to be oversubscribed with student demographics, including grade point average and GMAT scores that exceed targets, and student participation from 28 states and two non-U.S. countries. During its most recent AACSB accreditation review it was noted, "The Review team recognizes that offering a MSA program online at a major flagship university is unusual and innovative in accounting education. The faculty and students with whom we spoke were very positive about this educational approach and believe that it helps student to develop good research and teamwork skills" (AACSB Review Team, 2006, e-mail).

The MSA program currently admits approximately 115 students per year and most students complete the 30-credit degree within 18 months. The program launches in May each year with a traditional face-to-face in-residence week in which we foster a sense of community among the students and faculty and cover content that creates a level playing field for all students on a variety of topics, including information literacy. All remaining nine courses are conducted completely asynchronously online.

RELM: AN INTERDISCIPLINARY MODEL FOR INSTRUCTIONAL DESIGN

RELM had been applied successfully by this instructional designer initially in face-to-face delivery at several colleges and universities in courses ranging from accounting to zoology. At UConn, the model has been used to develop asynchronous online classes as part of the Insurance Law LLM offered by the School of Law, MSA, and business courses other than accounting (e.g., finance, health care).

The MSA course on information literacy, which has been designed specifically with an interdisciplinary approach in mind, engages students in information literacy including critical thinking, skepticism, and metacognition in general applications (e.g., car purchases, vacation planning) that are subsequently applied in a comprehensive case in the context of a specific discipline, which in this case is accounting. Thus, the front end of the course where the basic information literacy skills are first introduced and practiced can be applied to any discipline and a discipline-specific comprehensive case could be substituted for the accounting case.

Faculty–Librarian Collaboration

As described earlier, the RELM model is an ongoing partnership among the faculty content expert, instructional designer, librarian, media expert, and students. The importance of collaboration for faculty is explained well by Tagg (2003: 263) who argues:

> We cannot create genuine communities of practice for students until we allow faculty to participate too. Learning communities that bring together faculty members from across disciplines are a powerful way to address this challenge. Only if the teachers are learners too, and if they are seen to be learners, can they genuinely model deep learning for the apprentice learners in the community.

Although RELM is described in more detail in subsequent sections, the concept is to create a team of scholars to work together to develop faculty and produce a course where the scholars are from the disciplines of the content area (faculty member), curriculum and learning (instructional designer), information literacy (librarian), and technology (media specialist). RELM is a constructivist model for faculty development where the instructional designer works one on one with the faculty member to develop an active student-centered learning experience for students by engaging the faculty member in the same process to develop skills in constructivist learning (Lavoie, 2001; Lavoie and Rosman, 2007).

RELM begins with the faculty member and instructional designer teasing out the primary learning objectives and operational definitions which establish the knowledge and skills that students should be able to master by the end of the course. The librarian is brought into the design process at the appropriate point to identify relevant resources for the faculty member to consider as activities are designed to assess student learning. Because we had the good fortune of designing an entire degree program this way, the librarian has been able to create a resource directory as part of the UConn library website that has application beyond the MSA but clearly attends to the MSA program's information literacy needs (see http://classguides.lib.uconn.edu/accounting). Because faculty within the department have gone through the same design process, they are now able to use the same jargon, develop and share best practices, and assist one another in what amounts to an extension of the partnership that began with a faculty member, instructional designer, librarian, and media specialist to now include other content experts.

During the week-in-residence, which is a face-to-face course that launches each new class of students, the librarian leads a session on information literacy and demonstrates how resources are used across classes in the MSA. In a sense, she introduces the library resources as well as herself and establishes a connection with the students that extends to her contact information being listed on each course webpage.

PROGRAM PLANNING

Developing the initial online courses for the MSA took approximately three years. Several courses have been retired and others have been added to keep the curriculum current. Each time a course has been developed all tenured and tenure-track faculty have received curriculum development grants to enable them to participate in the instructional design process, which takes three to four months to complete. As courses were developed they were rolled out to students who were in our traditional face-to-face program until we had approval from the Department of Higher Education to offer the degree online. We admitted our first fully online class in May 2003.

Course refinement continues each time a course is taught, as faculty review summative surveys completed by students and then make appropriate changes. No additional funding is provided at this stage. However, funding is provided to hire teaching assistants each time a course is offered and to provide software (e.g., HTML editor) as needed. Otherwise, there are no other significant costs that are unique to the MSA program to deliver courses online.

CONCEPTUAL UNDERPINNINGS OF RELM

RELM is primarily a model of faculty development in which an instructional designer engages faculty in the process of developing an active student-centered learning course. The mentoring process that ensues is itself a form of active student-centered learning in which the faculty member is the student who is mentored by the instructional designer in constructivist theory, which contrasts with behaviorist theories of learning. The mentoring process is a best practice that is preferred by faculty over other approaches such as workshops and is shown to be highly effective (Taylor and McQuiggan, 2008).

Courses that are designed following a behaviorist approach are likely to focus on a faculty member using lectures to transfer knowledge and traditional objective question tests to assess learning. Constructivism, a competing approach, has given rise to the terms *student-centered* and *active learning*. As the term suggests, constructivism focuses more on course designs where students construct their own learning through activities that are matched to realize specific objectives or outcomes that are assessed using rubrics and that come to exist in a portfolio of their own learning. According to Boettcher (1999: 64):

> The current constructivist theory (or philosophy) of learning speaks in terms of students building concepts and constructing their knowledge base. This is an improvement over the blank slate model in which the faculty were expected to write on the blank slates of the minds of their students. Over the last 15 years, the constructivist model has had imagery creep in, generating related concepts. One of these is "scaffolding" learning, which provides temporary supports for learners as they acquire concepts.

Constructivist learning that exists with faculty individually interacting with students and with all students participating in a substantive way is difficult to achieve in the traditional physical classroom. Thus, the benefit of an asynchronous online environment to foster constructivist learning is clear because asynchronous learning is less constrained by time and physical space and has the capacity to transcend passive lecture-based learning.

The paradigm shift from "teacher-centered" to "student-centered learning" courses appears to be gaining momentum due to the attributes afforded by the characteristics of online learning environments. Students who participated in The National Survey of Student Engagement (NSSE) (2008), "Promoting Engagement for All Students: The Imperative to Look Within—2008 Results," reported more experience with deep learning in student-centered designed courses when enrolled in online courses now compared with earlier online courses that had simply transferred traditional face-to-face courses into the new medium. Whereas face-to-face learning can be more instantaneous with selective and reduced student interaction, one of the benefits of online learning is that it allows for reflection and participation by each individual in the class. The rhythm or cadence of an online course that is constantly in play allows students to set their pace for learning instead of being compartmentalized into blocks of time, which is considered a critical component of enabling deeper and more successful learning (Tagg, 2003).

Designing online learning to foster active learning is shown to provide a learning experience that is superior to face to face (U.S. Department of Education, 2009). Similarly, Bernard et al. (2009) conclude that active student-centered learning rather than learning online is the factor that contributes to high student achievement and that instructional design is an important factor in increasing the quality of online interaction.

These two metastudies together provide significant clarity for the future of online learning. The U.S. Department of Education study shows that it is design rather than the medium that contributes to increased learning, and the Bernard et al. study shows that active over passive student engagement, particularly actualized through instructional design, increases achievement of learning outcomes in distance learning. While others have come to the same conclusion, "Professional practice still lags woefully behind" in designing active student-centered learning into courses (Fink, 2003: xi). Spence (2001:

18) concludes that "we won't meet the needs for more and better higher education until professors become designers of learning experiences and not teachers," which is the principal issue addressed by RELM.

INSTRUCTIONAL DESIGN PROCESS RESULTING FROM RELM

The RELM instructional design process begins with a meeting between the faculty member and instructional designer. The focus of this initial meeting is to describe the instructional design model. The designer receives a copy of the course syllabus if there is an existing course and provides the faculty member with a few general readings about the subject of teaching online.

The instructional designer identifies an initial set of learning objectives to use to start a dialogue with the faculty member who typically has not thought of the course in terms of learning objectives. Some revisions are made and then the designer and faculty member develop an operational definition, which articulates what students are expected to be able to do and what knowledge they should possess at the end of the course. In other words, the learning objective and its operational definition document how the student is expected to "change" as a result of the course (Tagg, 2003). Working through several rounds of refining the operational definition in a reflexive way is where the course really begins to take shape, although the learning process for the faculty member is well underway.

With solid drafts of learning objectives and operational definitions complete, and realizing that they may be revisited throughout the design process, the faculty member and instructional designer create thematically discrete modules based on the operational definition. This evolving process is captured and made visual through storyboarding. The thematically unique modules, each representing a portion of the operational definition, consider that portion as a unique learning outcome. Having partitioned the operational definition into these modules, the next step is to begin to organize the readings and media that provide the base knowledge to achieve the individual module's outcome, which is the point at which the librarian typically becomes involved. Using an HTML editor to create the pages to storyboard the course means that the course pages, full of hyperlinks to different types of materials, are web ready.

Once the base level of the course is arranged (i.e., the session modules with the relevant reading and media, some of which are selected by faculty and some they need to create), the progression of the course design can continue. This is where a collection of scaffolded activities of increasing cognitive rigor that builds on the readings and media achieve the fulfillment of each module's learning outcome. These activities provide deliverables, which are artifacts that are a manifestation of a student's learning which come to exist in a course portfolio.

However, this instructional design process does not end with the planned activities. Such a student-centered learning pedagogy, assessing for learning more than for a grade, relies on a different form of assessment. The design process must assist faculty to develop these different forms. Once the activities for the course are completed, the next step is to introduce faculty to rubrics, both analytical and holistic, and instruct them to develop one for each activity.

Even then, the design process, which focuses on faculty development first and course development as an outcome or by-product of this process, is not complete. When the course is taught, three anonymous surveys (initial, formative, and summative) are completed by students. These surveys provide feedback to faculty while the course is ongoing as well as at the conclusion of the course to affect future versions. Meeting with the instructional designer subsequent to teaching the course allows for the refinement of the course design. The librarian may become involved as well, depending on the feedback received from the surveys. This process is usually repeated three times. After the design process is complete and the course has been taught twice, the third iteration is usually set, although minor changes including editing and keeping the course timely and relevant continues.

Differentiating Graduate and Undergraduate Learning

When the RELM design process is used with related courses that make up a curriculum, a student is exposed to information literacy in multiple contexts that collectively provide both depth and breadth. The librarian is better informed when making decisions about building the collection, and the faculty member has provided activities that contribute to lifelong learning.

What makes this collaborative effort easier to achieve at the graduate level is that course designs tend to focus on activities that are real-world problems and/or simulations. Hence, while searching for materials is necessary, compared to undergraduate efforts of information literacy that emphasize search, the graduate emphasis is more on evaluating information, which is a different part of the ACRL standards.

The focus on higher-order thinking has been brought about because of the technological ease with which to search and retrieve information. Access is less in question; rather, determining which resources are reliable is more like the vetting service provided by librarians and is the focus of graduate information literacy to overcome the lack of critical distinction among sources in the information deluge associated with the Internet. Graduate students need to possess the ability to evaluate information across a number of variables similar to the skills of a research librarian and to be able to transfer these skills to other courses and to their professional work settings.

A key factor in the success of RELM in incorporating information literacy across an entire curriculum is that faculty members have a common language and understanding of the challenges and opportunities of working online and can build on on another's incorporation of information literacy into a particular course. In this way, the initial collaborative effort of a faculty member, instructional designer, librarian, and media specialist becomes collaboration among many colleagues as well.

LIBRARIAN ROLE IN INFORMATION LITERACY

Once the course objectives have been defined and articulated, the librarian is brought into the process to further enhance and enrich the information literacy components in each course. This involves examining each learning activity (e.g., project, discussion thread, research paper) to identify information needs, research skills, and resources that students would need to successfully fulfill the learning objective. Sometimes the librarian must deconstruct a project to explicate specific research elements and to help connect the dots. The following are examples of learning activities that involve information literacy across five asynchronous online courses:

- **Developing a Global Comparative Framework and Testing a Multinational Profile.** This two-part project requires student groups to develop a global comparative framework based on national culture and subcultures (e.g., legal systems) that leads to testable expectations about differences in financial reporting across countries. The groups are assigned to two non-U.S. companies within an industry and collect critical data to test the expectations based on the global comparative framework. Students must find and analyze company and industry information, financial statements, and country information relating to subcultures including demographic, economic, political, and regulatory issues, as well as consult relevant statistics and ratings to undertake financial analysis.

- **Financial Reporting Analysis in the Financial Services Industry—Memo to the CEO.** Students play the role of an analyst assigned to investigate an insurance company that is a potential acquisition target. Assuming a management outlook, students investigate the target company from three perspectives: investor, consumer, and quality of assurance. Using data for the target company, they assess its financial health and make a recommendation to the CEO in a memo as to whether that company would make a good acquisition target with key reasons which led to that decision. This project requires in-depth research about the target company. Students engage in a series of individual and group activities to locate relevant data and apply the newly gained knowledge and skills to the project at hand. They are required to locate and consult financial statements, most recent 10-K filings, financial strength ratings, earnings forecasts, brokers' recommendations, and stock price data.

- **Balanced Scorecard.** Students create a balanced scorecard to measure the performance of a chosen company based on four perspectives: financial, customer perspective, internal business process, and learning and growth within the company. Through a series of readings and exercises students learn in detail how to use the balanced scorecard to analyze and evaluate a company's performance and how to identify a set of objectives and measures for each of the four perspectives. To guide this process, the librarian develops a basic presentation about balanced scorecards to clarify the types and sources of information that would be required to gather evidence for each metric. This includes researching the background information about the company, its products and services, productivity rate, market share, competitors, financial data, ratios, customer satisfaction, employee skill levels, and turnover rates. In addition to the main project, students engage in threaded discussions on topics such as use of balanced scorecard for external corporate reporting and metrics one can use to evaluate Internet businesses.

- **Audit Risk Analysis.** Students undertake a risk analysis for their client company based on inherent risks as well as business and industry risks. To complete the project, students need to locate and analyze information about the impact of economy, industry, and competitors on the client. It also requires investigating accounting and auditing issues such as specialized accounting practices, unusual transactions, and special disclosure requirements.

- **Evaluating Internal Controls**. Students write a paper about how the accounting profession might change in the years ahead. To complete this assignment, students need to find articles about the future of business, technology, and policy, and how these relate to accounting.

The discussed projects illustrate the nature of information literacy activities that students in the MSA program undertake. These projects incorporate inquiry, analysis, synthesis, and evaluation and often entail nuanced research and disciplinary discourse that require higher-order thinking skills.

Students entering the MSA have varied backgrounds in terms of when and where they got their last degree and their familiarity with research resources and skills. Therefore, before students work in the online environment, which constitutes 9 of the 10 courses to complete the degree, we conduct a traditional face-to-face in-residence experience to level set students. Among the activities is a library session that includes an overview of library collections, the authentication process for accessing the library's resources remotely, and library services such as document delivery and interlibrary loan. The remaining library session focuses on skills and resources that align with research activities inherent in various projects. Having scoured courses to identify specific research activities, the librarian is able to emphasize common threads and core competencies students would need to excel. The business librarian starts by illustrating sample projects to contextualize library research and training. Showcasing the research aspects of various projects also serves to communicate learning outcomes and expectations and helps students value the importance of good research skills.

Depending on the project, students' research needs vary from looking for key facts to seeking comprehensive knowledge about an industry, company, country, or market. They need to consult a variety of primary and secondary sources that provide varying levels of granularity to understand, corroborate, and evaluate issues at hand. To ensure that they understand which information source to use and when, the business librarian provides an overview of various databases, covering their scope and content, inherent biases, intent and methodology behind data, search interface, and research strategies. The library session takes place in a wired classroom where students are provided hands-on session on relevant resources. This is followed by a quiz that is administered within WebCT, the learning management system used by the university. The quiz reinforces the concepts and resources covered during the hands-on session. The questions on the quiz are based on actual research activities that students undertake for various projects in the online courses, giving them an opportunity to practice finding and retrieving information they will need for problem solving. In the most recent offering of this course the mean quiz score was 98.8 out of 100 (range 90–100). These scores are high as the quiz primarily focuses on searching and retrieval, foundational skills that would later lead to higher cognitive skills such as evaluating information content and using found information for a specific purpose assessed by faculty from students' final projects and assignments.

Consider the following three comments that were provided in an anonymous summative survey at the end of the course as they inform the faculty, instructional designer, and librarian about the success of the information literacy session:

- "The courses clearly induce an active learning environment. The information literacy lecture was helpful, and the quiz was even better at utilizing the tools for specific tasks."
- "The library presenter gave a great presentation on all the sites we can use to look up info which will not only help us during these courses but for years to come. Also, because this is a purely online program, it was apparent to me that we would be doing most of the learning ourselves with help from the professors through e-mails and discussion boards, and help with the groups I am assigned to."
- "This day and age, information literacy is key. The presentation on the library databases was eye opening as my previous undergraduate school had nothing that could hold a candle to Uconn's system...and I graduated Saturday, not 15 years ago! The ability to view financial statements of different publicly and privately traded companies is very relative to almost all of the courses, and the databases will absolutely help facilitate this."

To reinforce the concepts and resources introduced during the orientation week, students have access to a set of online subject guides that include tips, tutorials, websites, and databases relevant to conducting research involving accounting standards, companies, countries, industries, economics, finance, and marketing. These guides are linked from the course pages within WebCT and share common interface, structure, and navigation to promote consistency. The guides are Web 2.0 enabled to facilitate relevant RSS feeds, widgets, and other interactive tools. Based on student and faculty feedback, subject guides are constantly updated for content, ease of use, and functionality. For example, to ease student anxiety about which database to use for what, a company comparison chart was created that allows students to quickly compare key databases for the types of information they cover.

IMPACT ON STUDENT LEARNING: EXAMPLE OF MODEL APPLIED TO TWO COURSES

Information literacy consistent with RELM is evidenced in the MSA program on two levels: a standalone online course (Acct 5582, Research for Accounting Professionals) and integration into online courses. The latter will be demonstrated in this section by referring to Acct 5535 (Global Financial Reporting and Analysis).

Standalone Information Literacy Course: Acct 5582

Acct 5582 has been redesigned from a traditional research course that focused more on identifying resources to a RELM-based online course that explicitly takes students through each of the steps of the ACRL information literacy process. The learning objective and its operational definition are as follows:

- **Learning Objective**: Information Needs, Search Expectations, Accessing and Evaluating Systems and Data, A Synthesized Response, and Qualified Fulfillment

- **Operational Definition**: Posed with a scenario that requires a search for information, a student will be able to:

  I. precisely **define** and **articulate** the information need(s),

  II. **develop** expectations to formulate a search strategy to retrieve information given the defined need,

  III. **engage** information resource systems to **retrieve** information using the formulated search strategy,

  IV. subsequently, **evaluate** the pertinent resources and information effectively retrieved from the information resource systems,

  V. **determine** the fulfillment of the information need, and

  VI. **communicate** the information need and the fit of the search to fulfill it.

The learning objective and operational definition are deconstructed and then put into a calendar to ensure learning that fits within the time constraints imposed by the university. Each thematic topic, such as those above for the steps of the operational definition are considered to be a unique session of the course, and each session is then fit into the calendar; it is important to note that sessions do not necessarily need to equate with weeks. Outcomes are then constructed for each session and an assessment activity for each outcome is created.

To set the context for this class, students are introduced to readings and media in the first week that introduce the concepts of critical thinking, skepticism, and metacognition, which are then all tied into the broader construct of information literacy. As with all readings and media, students are assessed in terms of their mastery of knowledge and comprehension—the lower levels of Bloom's Taxonomy (Bloom, 1956)—through objective-question quizzes. Another written activity is used to assess higher-level cognitive outcomes for this session.

Students engage in online activities which enable them to produce work products (e.g., written assignments, discussion board posts) that allow the faculty member to assess their learning relative to the operational definition. For example, in session 2, students are presented with a narrative and are asked to develop a concept map to produce information needs in order to fulfill part I of the operational definition provided. The readings and media for this week include resources on how librarians interview people to determine information needs as well as how to interview people in general. Students engage information literacy in this stage of the course in the generic setting of vacation planning and then follow the information needs they develop in session 2 through the remaining steps (II through VI). A summative project follows in the second half of the course that deals with a much more complex case on sustainability which is contextualized to the MSA program (specifically, it deals with accounting, taxes, and related business issues).

A major tool used in documenting part of the information literacy process is referred to as an **evaluation template**. It is used in sessions 5 and 6 to record the process followed and judgments made by students to evaluate resources collected to address an informational need and is used again in the summative activity for the course. The four broad categories for which students will evaluate a resource are scope/coverage, content, usability, and bias. Each category has several subcategories, which total to 14 evaluation criteria. After each criterion is qualitatively evaluated students then complete a summative evaluation using a seven-point Likert scale. An example of the scope category for the evaluation template for a specific resource for vacation planning that was selected to address the information need "to identify the cost of off-season locations for the time of year we want to travel" is provided in Figure 7.1. The evaluation is used by students in session 6 to write up a memorandum that assesses whether the multiple resources selected collectively fulfill the information needs identified in week 2.

Evidence of the importance of information literacy in everyday and professional decision settings is provided in an excerpt from a discussion board thread that is captured in Appendix 7.1. Students have already responded to two questions in which they explained an information search strategy regarding a specific information need they generated from a relatively complex narrative about planning a vacation and reacted to other students' posts regarding their search strategy and results. The excerpt from Question 3 clearly documents the discovery nature of active learning in the course, which makes the point more salient to the students than if the faculty member had simply lectured on this point. The thread shows that the students "discovered" the weakness in relying on a particularly common information search strategy (i.e., simply use a single search engine), could construct solutions and alternative practices to correct for the discovered weakness, and could extend those practices from the everyday pedestrian example of vacation planning to conducting tax research in a professional setting. This activity provides evidence of the success of the course design in achieving the specified learning objectives.

Information Literacy Integrated into a Course: Acct 5535

Acct 5535 has been taught online since 2003. It has undergone multiple revisions as not only context has needed to change to remain current but also student feedback from summative surveys that are conducted at the end of each semester have suggested changes that needed to be made. The course's two learning objectives along with their operational definition are:

- **Learning Objective 1**: A Preparer's Global Perspective on Accounting, and Accounting-Related Information About Multinational Enterprises in a Principles-Based Decision Environment
- **Operational Definition 1**: Students will be able to construct and explain a preparer's perspective for financial reporting in a principles-based decision environment that is based on an analysis of a country's culture, legal system, economy, and political system.
- **Learning Objective 2**: A User's Global Perspective on Accounting, and Accounting-Related Information about Multinational Enterprises in a Principles-Based Decision Environment
- **Operational Definition 2**: Students will be able to examine the financial reports of non-U.S. companies by developing and testing expectations about the content of

Figure 7.1. Example of Evaluation Template for Scope/Coverage Criteria

EVALUATION CRITERIA (Session 5)	Click here to REFER TO "SESSION 5 NOTES/ NARRATIVE" FOR THINGS TO CONSIDER	SUMMATIVE EVALUATION (Session 6)			
Scope/ Coverage	Note: Your answer should address the "Things to Consider" from Session 5	Scope/ Coverage	Scale (Bounded by 1 and 7)		Decision
Scope	The site has a navigation bar at the top that includes forums, destinations, trip ideas, hotels, restaurants, cruises, deals, blog, and guidebooks. Their About Us statement claims to offer insights and tools "to experience the trip you want." Claims to offer recommendations for shopping, dining, hotel, and culture recommendations. Includes articles that "convey the essence of each destination" written by people who live there.	Based on the information evaluated, the **scope/ coverage** of this source is:	1 2 3 4 5 6 7 | | | | | | | Not at all complete Neutral Extremely complete		5
Breadth	While the navigation bar suggests a broad approach to travel, it seems focused more on destinations.	Based on the information evaluated, the **breadth** of coverage of this source is:	1 2 3 4 5 6 7 | | | | | | | Not at all broad Neutral Extremely broad		5
Depth	The material is descriptive and in-depth. The level of detail is quite good, especially for destinations.	Based on the information evaluated, the **depth** of coverage of this source is:	1 2 3 4 5 6 7 | | | | | | | Not at all deep Neutral Extremely deep		6
Virtual Scope	Very few links to resources outside of itself. Any such links are to just a few advertising promotions. It seems to be more the reverse. Many other sites link to it.	Based on the information evaluated, the **degree of connectedness** of this source is:	1 2 3 4 5 6 7 | | | | | | | Not at all connected Neutral Extremely connected		4

those reports based on an understanding of the preparer's perspective that is applied in a principles-based decision environment (i.e., impact on financial reporting of culture including national, professional, and firm-level; legal systems; economies; tax systems; and political systems on financial reporting).

Acct 5535 is used here as an example of an online course that incorporates information literacy to achieve its learning objectives, whereas Acct 5582 has information literacy as its learning objective. In Acct 5535, information literacy (consisting of critical thinking, skepticism, and metacognition) is applied as students learn to develop expectations about how national culture might affect financial reporting consistent with the learning objectives and operational definitions. Essentially, students are asking themselves whether a company from one culture would be more or less leveraged, profitable, and liquid than a well-matched competitor from another culture. Information needs are informed by the expectations and are refined as subcultures (e.g., legal systems) are evaluated to help resolve conflicts that might occur as national culture is applied to form expectations. As information needs are formed and refined, students retrieve resources and evaluate the data to test the expectations. As with Acct 5582, session outcomes are scaffolded according to Bloom's taxonomy, activities are created to assess session outcomes, and the model that is developed in the course is recast in two summative activities: a two-part group term project and final summative individual-level activity. In total, there are 21 assessment activities.

Grading rubrics are provided for students for each activity, and feedback is an integral part of the learning experience. Students receive detailed written feedback tailored to their deliverable when assignments are returned in the case of written documents or in comments through the learning management system in the case of discussion boards. Because the course is designed so that learning is scaffolded according to Bloom's taxonomy, and several level-setting activities are included, typically in a summative format, the feedback on earlier activities is critical to successful learning later on. That subsequent learning results from faculty-student interaction as well as from student-to-student interaction in discussion boards and in group projects.

Data collected from the summative course survey indicate that the information literacy component of the course has been successful. Students respond to "Has THIS COURSE increased your awareness of 'Information Literacy' (the ability to identify an information need; efficiently select potential information resources; effectively engage and retrieve pertinent information; critically analyze and synthesize the information into a response; and, coherently articulate the fit of that response back to the original need)?" Over the past three semesters since a major revision to the course took place, 80 percent of students responded "yes" to the question. Comments most indicative of how awareness of information literacy has been increased both in the classroom and workplace are included in Appendix 7.2.

ASSESSMENT OF ONLINE LEARNING

The role of assessment in a constructivist-designed course is different from that in a traditional passive lecture-based course. Huba and Freed (2000: 3) explain:

The idea of focusing on learning rather than teaching requires that we re-think our role and the role of students in the learning process. To focus on learning rather than teaching, we must challenge our basic assumptions about how people learn and what the roles of a teacher should be. We must unlearn previously acquired teaching habits. We must grapple with fundamental questions about the roles of assessment and feedback in learning.

Consistent with the approach taken to design courses in our MSA program, Acct 5582 and Acct 5535 focus on process more than on outcomes. Information literacy is a significant component of the process of learning and, therefore, is a significant focus of the assessment process in our courses. A goal of the MSA is provide students with the ability to master processes rather than outcomes. The distinction is that the former can be repeated and replicated in other classes to foster new learning and can be applied in the workplace to truly fulfill the goal of lifelong learning in a substantive way.

There are three implications of our focus on process for assessment. First, we must make our course designs completely transparent to the students because the design itself represents the application of critical thinking, metacognition, and skepticism in such a way that it produces a flow or process for learning that can be internalized and recalled at a later time in another context. In Acct 5535, for instance, the reason that each reading or media item has been selected is explained to students so that the students can fully comprehend the faculty member's rationale for its inclusion as a basis for understanding more cognitively complex processes and ideas. Readings and media are tested in objective-question quizzes that students can take twice with all resources available to them. Although graded, the primary goal of these quizzes is to ensure mastery of knowledge acquisition and comprehension from readings and media before moving on to more cognitively demanding tasks.

Once mastered, students can proceed to higher-level session outcomes with more challenging assessment activities that have been created to measure learning at the appropriate level of Bloom's taxonomy. In fact, students are instructed on Bloom's taxonomy and all session outcomes and activities are coded according to the taxonomy so that students can appreciate how learning has been layered or scaffolded. Again, transparency fosters a more complete understanding of the course design, which is a coordinated series of session outcomes and related assessments that are logically sequenced according to Bloom's taxonomy so that the students can come to internalize the logic of the progression of the course. The logic that underlies the course architecture does not need to be memorized but can be replicated when necessary because the intuition inherent in the design is a process that can be re-created (see Appendix 7.2 for evidence of the ability to articulate information literacy in Acct 5535). In essence, students are learning how to structure problem spaces that they encounter according to Bloom's taxonomy in order to be more successful at resolving whatever they might encounter in other courses and in their professional careers.

Second, assignment grading rubrics are explained up front, and feedback is provided to all students on each activity so that they are level set before continuing. That is, students are not left behind in order to move to the next topic or level of learning as dictated by a calendar. Feedback is also provided on the final activity, in contrast to most final exams, in which feedback—other than a grade—typically is not provided. Similarly, students provide feedback to faculty at three points in the course through an initial survey (week 1), a formative survey (week 4), and a summative survey (after the course is complete).

Third, courses are layered according to Bloom's taxonomy and are scaffolded so that activities are rolled up to summative activities where learning using components of various processes are aggregated and repeated. For example, in Acct 5535, the first learning objective (i.e., the preparer's perspective) is studied in the first four sessions of the course using two specific countries. Students work on individual activities and in discussion groups of 10 to 12 members until they come together in small groups (three to four students) to study two new countries in a comprehensive term project. They receive feedback on this summative activity and are expected to revise their work product based on comments before they move to the second stage of the term project. In session 6 they work individually to learn the user's perspective (i.e., the second learning objective), again in the context of the original two countries. In session 7 they get back together with their small groups and revise the first part of the term project based on feedback from the instructor and then complete the second part of the term project. Finally, in the summative activity that culminates the course, students work individually with yet a new (i.e., third) pair of countries and apply the processes learned in the course without direction, just with a simple prompt to engage them in re-creating the experiences learned in the course.

CONCLUSION

In the new global economy, change may be the only constant. Everyone needs to continually update his or her skills, knowledge, and social, cultural, and ethical sensibilities to stay relevant and competitive. Educational institutions that offer flexible, interactive, and timely programs will be able to adapt to the changing global environment. Advances in technology, particularly for online learning, enable us to teach from anywhere at any time. However, technology is only a means to a higher goal. It should be harnessed to deliver content which is relevant and which cultivates students' information literacy skills so that they can continue to learn.

The model for faculty and course development that we describe in this chapter, RELM, requires a concerted effort from all stakeholders to ensure that course design and information literacy are well balanced in terms of content, pedagogy, resources, and technology. This particular team approach to information literacy has enabled us to capitalize on our collective expertise, remove redundancies, and fill gaps. The return on this investment is evident in tangible ways for both faculty and students. We have developed a practical and scalable model that we are already applying to new courses in finance and health care management. Our students are engaged and learning how to learn within their disciplinary context. Working together has enabled us to develop an appreciation for and understanding of the role that each of us plays in maximizing students' online learning experiences. It has solidified our commitment to information literacy and what it takes to build and sustain a nationally recognized online program.

Future directions include studying how metacognitive characteristics, such as learning style, influence the way that students approach active student-centered learning in online courses. Determining whether such a relationship exists and how it might mitigate learning in online courses is an important step toward allowing students to take even more responsibility for their learning by being able to self-regulate how they reach their goals and those of each course. This information will help students become aware of when they might need help from faculty or classmates (e.g., to overcome difficulty engaging in group work online) and how to develop and apply those strategies. Ultimately, doing so will help students engage all facets of online courses more independently, including information literacy.

While some might argue that the collaboration we have described in this chapter is too costly in effort and time to follow for each individual online course, we would argue that pursuing a traditional model where faculty members singularly take on the challenge of teaching online and integrating information literacy into their courses is inefficient and likely to be ineffective. Rather, starting with the RELM approach for faculty development and course design, and involving librarians, media specialists, and students in the process, allows us to learn, grow, and progress together and provides us new insights into how information literacy can empower online education. The resulting economies of scale occur over time as faculty teach successive courses with the skill set to appropriately integrate information literacy to achieve course learning objectives. The result is a more sustainable model for achieving success in online education.

NOTE

1. This chapter considers "online" as a mode of delivery that could be mixed with face-to-face learning in a hybrid fashion or conducted exclusively online. However, whatever portion of the course is conducted online is considered to be so done asynchronously rather than synchronously.

REFERENCES

Allen, Elaine I., and Jeff Seaman. 2008. "Staying the Course: Online Education in the United States, 2008." *Sloan Survey of Online Learning.* http://www.sloanconsortium.org/sites/default/files/staying_the_course-2.pdf.

Allen, Maryellen. 2008. "Promoting Critical Thinking Skills in Online Information Literacy Instruction Using a Constructivist Approach." *College & Undergraduate Libraries* 15, no. 1/2 (March): 21–38.

American Library Association. 2000. *Information Literacy Competency Standards for Higher Education.* Chicago: The Association of College and Research Libraries. http://www.ala.org/al/Amgrps/divs/acrl/standards/standards.pdf.

American Philosophical Association. 1990. *Critical Thinking: A Statement of Expert Consensus for Purposes of Educational Assessment and Instruction.* "The Delphi Report," Committee on Pre-College Philosophy. ERIC Doc. No. ED 315 423.

Association to Advance Collegiate Schools of Business (AACSB) International. 2009. "Eligibility Procedures and Accreditation Standards for Accounting Accreditation." AACSB. http://www.aacsb.edu/accreditation/ACCOUNTING-STANDARDS-2009_Final.pdf.

Bernard, Robert M., Philip C. Abrami, Eugene Borokhovski, C. Anne Wade, Rana M. Tamim, Michael A. Surkes, and Edward Clement Bethel. 2009. "A Meta-Analysis of Three Types of Interaction Treatments in Distance Education." *Review of Educational Research* 79, no. 3: (September): 1243–1289.

Bloom, Benjamin S. 1956. *Taxonomy of Educational Objectives. Handbook I: The Cognitive Domain.* New York: David McKay.

Boettcher, Judith. 1999. "What Does Knowledge Look Like and How Can We Help It Grow?" *Syllabus Magazine* 13, no. 2 (September): 64+. http://tipsnews.org/newsletter/00-06/knowledge .html.

Donaldson, Christy A. 2004. "Information Literacy and the McKinsey Model: The McKinsey Strategic Problem-Solving Model Adapted to Teach Information Literacy to Graduate Business Students." *Library Philosophy and Practice* 6, no. 2 (Spring): 1–8.

Dutton, John, Marilyn Dutton, and Jo Perry. 2002. "How Do Online Students Differ from Lecture Students?" *Journal of Asynchronous Learning Networks* 6, no. 1 (July): 1–20.

Fink, L. Dee. 2003. *Creating Significant Learning Experiences: An Integrated Approach to Designing College Courses.* San Francisco: Jossey-Bass.

General Education Oversight Committee, University of Connecticut. 2003. "University of Connecticut General Education Guidelines." University of Connecticut. http://geoc.uconn.edu/ geocguidelines.htm.

George, Carole A., A. Bright, T. Hurlbert, E.C. Linke, G. St. Clair, and J. Stein. 2006. "Scholarly Use of Information: Graduate Students' Information Seeking Behaviour." *Information Research* 11, no. 4 (July): 1–23.

Grafstein, Ann. 2002. "A Discipline-Based Approach to Information Literacy." *Journal of Academic Librarianship* 28, no. 4 (July): 197.

Hrycaj, Paul L. 2006. "An Analysis of Online Syllabi for Credit-Bbearing Library Skills Courses." *College & Research Libraries* 67, no. 6 (November): 525–535.

Huang, Chun-Hung, and Ming Chuan. 2005. "Exploring Employed-Learners' Choice Profiles for VMBA Programs." *Journal of American Academy of Business* 7, no. 2 (September): 203–211.

Huba, Mary E., and Jann E. Freed. 2000. *Learner-Centered Assessment on College Campuses: Shifting the Focus from Teaching to Learning.* Needham Heights, MA: Allyn & Bacon.

Kerns, Lorna. 2006. "Adult Graduate Students in Higher Education: Refocusing the Research Agenda." *Adult Learning* 17, no. 1–4 (January): 40–42.

King, Alison. 1993. "From Sage on the Stage to Guide on the Side." *College Teaching* 41, no. 1 (December): 30–35.

Lavoie, David. R. 2001. "A Resource-Enriched Learning Model." *Educause Quarterly* 24, no. 2: 67–68.

Lavoie, David, and Andrew. J. Rosman. 2007. "Using Active Student-Centered Learning-Based Instructional Design to Develop Faculty and Improve Course Design, Delivery, and Evaluation." *Issues in Accounting Education* 22, no. 1 (February): 105–118.

Liao, Yan, Mary Finn, and Jun Lu. 2007. "Information-Seeking Behavior of International Graduate Students vs. American Graduate Students: A User Study at Virginia Tech 2005." *College & Research Libraries* 68, no. 1 (January): 5–25.

National Survey of Student Engagement (NSSE). 2008. "Promoting Engagement for All Students: The Imperative to Look Within—2008 Results." Indiana University. http://nsse.iub.edu/NSSE_ 2008_Results/.

Orr, Debbie, Margaret Appleton, and Margie Wallin. 2001. "Information Literacy and Flexible Delivery: Creating a Conceptual Framework and Model." *Journal of Academic Librarianship* 27, no. 6 (November): 457.

Parry, Marc. 2009. "They Thought Globally, But Now Colleges Push Online Programs Locally." *The Chronicle of Higher Education* (July 10).

Spence, Larry D. 2001. "The Case Against Teaching." *Change Magazine* 33, no. 6 (November–December): 10–19.

Tagg, John. 2003. *The Learning Paradigm College.* Bolton, MA: Anker Publishing.

Taylor, Ann, and Carol McQuiggan. 2008. "Faculty Development Programming: If We Build It, Will They Come?" *Educause Quarterly* 31, no. 3 (July–September): 29–37.

U.S. Department of Education. 2009. "Evaluation of Evidence-Based Practices in Online Learning: A Meta-Analysis and Review of Online Learning Studies." Washington, DC: U.S. Department of Education. http://www2.ed.gov/rschstat/eval/tech/evidence-based-practices/finalreport.pdf.

Appendix 7.1. Information Literacy Evidenced in a Discussion Board Thread	
Example 1	
Subject: Question 3	*Author: Faculty*
Comment on what was found in the multiple searches for each of the information needs, making sure to contrast search engines, meta search engines, and directories. Are there benefits from using multiple search strategies? Discuss.	
Subject: Re: Question 3	*Author: Student MM*
I thought I would get us started on some discussion about the results. First, this has been an eye-opening exercise, as someone who uses Google almost exclusively. I have it set as my homepage, and it's my "default" information source and not necessarily because I think it's the best; it's just comfortable to go back to the same place. Seeing the different ways (other search engines, meta search engines, and directories) to get information is important to understand that there are other options. However, for me it has highlighted the importance of developing search-term skills with some degree of precision because of the sheer amount of information that is gathered. Before this class, I did not spend much time on search terms. In fact, I usually just typed my search as a question. Running searches with different search terms, using connectors, and truncating really affects the results as we saw from some trial and error on the discussion board.	
Subject: Re: Question 3	*Author: Student LJ*
I have to agree with you. I use Google all the time and have never really considered the limitations of Google or the possibility that there are better options out there. In the future I will probably still use Google for the most part, because as you said, it's comfortable to go with what you're used to, but I will probably start checking out some different sites just to compare the types of results I am getting. Lately I have been doing a lot of tax research at work, and it has made me realize the importance of using a good search term. I rely a lot on trial and error to narrow my search results down to find what I am looking for. And even though we have paid research resources, I find that I also use Google a lot to narrow down to specific tax code sections or court cases, which I then look up in the tax research software.	
Subject: Re: Question 3	*Author: Faculty*
I like the discussion so far and suggest that, in response to the observation about how important it is to really focus on search terms, it brings us back to the importance of focusing on information needs. If we do a good job identifying the information need we are much more likely to be able to identify the appropriate search strategy and search terms.	
Subject: Re: Question 3	*Author: Student MM*
Thanks for adding that. I don't think I had made that connection. I was thinking of the search terms as more of a mechanical exercise, but I see how developing a precise information need gets you pretty far down the road on precise search terms with the understanding that the connectors/truncating, etc. just put an even sharper point on things.	
Subject: Re: Question 3	*Author: Student JG*
I also have to agree that before this week's readings I was an exclusive Google user. I used Google for everything, including looking up medical questions and other important topics. When doing this I can usually get to some medical-based material, such as WebMD or Mayo Clinic, etc, but I also come across many people's blogs or wiki answer type databases. These can be good, but I would like to avoid them sometimes because when you are trying to find an answer about something it is easy to be persuaded by what other people are saying (which sometimes have no fact base).	

(Continued)

Appendix 7.1. Information Literacy Evidenced in a Discussion Board Thread *(Continued)*

Example 1 *(Continued)*

Subject: Re: Question 3 (Continued)	*Author: Student JG (Continued)*

I think I will start using clusty.com a lot more for searching since it has the groupings on the side so that you can limit the type of resources that you are reading. I also like the fact that you can open the search result in a new window and not lose the list of search results in the process.

I definitely will start using more search engines when doing research from now on. I had never thought about the information need aspect of researching before this class and this exercise.

Subject: Re: Question 3	*Author: Student MM*

A couple of other observations from looking at the search results-I'm going to make a meta-search engine my starting point for all purposes and get a feel for how that is different. It seems to me there is no reason not to do that (unless the meta-search engine excludes Google, like clusty) because you can draw from more sources. You need to be sensitive to the "sponsored by" links in the case of dogpile. Another observation is the potential power in the directory. I think Ron's use of the directory was interesting. One of the directories had concise subtopics (B2B) that were organized by name of travel company and geography. I thought that was helpful. I also found that I was more aware of the commercial nature of many of the search results and was thinking that more news or magazine articles, or blogs, etc., with more analysis/commentary was more of what I would like to read than the information from travel companies' sites. Dogpile, in particular, appeared to have lots of commercial sources.

Example 2

Subject: Re: Question 3	*Author: Student SC*

When you are talking about using longer search phrases, the other thing that I learned this week was the importance of using quotes, AND, OR, and others. I have always known that they were available to use, but when I think back, I never really used them in any of my searches. When we were talking about low-cost vacations in one of the searches, it did make a different when putting "low cost" in quotes to ensure that the query looked for that exact term. I will definitely be more conscious of using them going forward.

In Reply to: Student SC

Subject: Re: Question 3	*Author: Student AS*

The ability to retrieve so many different results from each search engine/method is what stands out most to me. Like most people I am a Google junkie and usually have no need to go past the first page or look elsewhere, and for most of my Internet searching that is okay. However, when I am in need of solid research links there is no doubt in my mind now that you have to spend time with other search engines and methods.

Before this exercise I never even considered the possibility of valuable information from meta-search engines. I figured that I could find whatever I wanted just fine through Google or another one, but it is clear that even though they pull from common search engines the results will not always be the same, and there is value in that. I really liked the way that Clusty presents information and how Dogpile doesn't show you hundreds of thousands of links, which makes it possible to actually scroll through all the results.

Lastly, as was mentioned in a previous post, the directories we searched are not best utilized by looking up nonscholarly topics. However, after scanning through the results it is easy to see that there is value because you get an entirely different set of results. Overall, I think the big idea is that because there is such a vast amount of information available through the Internet using only one type of searching and limiting your research to one site hinders the possibility of finding valuable information.

Appendix 7.2. Acct 5535 Responses to Information Literacy Summative Survey Question

1. During the first project, we needed some other research to confirm our expectations. Someone else in the group had found "Control of Corruption" indices for our countries. Because of this available data, I tried to find information linking corruption to profit, and was successful. We included this research in our final paper; this research linked corruption to profit.

2. I recently "activated" the segment analysis information (regarding goodwill impairment) during one of my international audits.

3. I consolidate our financials from multiple foreign subs and branches. This class really got me to realize how some of the foreign subs may have tendencies to report in certain ways (i.e., our new China joint venture).

4. Within the class, the process of searching, obtaining, and using the Thomson One data was a useful increase in my "Information Literacy." It was simple to learn to use and supplied a wealth of useful information that I had not thought available in a single location. In the class, by reviewing a number of Hungarian and Spanish Pharma firms, I gained insight into the assignment and was able to develop a hypothesis of the firms used. Going forward I expect to use the skills gained at work to understand our vendor partners better. It will also enhance my abilities as an individual investor.

5. The readings assigned were excellent sources of information. However, in this course we learned not just to read them but to evaluate to what extent they can be used. As a result we were able to learn when the information fit our objective and when we needed to consider alternatives.

6. The term projects helped focus on information literacy. We realized that our expectations were not being supported and the data was not enough information. We realized the need for more information and how it can be frustrating to users of these statements.

7. Like most things, I felt I struggled in the beginning to locate the necessary resources to provide a compelling argument, but by the end of the course I had a strong grasp of the material and what was expected of participating students.

8. I performed a financial analysis on my company compared to those in the States. Even though my company is a government-run company, we have a lot of impact from the local Japanese economy. Compared to all of the MCCSs across the nation, we are the most profitable and do the best on audits. Most of our employees are Japanese. I would say 70 percent are Japanese.

9. In my everyday experience of working with various teams worldwide, we often come across conflicts of opinion with our Japanese colleagues regarding independence impairing engagements. After going through this course, I learned that the culture plays an important role in accounting and interpreting different financial rules. Therefore, I did some research on Japanese accounting rules and their culture and realized that it'll take a long time to get everyone to adhere to one set of global rules without encountering differences of opinion that have to be resolved.

10. I think the entire final project was a good example of this. Also the Term Project. We needed to identify subcultures to support the primary or alternative expectation. We were able to retrieve the needed information and use it to support our expectations or explain why our expectations were incorrect.

8

Working Outside the Org Chart
A Faculty–Librarian Partnership to Design an Online Graduate Course

Susan M. Frey and Rebecca L. Fiedler

INTRODUCTION

In thinking about teaching partnerships, it may be axiomatic to note that trust, the facility to share professional identities, and the aspiration to seek common ground are all requisite elements in successful collaborations. However, these qualities remain elusive. Such qualities are difficult to measure and replicate, and are often the obscure, neglected dimension of productive faculty–librarian relationships. Since librarians began to formally offer library instruction in the academy they have been experimenting with different forms of collaboration with faculty. This exploration can be viewed in positive and negative terms. While it could be said that librarians are grappling with ways to make their instruction relevant, others claim that experimenting with different forms of collaboration has allowed for the emergence of robust best practices. Many relationships between instructional librarians and teaching faculty center on various types of client-based liaison models in which the librarian provides instructional support for the professor's class. Some take the relationship a step further and involve activities such as collaborative instructional design and team teaching.

Although collaboration between faculty and librarians exists within a variety of frameworks, in these relationships the librarian is usually the information guide and consultant, while the professor has the responsibility for teaching within his or her discipline. Thus a division of labor, defined by expertise and job function, helps to define the relationship. While these distinctions are not, in and of themselves, detrimental to the implementation of successful instruction, they can have the potential to constrain behavior to the point that *who* is suggesting a good idea is more important than *what* is being suggested. As in any working environment, professional self-image, lack of communication, politics, and bureaucracy can complicate and damage relationships in faculty–librarian collaborative endeavors.

This chapter describes the creation of a fully online graduate course in information literacy designed for the Bayh College of Education at Indiana State University (ISU). A reference and instruction librarian with faculty status designed the course in partnership with an assistant professor of curriculum, instruction, and media technology. In this collaboration the librarian became the subject matter expert (SME) and course designer, while the professor assumed the role of instructional design consultant.

RELATED LITERATURE

Librarians have long been aware of their teaching mission. As far back as 1876 Otis Robinson wrote, "A librarian should be more than a keeper of books; he should be an educator.... If we can send students out self-reliant in their investigations, we have accomplished very much" (p. 124). Although the librarian's role of information guide and provider is firmly entrenched in the professional and popular imagination, the librarian-as-teacher has been harder to define in the academy. Formal information literacy instruction is an established service of the profession; however, the classic one-shot library instruction session is no longer seen as an effective means of addressing the educational needs of students (Cunningham and Lanning, 2002; Dorner, Taylor, and Hodson-Carlton, 2001; Gandhi, 2004). Instead, collaboration with faculty to assimilate library and information literacy instruction into the curriculum is seen by librarians as imperative in preparing students to be information-literate, lifelong learners (Cohen, 1995; Nimon, 2001; Paglia and Donahue, 2003; Walter, 2000; Warmkessel and McCade, 1997).

With the challenge of promoting greater integration of information literacy instruction into course design, models of collaboration have emerged that place librarians and faculty in a wide variety of complementary roles. Himmelman (1996) provides helpful categories for conceptualizing these activities, which are distinguished by increasing levels of intensity. These are networking (encompassing the exchange of information between parties); coordination (individuals working together to solve a problem); and collaboration (an extended, structured relationship of shared or harmonizing actions). Similarly, Montiel-Overall (2005) outlines four levels of collaboration: coordination, cooperation, integrated instruction, and integrated curriculum. Though there is evidence that collaboration between faculty and librarians is on the increase (Raspa and Ward, 2000), some note that these successes are isolated and such partnerships have not yet become an established part of the campus culture (D'Angelo and Maid, 2004).

In spite of some successful collaborative initiatives, librarians are not routinely included in curriculum planning or course-integrated information literacy instruction (Bell and Shank, 2004; Lindstrom and Shonrock, 2006; Winner, 1998). This condition appears to persist in spite of administrative commitment to information literacy instruction. Bennett (2007) describes a series of workshops on information literacy for almost 160 institutions of higher learning sponsored by the Council of Independent Colleges and the National Institute for Technology and Liberal Education that were held from 2004 to 2006. Teams from each institution comprised a chief academic officer, a library director, and a faculty member or information technologists. These teams worked together to define how they would advance information literacy at their institutions. Data culled from the almost 500 participants reveal that while 80 percent of these institutions employ librarians with teaching responsibilities, only 58 percent of them create opportunities for their librarians to be involved in curriculum development planning (Bennett, 2007: 152).

This disconnect between the perceived importance of librarian involvement in the curricula and the opportunities for real collaboration means that librarians are forced into playing the role of promoter when attempting to establish their teaching potential within the university infrastructure. The library literature is replete with advice for librarians to be strategic, proactive, and vigilant in creating opportunities to engage with faculty (Gilson and Michael, 2002; Iannuzzi, 1998: Mackey and Jacobson, 2005; Saunders, 2008; Smith, 2001; Thaxton, Faccioli, and Mosby, 2004), to strive for "constant collaboration" outside the library (Dewey, 2004: 5), and to provide reminders that "the battle is not yet won" (Farber, 1999: 229) on the collaboration front.

Maintaining this position of tireless advocacy is seen by librarians as a response to institutional neglect of their teaching mission (Mackey and Jacobson, 2005: McCarthy, 1985). One problem identified by librarians is that the greater academic community does not take widespread notice of successful faculty–librarian collaboration in the academy. As librarians celebrate their collaborative achievements in the library literature, many faculty are unaware of these teaching partnerships because they do not read library journals (Stevens and Campbell, 2007; Still, 1998).

The factors affecting the faculty–librarian dynamic are seen as myriad and diverse. Librarians can feel out of their depth in the role of teacher (Albrecht and Brown, 2002). Unfortunately, the current library graduate school curriculum does not include the pedagogy of teaching and learning or the principles of instructional design (Albrecht and Brown, 2002; Bell and Shank, 2004; Campbell, 2009; Peacock, 2001). It certainly can be argued that the majority of teaching faculty are like librarians in that they do not have formal training in pedagogy. But by tradition, faculty enjoy the prestige and credibility of officially owning the educative role in the academy. They have also had problems in thinking of librarians as equal partners because librarians do not customarily have the advanced degrees, teaching experiences, and publication output similar to their own (Cook, 1981; Divay, Ducas, and Michaud-Ostryk, 1987; Hardesty, 1991; Haynes, 1996; Ivey, 1994; Oberg, Schleiter, and Van Houten, 1989).

The self-image of the professoriate is critical in understanding the potential for inequality in the faculty–librarian relationship. A workshop conducted in 2000 focusing on enhancing collaboration between faculty, librarians, information technologists, and students was conducted involving nine institutions of higher learning. Teams of representatives from each community discussed how they might work together to integrate technology into the classroom. In an ethnographic study of what transpired it was found that for the faculty attending the workshop, sharing the decision-making process with others about what would happen in their classroom required "a profound reexamination of their pedagogical identities" (Church, 2000: 3). Clearly, for successful collaboration between faculty and librarians to work there must be this recognition of professional identity and the willingness to sometimes negotiate beyond it.

Because the professional identities of faculty and academic librarians are shaped by different qualifications, research expectations, and communities of practice, it can be challenging for some to see commonalities. But instead of librarians courting faculty, a more profound collaboration can blossom from equal partnership. Such a partnership should be defined not by job titles or qualifications but by the shared purpose of educating students. Raspa and Ward describe the elusive quality of successful collaboration between librarians and faculty in the academy:

> Successful collaboration requires substance from the participants. It cannot be mandated or assumed. It cannot be undertaken unilaterally or coaxed into existence. By nature, collaboration is a fragile relationship possibly destined for greater achievements. But the powerful collaboration requires significant effort, lots of time, and a desire to make things happen. Above all else, it requires space for listening: listening to our self and to the "other." It requires space for exploration without the pressure of immediate results. Good results will come, but they will come later. (Raspa and Ward, 2000: 7)

If it is true that successful collaboration cannot be "mandated" or "coaxed into existence," then a bottom-up approach to collaboration may be central to establishing effective teaching partnerships. For such projects to be truly collaborative, both parties must have the desire to share not just duties and responsibilities but professional identities.

INSTITUTIONAL CONTEXT AT INDIANA STATE UNIVERSITY

Indiana State University (ISU) is an open-access institution serving approximately 10,000 students—20 percent of them graduate students. About 78 percent of ISU's students are from Indiana. The collaboration described in this chapter involved the Curriculum, Instruction, and Media Technology (CIMT) department located in the Bayh College of Education. The CIMT department awards two master's degrees—a master of science in educational technology and a master of education in curriculum and instruction. Students may complete a traditional master of science in educational technology degree or enroll in a track within the master of science in educational technology that prepares them to become school library media specialists. The department also awards PhD degrees in 12 areas of specialization as follows:

- Early Childhood Education
- Educational Technology
- Elementary Education
- English Education
- History Education
- Industrial Technology Education
- Language Education
- Math Education
- Secondary Education
- Science Education
- Special Education
- Teaching and Learning

Many courses offered by the CIMT department are fully online or in hybrid format. All courses in the school library media specialist track are fully online, and students participate from all over the world.

Similar to most universities in the United States, ISU faces serious budgetary constraints that have been exacerbated by the recent downturn in the U.S. economy. Consequently, there is an increasing focus on student retention at the university and department levels. In reviewing departmental efforts, CIMT faculty realized that many of the international students and returning nontraditional students lacked sufficient background in information retrieval and were unfamiliar with current resources, such as electronic databases. Personnel changes within CIMT reopened a dialogue about the research classes within the department. Professors discussed the challenges of teaching students how to do a literature review. In particular, they noticed students lacked basic search skills; familiarity with information resources beyond the World Wide Web; skills to evaluate and manage the information they did find; and the ability to synthesize the information they read. CIMT professors also noted students' lack of persistence in following a trail of publications and citations to flesh out their own understanding of the field. These observations led faculty to believe that they were not creating enough opportunities for students to hone these essential skills. It was within this environment that the need for courses like the one described in this chapter became apparent to the authors and their colleagues in CIMT.

INTERDISCIPLINARY PERSPECTIVES

In the following year, faculty–librarian discussions about the information literacy needs of ISU students informed the development of the course, Accessing Information with Technology. This course is an elective for master's degree and doctoral students studying curriculum and instruction, instructional design, or library media services. Students in library media services are becoming certified to serve in schools that teach kindergarten through twelfth grades, both public and private. As such, these students need to become information service professionals. In contrast, students in curriculum and instruction and instructional design desire information skills primarily in service of their own research needs and those of collaborators. This course has the potential to reach all students in CIMT and directly responds to the challenges identified by the CIMT department by focusing on the students' information-seeking skills. The course also needed an update because of today's rapidly changing information technology, especially related to the advent of Web 2.0 and social media. The librarian, who was also a graduate student in CIMT, received three hours of practicum credit for her involvement in the redesign of this course.

For this collaboration, the librarian tended to focus more on the front-end process of bibliographic and online research. At ISU, reference librarians normally see students at the reference desk, where the information-seeking process is usually just beginning. Librarians think in terms of teaching students how to define their information needs and then help them to find the resources to meet those needs. For the professor, the focus centers on the back-end of students' analysis and synthesis efforts. CIMT professors read a wide variety of student papers such as literature reviews, case studies, essays, theses, and dissertations. Professors concentrate on how well students demonstrate their understanding of various subspecialties in education by the quality of the information cited and how the information is represented in their writing. Where a librarian may teach a student how to tease the right articles out of a journal database, the professor will teach that same student how to synthesize information culled from journal articles into a literature review. Thus the librarian and the professor have different but corresponding perspectives of students' research processes. The complementary quality of this shared teaching experience proved to be a building block on which the collaborators designed the online course.

FACULTY–LIBRARIAN COLLABORATION

The ISU Library uses the liaison model and both authors of this chapter have a good working relationship with the education librarian. But for this project, the authors stepped out of the established liaison model because of a unique overlap of interests. This collaboration reflects the deeper relationships reported by Himmelman (1996) and Montiel-Overall (2005) because it exemplifies a level of collaborative intensity that allows for a mutual sharing of professional identities. The collaborating librarian holds an MS degree in library science and is studying instructional design at ISU. The professor's primary specialization is instructional design, but she has a particular interest in fostering students' information literacy skills because of the research classes she also teaches. What brought the collaborators together was the librarian's enrollment in the professor's course on the technology of distance education. As the librarian studied online pedagogy with this professor, an overlap of interests emerged which led to the redesign of the Accessing Information with Technology course. Each partner in the collaboration served multiple roles but coached the other in their domains of expertise. For the most part, the librarian developed the course on her own with some oversight from the professor on the practical matters of pedagogy. This was the librarian's opportunity to put into practice what she had learned in her instructional design studies. In effect, the librarian was a SME for matters of information literacy, while the professor mentored the librarian in instructional design and online pedagogy.

To accomplish the goals of this project, the collaborators reviewed a previous version of the course and course syllabus. After that, they met to discuss what they thought should be retained from the old course and what could be reduced or eliminated. In this meeting, the professor outlined a few of her goals for the course and typical policies to which she wanted students to adhere. The collaborators determined that the librarian would screen potential textbooks for the professor's approval and provide recommendations for textbook adoption. The librarian also volunteered to sketch the initial plans for student assessment activities. Between meetings, the authors used e-mail to discuss progress, ask clarifying questions, and discuss ideas they were considering. At another meeting, the professor reviewed the librarian's progress on developing student assignments and suggested modifications to make them more pedagogically sound. She also shared rubrics to use or modify for the course. Despite the librarian's extensive involvement in the academic content of the course, neither participant wanted the professor to abdicate her academic responsibilities. All decisions were subject to her approval.

What the professor gained from the collaboration was a more sophisticated mastery of information seeking for herself and her students and greater awareness of the diversity of information resources available today. For the librarian, this was an opportunity to learn online pedagogy. For the education students, this collaboration offers them an opportunity to learn information literacy at an advanced level by taking the course. This collaboration was fruitful because neither librarian nor professor was limited by her job description. In essence, the professor saw the librarian as an educator, while the librarian viewed the professor as an instructional design consultant. The two soon realized that this is a reversal of typical librarian–faculty collaborations in which the professor owns the role of educator and the librarian usually serves a supportive role of consultant or guide.

COURSE PLANNING AND ONLINE LEARNING MODEL

Accessing Information with Technology is a three-credit graduate course in the CIMT department. The course is one semester long (approximately 16 weeks) and is fully online. All activities are asynchronous because many CIMT students are working professionals and are distributed across the country and the world. Time zone challenges for synchronous events are nearly insurmountable. Though some students taking this course aspire to be school media specialists, others are following career paths to educational administration, elementary or secondary education, higher education, or educational technology. Course content is informed by traditional subjects embedded in library and information science programs; however, the librarian and professor placed emphasis on relating these subjects to the education environment. This was a conscious decision. Though Accessing Information with Technology might first appear like a traditional course in an MLS program, it is designed as an advanced information literacy course for those studying in the field of education. As such it has the potential to be adapted to other disciplines in the academy.

Course content introduces students to well-respected information resources in their field. However, it also challenges them to study topics and issues that are normally the purview of librarians and information scientists, such as profiling users' information needs, advanced Boolean operation, information-seeking behavior, and collection building. Students are not only expected to learn how to define their own information needs as education students, they are also encouraged to learn the process of how to define information and information needs in general. They are not just asked to learn how to effectively search for information but are challenged to analyze the research of information-seeking behavior. The librarian-course designer includes tool-related topics (such as blogs, portals, indexes, etc.) and cognitive-based topics (such as locating and evaluating information).

The course is delivered via the university's Blackboard server, and students need access to a computer and the Internet. The technological structure of this course is atypical of most Blackboard classes. The course uses only some of the functions of the Blackboard course management software and provides a large amount of course material on custom webpages that were created in HTML by the collaborators. Blackboard features are utilized, such as weekly announcements, weekly discussion boards, an assignment submission tool, and the class grade book. However, most of the course is on webpages that reside on another university server, under the instructor's individual faculty account. This integration is seamless to students because the HTML webpages load within the Blackboard menu frame, and look as if they are part of the Blackboard environment.

The reasons for constructing the course in this way are twofold: In Blackboard, updating material in several sections of the same course requires one to go into each class section and make multiple updates. This can be tedious and encourages mistakes.

However, with this technological structure, all sections of the same course can be updated by making one edit to only one HTML webpage, because all course sections link to the one webpage. This efficiency saves time and guarantees uniformity. In addition, once the semester ends, Blackboard shuts students out of the course. But since the bulk of the course is on the webpages, an instructor has the option of allowing students to have access to the course after the semester ends by providing them with the URLs to the webpages. For doctoral students especially, this can be useful in helping them review what they have learned as their studies in the program progress. These webpages can be divided into several categories, which are described in detail in the sections that follow: topics pages; assignment pages; lecture notes; and anchoring pages.

Weekly Lessons

Embedded into ISU's 16-week semester are two weeks in which the university mandates that no classes meet: a study week and finals week. The course is divided into 14 separate lessons called *topics*. Each week is devoted to one topic, which is presented on its own topic webpage. The topics, in chronological order, are Getting Acquainted & Internet History, in which students learn to navigate the Blackboard site, greet their fellow students, and become familiar with the history of the Internet; Information Seeking & Retrieval, where students are introduced to studies on information-seeking behavior and information retrieval and learn how these subjects relate to information literacy and instructional design; Directories & Portals introduces students to the capabilities and characteristics of portals, directories, and the invisible web; Search Engines & Search Strategy covers search engine construction, functionality, and Boolean logic; Evaluating & Managing Information reviews how to evaluate information resources and examines current issues in information management; Indexes & Journals reviews distinctions between free, subscription, and pay-per-view services, and government-funded digital libraries; E-Books and E-Reference Collections helps students become familiar with the ISU library's e-book collections and freely available electronic books and explores the open-textbook movement; Web 2.0 reviews interactive information and knowledge sharing via the Internet and explores how collaborative online tools can aid in information gathering; Images & Audio describes how to search for images and audio on the Internet, reviews copyright issues, and explores the use of such files as a teaching tool.

Online Information Services reviews common distinctions between ready reference and in-depth research consultation, explores the online reference services of the ISU library, and compares fee-based and free references via the Internet; Apps and Going Mobile explores how mobile technology is affecting information-seeking and teaching experiences; Newspapers, Newsgroups, and Newslogs covers news aggregators, news blogs, newspaper websites, and news alert services, and explores citizen journalism; Plagiarism and Copyright reviews the academic honesty and copyright policies at ISU, covers plagiarism issues in the classroom, and introduces students to the Creative Commons movement; Information Literacy reviews information literacy standards worldwide and examines the role that information literacy plays in different work and learning environments. The semester ends with study week and finals week for students to complete assignments and evaluations for the course.

All topic webpages are presented in a standard format using graphical icons to mark sections. The sections in the topic pages include the learning objectives for the week; a listing of that week's reading assignments with instructor notes on what to look for in the readings; links to any web resources or online articles with instructor notes on what to look for in the readings; a list of weekly class activities to reinforce concepts covered in the reading materials; a self-reflection section listing thought-provoking discussion questions for students to review; and notes of any graded assignments that are due that week. For some weekly lessons, links to separate lecture note webpages provide additional information. These lecture note pages are used when the textural content is too lengthy for the standard topic webpage format.

Course Materials

In addition to topic webpages there are two anchoring pages for the course. An index webpage provides links to every topic webpage in the course. To allow for smooth navigation, all course pages link back to this index page. The general information webpage links to descriptions of each graded course assignment and to other supporting material, including templates for papers in MS Word. Also included on this page are links to helpful resources for online and distance learners such the ISU Library Distance Education webpage, the ISU Writing Center webpage, and the campus Student Technology Guide. Links to online advice columns on such subjects as discussion board etiquette, how to manage personal electronic folders, and time management are also available.

The class uses three print textbooks. To assist students in learning the variety of Internet resources available to them, Randolph Hock's (2007) *The Extreme Searcher's Internet Handbook* and Nicholas Tomaiuolo's (2004) *The Web Library* are required reading. Both books are written from a practical standpoint by listing annotations to resources organized by broad subject and media categories. These authors update the printed information by hosting freely available websites to complement their books. Links to the sites are on the general information webpage. The third book, Joyce Kasman Valenza and Reva Basch's (2005) *Super Searchers Go to School*, offers valuable insight on the state of information literacy in the K–12 environment by featuring interviews with teachers, librarians, and administrators on such topics as pedagogy, policy, and coworker relations. These three books were chosen to help students learn about specific information resources and become aware of the educational environment in which such resources are used and taught. Additional assigned readings are accessible either through embedded links in the topic webpages, through the ISU library's Electronic Reserves service, or via the ISU library subscriptions to full-text journal databases. Web resources, such as blogs, wikis, portals, interactive tutorials, and guides are embedded in the topic webpages. A course assignment checklist and the syllabus, both available in PDF format, are linked from the general information webpage.

Discussion Boards

There is a separate discussion board set up within Blackboard for each of the weekly lessons. Each board is labeled to correspond to the weekly lessons. The instructor facilitates learning by moderating students' required posts to the weekly boards. Students are informed that three thoughtful posts per week also serve as weekly attendance in the class. The writing prompt for each weekly discussion board is inspired by that week's class activities and discussion questions made available on the topic webpage. The course instructor monitors weekly postings and may join the class discussion.

Both the librarian and professor designing this course believe that in online courses it is important to provide a space for students to get to know one another and their professor. In Accessing Information with Technology, the instructor sets up a discussion board called Meet and Greet and requires all students to introduce themselves and to greet others at the start of the course. Experienced online professors provide social spaces with titles such as CyberCafe or At the Water Cooler (Collison et al., 2000) to satisfy students' social needs that extend beyond the first weeks of class. In the Accessing Information with Technology course, the social space is called Hallway Hangout because the space is meant to simulate the hallway where casual conversations and serendipity naturally occur in a face-to-face class. Students often share news about important life events or amusing anecdotes, which helps to establish camaraderie.

ASSESSMENT OF ONLINE LEARNING

Students in Accessing Information with Technology are assessed on a variety of assignments and activities. The research paper project, which accounts for a large portion of their course grade, is divided into developmental, iterative stages that are graded separately. This iterative approach is commonly recommended as a deterrent to plagiarism. Students choose a paper topic on a subject relating to information literacy. This topic must be submitted to the instructor for approval. Students then gather sources and submit an original annotated bibliography. This step serves several purposes. By collecting their sources early in the semester, students learn valuable research habits. The development of writing annotations compels them to carefully examine each resource to properly synthesize and evaluate the research before including it in their papers. The annotated bibliography is especially effective as an antiplagiarism device because it requires students to provide analyses of sources before the paper is actually written. After the bibliography is submitted, students have time to write their research papers, which they peer-review before submitting to the professor for grading. Students also provide their fellow classmates with a presentation of their research for review and comment. Many students choose to do this by uploading narrated PowerPoint presentations to Blackboard, but other presentation formats are also accepted.

Another major assignment is the website evaluation, in which students write a detailed, evaluative essay on the informative value of a selected website. This project is also iterative, and each stage is graded separately. For this project, students submit their website selection to the instructor for approval, develop an evaluation rubric, write an evaluative essay, and critique one another's essays. In the resource library assignment students profile a hypothetical user with information needs different from their own. They then compile and annotate a variety of Internet resources for their designated user. The graded components to this assignment include a user profile; an annotated library uploaded to a freely available web space, such as Delicious; and reflections posted to a discussion board. In the search interface comparison assignment, students choose two search interfaces of proprietary databases, such as ProQuest and EBSCOHost, and write a five-page paper comparing such elements as database content, search functionality, and graphic design. Each of these assignments is described in detail on separate assignment webpages that are linked on the general information webpage. Rubrics outlining important assignment elements are provided to students.

CONCLUSION

While the authors maintain that the newly redesigned Accessing Information with Technology course can serve as a model for advanced information literacy courses for graduate students outside of the field of education, they concede that replicating the quality of their collaboration is harder to pin down. Having an experienced instruction librarian serve as a course designer for another department is one way of embedding information literacy instruction into a graduate program—but it is just one way. The initiative described in this chapter was bottom-up and can be viewed as either *circumnavigating* or *violating* established reporting lines and practices. Fortunately, the authors' desire to collaborate outside of the organizational chart was supported by their university, to the benefit of the students. Institutions advocating for robust information literacy course development should examine how well interdisciplinary and interdepartmental collaboration is tolerated and take steps to create safe spaces for experimentation and discovery.

If we accept the position that embedding information literacy into the curriculum is necessary for preparing students to be lifelong learners, then faculty–librarian collaborations that exist on many levels and in many forms can provide us with an infinite array of possibilities for building learning experiences. Collaborating to create an online course provides ongoing benefit to students who take the course in subsequent semesters. The reusability of an online course allows the institution to offer the advantages of collaborative course development and design to students without the intense human resource demands that would be required to allow faculty and librarians to team-teach face-to-face classes. Thus the benefit extends beyond the initial collaboration.

In the authors' case, collaboration grew out of a teacher-student relationship and blossomed into one in which both professionals merged their talents and shared goals while viewing each other as equals. In the end, they learned that the most profound collaboration comes from a position of reciprocal appreciation and respect. Church writes, "Forging professional identities where authority and expertise is shared and acknowledged requires a mutual accounting where investments are made of the self without the disenfranchisement of the other" (2000: 8). As faculty and librarians continue to collaborate in the academy, it is hoped that the practice of sharing authority and identity is fluid and comes from a place of trust.

REFERENCES

Albrecht, Rebecca, and Sara Brown. 2002. "The Politics of Pedagogy: Expectations and Reality for Information Literacy in Librarianship." *Journal of Library Administration* 36, no. 1: 71–96.

Bell, Stephen P., and John Shank. 2004. "The Blended Librarian: A Blueprint for Redefining the Teaching and Learning Role of Academic Librarians." *College and Research Library News* 65, no. 7: 372–375.

Bennett, Scott. 2007. "Campus Cultures Fostering Information Literacy." *Libraries and the Academy* 7, no. 2: 147–167.

Boote, David N., and Penny Beile. 2005. "Scholars Before Researchers: On the Centrality of the Dissertation Literature Review in Research Preparation." *Educational Researcher* 34, no. 6: 3–15.

Campbell, M. 2009. "Information, Knowledge and Wisdom: Collaboration between Librarians and Faculty in a Digital Age." *The Hispanic Outlook in Higher Education* 19, no. 22: 8–9.

Church, John. 2000. "Reimagining Professional Identities: A Reflection on Collaboration and Techno-Pedagogy." Bryn Mawr, PA: Bryn Mawr College. http://serendip.brynmawr.edu/talking/ReimagProID.pdf.

Cohen, Charlotte. 1995. "Faculty Liaison: A Cooperative Venture in Bibliographic Instruction." *Reference Librarian*, 51/52: 161–169.

Collison, George, Bonnie Elbaum, Sarah Haavind, and Robert Tinker. 2000. *Facilitating Online Learning: Effective Strategies for Moderators*. Madison, WI: Atwood Publishing.

Cook, M. Kathy. 1981. "Rank, Status Contribution of Academic Librarians as Perceived by the Teaching Faculty at Southern Illinois University, Carbondale." *College and Research Libraries* 42, no. 3: 214–223.

Cunningham, Thomas H., and Scott Lanning. 2002. "New Frontier Trail Guides: Faculty-Librarian Collaboration on Information Literacy." *Reference Services Review* 30, no. 4: 343–348.

D'Angelo, Barbara, and Barry M. Maid. 2004. "Moving Beyond Definitions: Implementing Information Literacy Across the Curriculum." *Journal of Academic Librarianship* 30, no. 3: 212–217.

Dewey, Barbara I. 2004. "The Embedded Librarian: Strategic Campus Collaborations." *Resource Sharing and Information Networks* 17, no. 1/2: 5–17.

Divay, Gaby, Ada Ducas, and Nicole Michaud-Ostryk. 1987. "Faculty Perceptions of Librarians at the University of Manitoba." *College and Research Libraries* 48, no. 1: 27–35.

Dorner, Jennifer L., Susan E. Taylor, and Kay Hodson-Carlton. 2001. "Faculty-Librarian Collaboration for Nursing Information Literacy: A Tiered Approach." *Reference Services Review* 29, no. 2: 132–140.

Farber, Evan. 1999. "Faculty-Librarian Cooperation: A Personal Retrospective." *Reference Services Review* 27, no. 3: 229–234.

Gandhi, Smiti. 2004. "Faculty-Librarian Collaboration to Assess the Effectiveness of a Five-Session Library Instruction Model." *Community and Junior College Libraries* 12, no. 4: 15–48.

Gilson, Caroline, and Stephanie Michael. 2002. "Fishing for Success: Faculty/Librarian Collaboration Nets Effective Library Assignments." In *Making the Grade: Academic Libraries and Student Success*, edited by Maurie Caitlin Kelly and Andrea Kross, 57–70. Chicago: Association of College Research Libraries.

Hardesty, Larry. 1991. *Faculty and the Library: The Undergraduate Experience*. Norwood, NJ: Ablex.

Haynes, Evelyn B. 1996. "Librarian-Faculty Partnerships in Instruction." *Advances in Librarianship* 20: 191–222.

Himmelman, Arthur Turovh. 1996. "On the Theory and Practice of Transformational Collaboration: From Social Service to Social Justice." In *Creating Collaborative Advantage*, edited by Chris Huxham, 19–43. London: Sage.

Hock, Randolph. 2007. *The Extreme Searcher's Internet Handbook: A Guide for the Serious Searcher*, 2nd ed. Medford, NJ: CyberAge Books.

Iannuzzi, Patricia. 1998. "Faculty Development and Information Literacy: Establishing Campus Partnerships." *Reference Services Review* 26, no. 3/4: 97–102.

Ivey, Robert T. 1994. "Teaching Faculty Perceptions of Academic Librarians at Memphis State University." *College and Research Libraries* 55: 69–81.

Lindstrom, Joyce, and Diana D. Shonrock. 2006. "Faculty-Librarian Collaboration to Achieve Integration of Information Literacy." *Reference and User Services Quarterly* 46, no. 1: 18–23.

Mackey, Thomas P., and Trudi E. Jacobson. 2005. "Information Literacy: A Collaborative Endeavor." *College Teaching* 53, no. 4: 140–144.

McCarthy, Constance. 1985. "The Faculty Problem." *Journal of Academic Librarianship* 11: 142–145.

Montiel-Overall, Patricia. 2005. "A Theoretical Understanding of Teacher and Librarian Collaboration (TLC)." *School Libraries Worldwide* 11, no. 2: 24–48.

Nimon, Maureen. 2001. "The Role of Academic Libraries in the Development of the Information-Literate Students: The Interface between Librarian, Academic and Other Stakeholders." *Australian Academic Research Libraries* 32, no. 1: 43–52. http://alia.org.au/publishing/aarl/32.1/full.text/mnimon.html.

Oberg, Larry R., Mary Kay Schleiter, and Michael Van Houten. 1989. "Faculty Perceptions of Librarians at Albion College: Status, Role Contribution and Contacts." *College and Research Libraries* 50, no. 2: 215–230.

Paglia, Alison, and Annie Donahue. 2003. "Collaboration Works: Integrating Information Competencies into the Psychology Curricula." *Reference Services Review* 31, no. 4: 320–328.

Peacock, Judith. 2001. "Teaching Skills for Teaching Librarians: Postcards from the Edge of the Educational Paradigm." *Australian Academic and Research Libraries* 32, no. 1. http://alia.org.au/publishing/aarl/32.1/full.text/jpeacock.html.

Raspa, Dick, and Dane Ward. 2000. "Listening for Collaboration: Faculty and Librarians Working Together." In *The Collaborative Imperative: Librarians and Faculty Working Together in the Information Universe*, edited by Dick Raspa and Dane Ward, 1–18. Chicago: Association of College and Research Libraries.

Robinson, Otis H. 1876. "Proceedings." *American Library Journal* 1 (November 30): 123–124.

Saunders, Laura. 2008. "Perspectives on Accreditation and Information Literacy as Reflected in the Literature of Library and Information Science." *Journal of Academic Librarianship* 34, no. 4: 305–313.

Smith, Kenneth. 2001. "New Roles and Responsibilities for the University Library: Advancing Student Learning through Outcomes Assessment." *Journal of Library Administration* 35: 29–36.

Stevens, Christy R., and Patricia J. Campbell. 2007. "The Politics of Information Literacy: Integrating Information Literacy into the Political Science Curriculum." In *Information Literacy Collaborations That Work*, edited by Trudi E. Jacobson and Thomas P. Mackey, 123–145. New York: Neal-Schuman Publishers.

Still, Julie. 1998. "The Role and Image of the Library and Librarian in Discipline-Specific Pedagogical Journals." *Journal of Academic Librarianship* 24: 225–231.

Thaxton, Lyn, Mary B. Faccioli, and Anne P. Mosby. 2004. "Leveraging Collaboration for Information Literacy in Psychology." *Reference Services Review* 32, no. 2: 185–189.

Tomaiuolo, Nicholas G. 2004. *The Web Library: Building a World Class Personal Library with Free Web Resources.* Medford, NJ: Information Today.

Valenza, Joyce Kasman, and Reva Basch. 2005. *Super Searchers Go to School: Sharing Online Strategies with K-12 Students, Teachers, and Librarians.* Medford, NJ: CyberAge Books.

Walter, Scott. 2000. "Engelond: A Model for Faculty-Librarian Collaboration in the Information Age." *Information Technology Libraries* 19, no. 1: 34–41.

Warmkessel, Marjorie M., and Joseph M. McCade. 1997. "Integrating Information Literacy into the Curriculum." *Research Strategies* 15: 80–88.

Winner, Marian C. 1998. "Librarians as Partners in the Classroom: An Increasing Imperative." *Reference Services Review* 26, no. 1: 25–29.

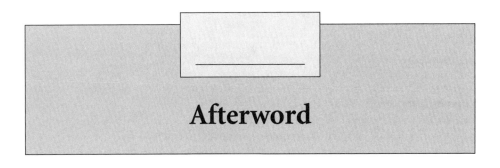

Afterword

In his foreword to this book Terry Anderson explored the changes we have seen in teaching and learning through networked culture and the web. These changes are evident in classrooms and libraries, in actual and virtual spaces, and in the ways instructors, scholars, librarians, and lifelong learners understand, produce, and share knowledge. Anderson refers to plural information literacies, accurately noting the multiplicity of this term, especially within online environments mediated by Web 2.0, social media, and social networking. He describes the models in this book as *interventions* for practice and, in developing our own information literacies, reinforcing the active nature of this work to spark further innovations.

The advantage of an edited volume such as this one is that readers have the chance to investigate multiple approaches to teaching information literacy based on real-world experience and practice. Each chapter asserts an active *collaborative intervention*, to use Anderson's term to generate new ideas and new methods for learning in online environments. As we have seen, the faculty-librarian teams in this book presented forward-thinking methodologies from disciplinary and interdisciplinary perspectives at the undergraduate and graduate levels. The technology formats have also varied and include reusable learning objects, learning management systems, avatars, and virtual islands in Second Life, open learning environments, wikis, interactive modules, digital images and documents, and online discussions. The technologies are always framed within pedagogical concepts, very often constructivist approaches, and are combined with issues related to faculty development, collaboration, and assessment.

Along with the multiplicity of practices, we have seen common goals in each chapter based on learner success and collaborative instructional design. The faculty-librarian authors in this book initially partnered to develop, expand, or revise blended and online courses that meet the needs of learners. This approach led to the active models we read about:

- Moving humanities courses into the digital age
- Expanding online offerings for working adults
- Developing a multiliteracy framework for information literacies
- Transitioning a collaborative history project online
- Combining information literacy (IL) and information and communication technology (ICT) instruction through supported open learning
- Teaching IL through a virtual library in Second Life

- Designing an asynchronous online program for graduate students
- Rethinking traditional professional roles to advance online learning

The overall structure of the book demonstrates the many choices available to instructors, librarians, and instructional designers to explore or expand flexible online learning models. Each chapter was organized to provide continuity, with an introduction, literature review, institutional context, disciplinary perspective, faculty-librarian collaboration, program planning, online learning model, and assessment. As we have seen, the development of information literacies online crosses the boundaries of discipline, location, and time. It also scales to meet the needs of traditional-age undergraduate and graduate students as well as nontraditional adult learners and lifelong learners.

The models in this book exemplify another key point about online learning. This process is not about moving content online, or marking up a syllabus in HTML, or even enhancing course documents with video lectures. Online learning involves interactivity, communication, dialogue, collaboration, and placing the learner at the center of active research, the production of digital information, and the codevelopment of new knowledge. Online environments must be flexible and user centered, allowing for a seamless experience moving from one application to another and in enabling a free-flowing conversation among students, faculty, and librarians. Today's online environments also impact our understanding of copyright and intellectual property, individual and virtual identity, information ethics, and information access. All of these issues intersect with and reinforce the need for a deep and coherent understanding of information literacy and ways of knowing in a digital age.

As the authors in this book make clear, teaching information literacy online is an opportunity to reinvent teaching practices and to redefine learning in a new way. Open and online learning environments provide active collaborative spaces for students to work together, to engage with information in a range of new media formats, to connect with other learners synchronously and asynchronously, and to do so in different time zones and from diverse cultural perspectives. Online learners explore virtual identities, produce digital projects, and share ideas through social networks. These activities align well with plural information literacies focused on finding, evaluating, synthesizing, understanding, organizing, and using information. Online environments also push the bounds of traditional information literacy definitions to include a necessary emphasis on the learner-centered production of digital information and sharing of new knowledge through social media.

We agree with Terry Anderson that "it is only a matter of time" before you design your own blended or online course, if you have not done so already. By exploring the chapters in this book you are well on your way to your own *collaborative intervention*. We wish you well in this venture, and we are confident it will be as engaging and rewarding as the innovative models from this book suggest.

About the Editors
and Contributors

Thomas P. Mackey, PhD, is the Interim Dean at the Center for Distance Learning at SUNY Empire State College in Saratoga Springs, New York. His teaching and research interests include information literacy, blended and online learning, social networking, Web 2.0, and social and community informatics. He has published three coedited books with Trudi E. Jacobson for Neal-Schuman Publishers, *Collaborative Information Literacy Assessments: Strategies for Evaluating Teaching and Learning* (2010), *Using Technology to Teach Information Literacy* (2008), and *Information Literacy Collaborations That Work* (2007). His research articles have been published in *College & Research Libraries, Computers & Education, The Journal of General Education, College Teaching, Rhizomes, The Journal of Information Science, The Journal of Education for Library and Information Science*, and the *Journal of the Library Administration and Management Section (JLAMS)* of the New York Library Association. Tom has presented his research at such conferences as the American Society for Information Science & Technology Annual Meeting, The Sloan-C International Conference on Online Learning, and the Sloan-C International Symposium: Emerging Technology Applications for Online Learning. He may be contacted by e-mail at Tom.Mackey@esc.edu.

Trudi E. Jacobson, MLS, MA, is the Head of User Education Programs at the University at Albany, SUNY. She coordinates and teaches in the undergraduate Information Literacy course program. Her interests include the use of critical thinking, active learning, and team-based learning in information literacy courses. She is the co-author, with Lijuan Xu, of *Motivating Students in Information Literacy Classes* (2004), and co-editor, with Thomas P. Mackey, of *Collaborative Information Literacy Assessments: Strategies for Evaluating Teaching and Learning* (2010), *Using Technology to Teach Information Literacy* (2008), and *Information Literacy Collaborations That Work* (2007). She also co-edited or edited *Teaching the New Library to Today's Users* (2000), *Teaching Information Literacy Concepts: Activities and Frameworks from the Field* (2001), and *Critical Thinking and the Web: Teaching Users to Evaluate Internet Resources* (2000). She has published articles in a number of journals, including *The Journal of General Education, College & Research Libraries, portal, Journal of Academic Librarianship, Research Strategies, College Teaching, and The Teaching Professor*. She is the editor of *Public Services Quarterly*. In 2009, Trudi won the Association of College and Research Libraries Instruction Section's Miriam Dudley Instruction Librarian Award. She may be contacted by e-mail at tjacobson@uamail.albany.edu.

. . .

Kristina DuRocher, PhD, received her PhD from the University of Illinois at Urbana Champaign. She is currently an Assistant Professor of History at Morehead State University. Her first book, *Lessons in Black and White: The Racial and Gender Socialization of White Children in the Jim Crow South, 1890-1939*, is forthcoming in 2011. She can be reached at k.durocher@moreheadstate.edu.

Rebecca L. Fiedler, PhD, was an Assistant Professor of Curriculum, Instruction, and Media Technology at Indiana State University and is now building her own consulting business. Dr. Fiedler's research focuses on distance education, and she is a frequent collaborator in software testing education and professional development. She can be reached at fiedler@beckyfiedler.com.

Ian Fishwick, PhD, BA PG Dip LIS, earned his doctorate from the University of Durham and has responsibility for Education within the Social Sciences team at the John Rylands University Library at the University of Manchester. He can be reached at ian.fishwick@manchester.ac.uk.

Susan M. Frey, MS (Library Science), MLS (Liberal Studies), is a Reference/Instruction Librarian and Interim Chair of Circulation at Indiana State University, where she is also a graduate student in the university's Curriculum and Instruction program. Ms. Frey's research interests are best practices in information literacy instruction, and the social and cultural studies of information. She can be reached at susan.frey@indstate.edu.

Katheryn Giglio, PhD, is a former Assistant Professor of Renaissance Literature at the University of Central Florida. Her scholarship has focused on education, literacy, illiteracy, and representations of the book in early English drama. These topics served as an inspiration to explore new kinds of literacy using contemporary technologies. She is currently working as a communications analyst at a nonprofit institution. She can be reached at kgiglio@mail.ucf.edu.

Clarissa Gosling, MPhys (Oxon), MSc, MCLIP, has worked in The Open University Library in the United Kingdom for the past five years and is currently the Head of Faculty Team for the Faculty of Maths, Computing, and Technology and The Open University Business School. She previously worked in the same institution as a Learning and Teaching Librarian for the Faculty of Science and the Faculty of Health and Social Care. In this role she was the key liaison between the library and the social work department and worked closely with them in the development of their new degree program. Prior to this she also worked in the libraries of a pharmaceutical company, a Catholic seminary, and an international charity. She may be contacted by e-mail at c.h.gosling@open.ac.uk.

Jenna Kammer, MA Ed, MLS, is an online instructor for NMSU–Alamogordo, NMSU–Dona Ana and UNM–Gallup in the computer and library science departments. She teaches web design, MS Office software, keyboarding, and information literacy. She obtained her Master's of Education with a specialization in Learning Technology from

New Mexico State University and Master's of Library Science from the University of Arizona. Jenna's primary research interests include information literacy and information seeking behavior in electronic environments. Jenna can be reached at jkammer @nmsu.edu.

David Lavoie, PhD, MLIS, is Director of Instructional Design and Assessment within the School of Business at the University of Connecticut and principal designer working with the accounting faculty concerning the master's degree in accounting. Prior to his present position, Dr. Lavoie was the Director of the Instructional Design and Development unit within the Institute for Teaching and Learning at the University of Connecticut. Before his employment at the University of Connecticut, Dr. Lavoie was an Information Fellow at Connecticut College. Dr. Lavoie completed his PhD in Curriculum and Instruction, with an emphasis in educational technology, within the School of Education at the University of Wisconsin, Madison, in 1999. He graduated with his MLIS from the University of Rhode Island in 1991 and his BA from Rhode Island College in 1984. In addition to his instructional design as faculty development effort for the MSA in Accounting, Dr. Lavoie works with the Finance faculty to develop the Master's Degree in Global Health Care Management and the faculty in the School of Law to develop their LLM in Insurance courses for online delivery. David may be reached by e-mail at David.Lavoie@business .uconn.edu.

Elizabeth Lehr, MA (Professional Writing), MA (Gender and Cultural Studies), earned two MA degrees: the first in Professional Writing from the University of Massachusetts Dartmouth (2000) and the second from Simmons College in Gender and Cultural Studies (2009). She embraces effective pedagogical use of technological innovations in both face-to-face and online classes. Her research interests meet at the intersection of language, history, and gender. She may be contacted by e-mail at elehr@umassd.edu.

Steve McIndoe, BA PgDip, is the Information Skills Coordinator at the John Rylands University Library, with responsibility for the development of the library's information skills strategy and the provision of its research support training program. He has worked at the University of Manchester since 2002, having previously worked in other higher education, government, and corporate libraries. Steve can be reached at Steve .Mcindoe@manchester.ac.uk.

Kari Mofford, MS, is the English Language and Literatures Librarian at the University of Massachusetts Dartmouth. She also serves as Liaison to Women's Studies, Liberal Arts, and African-American and Judaic Literatures. She recently copresented a Magna Online Seminar with Marilyn Steinberg, "Librarians and Faculty As Partners: Collaborations at Work." She received her MS in 1999 from the Simmons College Graduate School of Library and Information. Kari may be reached at kmofford@umassd.edu.

Lisa Nichols, MATESL, MSLIS, graduated from the University of Illinois at Urbana–Champaign Graduate School of Library and Information Science in 2005. She is enjoying her second career as a librarian after a 10-year stint of teaching English and English As a

Second Language in the public school system. Formerly the Head of Instructional Services at Morehead State University, she is currently the Public Services Librarian at Transylvania University in Lexington, Kentucky. She can be reached at lnichols@transy.edu.

Ingrid Nix, BA Hons, MA, PGCODE, is Lecturer in Learning and Teaching Technologies in the Faculty of Health and Social Care at The Open University, Milton Keynes, England. Since 2000 she has worked with faculty course teams and associated OU colleagues, leading and coordinating production to develop and enhance learning, teaching, and assessment using appropriate technology. She was responsible for designing and implementing the ICT skills strategy for the Open University Social Work degrees to meet the professional competencies required for Scotland, Wales, and England. Her current research interests include the role of technology-enhanced learning in preparing students for technology-enhanced (work) practice. She may be reached via e-mail at i.nix@open.ac.uk.

Jeannette E. Riley, PhD, received her PhD in English in 1998 from the University of New Mexico. Riley's research interests focus on women's literature, with an emphasis on contemporary women writers and feminist theory, and she has published articles on Eavan Boland, Terry Tempest Williams, Adrienne Rich, and Toni Morrison, among others. In addition, Riley has also published on feminist pedagogy and online learning. She may be contacted by e-mail at j1riley@umassd.edu.

Andrew Rosman, PhD CPA, is an Associate Professor at the University of Connecticut and a University Teaching Fellow. He has been at the University of Connecticut since 1989 and teaches a course on global financial reporting and analysis and another on information literacy, both of which are conducted asynchronously online. He has served as the Director of the MS in Accounting Program since 1998. In 2002, this program became the University of Connecticut's first online graduate degree. Andy now also serves as the Executive Director of Online Education for the School of Business. His primary research focus has been on how decision makers use information with the objective of identifying ways to improve decision behavior for business professionals' use of information in business-related activities as well as students in educational settings. He has published research in the *Journal of Accounting and Economics*; *Journal of Accounting, Auditing and Finance*; *Auditing: A Journal of Theory and Practice*; *Academy of Management Journal*; *Journal of Behavioral Decision Making*; *Journal of Business Venturing*; *Journal of Business Research*; *Issues in Accounting Education*; and *Research in Accounting Regulation*. He may be reached via e-mail at Andrew.Rosman@business .uconn.edu.

Shikha Sharma, MA, MLIS, is the Social Sciences Team Leader and the Business, Economics, and Legal Studies Librarian at the University of Connecticut Libraries. Her work and research interests revolve around issues related to instruction, information literacy, teaching methods, assessment, user-centered collections and services, and the impact of emerging technologies on teaching and scholarship. Shikha can be contacted at shikha.sharma@uconn.edu.

Matthew C. Sylvain, MLS, is eLearning Librarian and Online Support Coordinator at the University of Massachusetts Dartmouth. His responsibilities include the development and management of the library's eLearning program. He serves as liaison and subject specialist for the departments of Political Science and Sociology, Anthropology, and Crime & Justice Studies. He received his MLS in 1999 from the University of North Carolina at Chapel Hill. He may be contacted by e-mail at msylvain@umassd.edu.

Tracey Thompson, MLS, BSc, is the Acquisitions Librarian at New Mexico State University Library. She obtained her Master of Science in Library and Information Science from Drexel University and her Bachelor of Science in Computer Science from Central Missouri State University. Her research interests include management of electronic resources, virtual worlds such as Second Life, social networking, and the future of libraries. She is the recipient of a 2009 Amigos Fellowship Grant to study the impact of virtual worlds such as Second Life on information and libraries. Tracey can be reached at tthompson@metrolibrary.org.

John Venecek, MA, MLS, is the Humanities Librarian at the University of Central Florida. Prior to his arrival at UCF, John spent several years teaching English at the College of DuPage in suburban Chicago and also taught English at a small university in Yekaterinburg, Russia, while serving as a Peace Corps volunteer (1996–1998). His main area of interest is exploring how new and emerging technologies can be used to enhance information literacy instruction and promote faculty/librarian collaborations. John can be reached at jvenecek@mail.ucf.edu.

Andrew Whitworth, PhD, BA, PgDip, CMALT, has published widely in the field of e-learning and information literacy. In 2009 he published the book *Information Obesity*, which analyzed the state of ICT and information literacy education. He is the Program Director for the MA: Digital Technologies, Communication, and Education at the University of Manchester. He can be reached at Drew.Whitworth@manchester.ac.uk.

Index